HISTORY OF
MUGHAL EMPIRE

RITURAJ SARKAR

Published by

Hawk Press
4836/24, Ansari Road, Daryaganj
New Delhi – 110 002
Phones : 9643330713, 91-11-23278618, 91-11-35676207
E-mail: thehawkpress@gmail.com
www.thehawkpress.com

Copyright © 2022, *Editor*
ISBN : 978-93-95034-36-4
All rights reserved.

No part of this book may be reproduced, stored in a retrieval system, transmitted or utilised in any form or by any means, electronic, mechanical, photocopying, recording or otherwise, without the prior permission of the copyright owner. Application for such permission should be addressed to the publisher.

Contents

Preface (iv)

1. Rise of Mughal Empire 1
2. The Founder of Mughal Empire: Babur 40
3. The Reign of Humayun 73
4. Akbar the Great 88
5. Jahangir 123
6. Shah Jahan 138
7. Rise of Aurangzeb 157
8. Administration of the Mughals 191
9. Causes and Decline of Mughal Empire 237
   Bibliography 257
   Index 259

Preface

The Mughal Empire at its zenith commanded resources unprecedented in Indian history and covered almost the entire subcontinent. From 1556 to 1707, during the heyday of its fabulous wealth and glory, the Mughal Empire was a fairly efficient and centralized organization, with a vast complex of personnel, money, and information dedicated to the service of the emperor and his nobility.

The dynasty was founded by a Chagatai Turkic prince named Babur (reigned 1526–30), who was descended from the Turkic conqueror Timur (Tamerlane) on his father's side and from Chagatai, second son of the Mongol ruler Genghis Khan, on his mother's side. Babur's father, ?Umar Shaykh Mirza, ruled the small principality of Fergana to the north of the Hindu Kush mountain range; Babur inherited the principality at a young age, in 1494.

Much of the empire's expansion during that period was attributable to India's growing commercial and cultural contact with the outside world. The 16th and 17th centuries brought the establishment and expansion of European and non-European trading organizations in the subcontinent, principally for the procurement of Indian goods in demand abroad. Indian regions drew close to each other by means of an enhanced overland and coastal trading network, significantly augmenting the internal surplus of precious metals. With expanded connections to the wider world came also new ideologies and technologies to challenge and enrich the imperial edifice.

The individual abilities and achievements of the early Mughals—Babur, Humayun, and later Akbar—largely charted this course. Babur and Humayun struggled against heavy odds to create the Mughal domain, whereas Akbar, besides consolidating and expanding its frontiers, provided the theoretical framework for a truly Indian state. Picking up the thread of experimentation from the intervening Sur dynasty (1540–56), Akbar attacked narrow-mindedness and bigotry, absorbed Hindus in the high ranks of the nobility, and encouraged the tradition of ruling through the local Hindu landed elites. This tradition continued until the very end of the Mughal Empire, despite the fact that some of Akbar's successors, notably Aurangzeb (1658–1707), had to concede to contrary forces.

After Aurangzeb died in 1707, the empire started a slow and steady decline in actual power, although it maintained all the trappings of power in the Indian subcontinent for another 150 years. In 1739 it was defeated by the army of the Persian shah, Nadir Shah (1688-1747). In 1756 Ahmad Shah (1747-1772) of Afghanistan looted Delhi. Complacent in their military superiority, the Mughals failed to modernize their technology. While no Indians could challenge their cannon, outsiders could. Increasingly, the Mughal emperors grew less interested in good governance and more interested in maintaining their lavish lifestyle and expensive court. Hence, the emperors up to Aurangzeb are called the "greater," after him the "lesser." This is very similar to the pattern that emerged in the Ottoman Empire, where the rulers grew increasingly disinterested in good governance and repeated the pattern of their predecessors, the Afghan Lodi Sultans.

The mughal government was essentially a police government and confined its attention mainly to the maintenance of internal and external order and collection of revenue. The mughals failed to effect a fusion between Hindus and muslims and create a composte nation.

The death of Alamgir in 1707 is generally regarded as the beginning of the gradual decline, and ultimately fall, of the once extensive, prosperous and powerful Mughal Empire. Although it took nearly 150 years before the House of Babur finally disappeared from the scene, the cracks that had appeared at Alamgir's death widened.

The present book accounts all the major factors responsible for the downfall of Mughal empire.

—Author

1

Rise of Mughal Empire

The Mughal Empire was an empire that at its greatest territorial extent ruled parts of what is todays Afghanistan, Pakistan and most of the Indian Subcontinent, then known as Hindustan, between 1526 and 1707. The empire was founded by the Timurid leader Babur in 1526, when he defeated Ibrahim Lodi, the last of the Delhi Sultans at the First Battle of Panipat. "Mughal" is the Persian word for "Mongol". The religion of the Mughals was Islam.

The territory was largely conquered by the Afghan Sher Shah Suri during the time of Humayun, the second Mughal ruler, but under Akbar it grew considerably, and continued to grow until the end of Aurangzeb's rule. Jahangir, the son of Akbar, ruled the empire between 1605–1627. In October 1627, Mughal Emperor Shah Jahan, son of Jahangir, "succeeded to the throne", where he "inherited a vast and rich empire" in India; and "at mid-century this was perhaps the greatest empire in the world". Shah Jahan commissioned the famous Taj Mahal (between 1630–1653), in Agra.

The Mughals faced stiff competition from the Marathas, and after Aurangzeb died in 1707, the empire started to decline in actual power, giving way to the rise of the Hindu Maratha Empire.

The Mughals however managed to maintain some trappings of power in the India for another 150 years. In 1739 it was defeated by an army from Persia led by Nadir Shah. In 1756 an army of Ahmed Shah Abdali took Delhi again. The British Empire finally dissolved it in 1857, immediately prior to which it existed only at the sufferance of the British East India Company.

RELIGION

The Mughal ruling class were liberal-minded Muslims, although most of the subjects of the Empire were Hindu. Although Babur founded the Empire, the dynasty remained unstable (and was even exiled) until the reign of Akbar, who was not only of liberal disposition but also intimately acquainted, since birth, with the mores and traditions of India.

The Great Mughal Emperors

Emperor	Reign start	Reign end
Babur	1526	1530
Humayun	1530	1540
Interregnum*	1540	1555
Humayun	1555	1556
Akbar	1556	1605
Jahangir	1605	1627
Shah Jahan	1627	1658
Aurangzeb	1658	1707

Under Akbar's rule, the court abolished the jizya (the poll-tax on non-Muslims) and abandoned use of the lunar Muslim calendar in favour of a solar calendar more useful for agriculture. One of Akbar's most unusual ideas regarding religion was Din-i-Ilahi ("Faith-of-God" in English), which was an eclectic mix of Hinduism, panthiestic versions of Sufi Islam, Zoroastrianism and Christianity. It was proclaimed the state religion until his death. These actions however met with stiff opposition from the Muslim clergy. However, the orthodoxy regained influence only three generations later, with Aurangzeb, known for upholding doctrines of orthodox Islam; this last of the Great Mughals retracted nearly all the liberal policies of his forbears.

ESTABLISHMENT AND REIGN OF BABUR

In the early 16th century, Muslim armies consisting of Mongol, Turkic, Persian, and Afghan warriors invaded India under the leadership of the Timurid prince Zahir-ud-Din-Mohammad Babur.

Babur was the great-grandson of Mongol conqueror Timur Lenk (Timur the Lame, from which the Western name Tamerlane is derived), who had invaded India in 1398 before retiring to Samarkand who himself claimed descent from the Mongol ruler, Genghis Khan. Babur was driven from

Samarkand by the Uzbeks and initially established his rule in Kabul in 1504. Later, taking advantage of internal discontent in the Delhi sultanate under Ibrahim Lodi, and following an invitation from Daulat Khan Lodi (governor of Punjab) and Alam Khan (uncle of the Sultan), Babur invaded India in 1526.

Babur, a seasoned military commander, entered India in 1526 with his well-trained veteran army of 12,000 to meet the sultan's huge but unwieldy and disunited force of more than 100,000 men. Babur defeated the Lodi sultan decisively at the first Battle of Panipat. Employing gun carts, moveable artillery, and superior cavalry tactics, Babur achieved a resounding victory and the Sultan was killed.

A year later (1527) he decisively defeated, at the battle of Khanwa, a Rajput confederacy led by Rana Sanga of Chittor. A third major battle was fought in 1529 when, at the battle of Gogra, Babur routed the joint forces of Afghans and the sultan of Bengal. Babur died in 1530 at Agra before he could consolidate his military gains. He left behind as his chief legacy a set of descendants who would fulfill his dream of establishing an empire in the Indian subcontinent.

Early Sikh Gurus' perception of the Mughal Empire Babur's reign was witnessed by the first Sikh Guru Nanak Dev Ji. His Raag Asa Guru records Nanak's observations and thoughts in his poems. It says:

"Having attacked Khuraasaan, Babar terrified Hindustan. The Creator Himself does not take the blame, but has sent the Mugal as the messenger of death. There was so much slaughter that the people screamed. Didn't You feel compassion, Lord?" pg (360) On the condition of Hindu women in Babur's rule:

"Those heads adorned with braided hair, with their parts painted with vermilion - those heads were shaved with scissors, and their throats were choked with dust.They lived in palatial mansions, but now, they cannot even sit near the palaces.... ropes were put around their necks, and their strings of pearls were broken. Their wealth and youthful beauty, which gave them so much pleasure, have now become their enemies. The order was given to the soldiers, who dishonored them, and carried them away. If it is pleasing to God's Will, He bestows greatness; if is pleases His Will, He bestows punishment" pg (417-18) On the nature of Mughal rule under Babur:

"First, the tree puts down its roots, and then it spreads out its shade above. The kings are tigers, and their officials are dogs; they go out and awaken the sleeping people to harass them. The public servants inflict wounds with their nails. The dogs lick up the blood that is spilled." Source: Rag Malar, Strangely enough, the land on which the Sikh Golden temple now stands, was actually donated by Mughal emperor Akbar.

REIGN OF HUMAYUN

When Babur died, his son Humayun (1530–56) inherited a difficult task. He was pressed from all sides by a reassertion of Afghan claims to the Delhi throne and by disputes over his own succession. He fled to Persia, where he spent nearly ten years as an embarrassed guest of the Safavid court of Shah Tahmasp. During Sher Shah's reign, an imperial unification and administrative framework were established; this would be further developed by Akbar later in the century. In 1545, Humayun gained a foothold in Kabul with Safavid assistance and reasserted his Indian claims, a task facilitated by the weakening of Afghan power in the area after the death of Sher Shah Suri in May 1545. He took control of Delhi in 1555, but died within six months of his return, from a fall down the steps of his library.

REIGN OF AKBAR

Humayun's untimely death in 1556 left the task of conquest and imperial consolidation to his thirteen-year-old son, Jalal-ud-Din Akbar (r.1556–1605). Following a decisive military victory at the Second Battle of Panipat in 1556, the regent Bayram Khan pursued a vigorous policy of expansion on Akbar's behalf.

As soon as Akbar came of age, he began to free himself from the influences of overbearing ministers, court factions, and harem intrigues, and demonstrated his own capacity for judgment and leadership.

A workaholic who seldom slept more than three hours a night, he personally oversaw the implementation of his administrative policies, which were to form the backbone of the Mughal Empire for more than 200 years. He continued to conquer, annex, and consolidate a far-flung territory bounded by Kabul in the northwest, Kashmir in the north, Bengal in the east, and beyond the Narmada River in central India.

Akbar built a walled capital called Fatehpur Sikri (Fatehpur means "town of victory") near Agra, starting in 1571. Palaces for each of Akbar's senior queens, a huge artificial lake, and sumptuous water-filled courtyards were built there. However, the city was soon abandoned and the capital was moved to Lahore in 1585. The reason may have been that the water supply in Fatehpur Sikri was insufficient or of poor quality; or, as some historians believe, that Akbar had to attend to the northwest areas of his empire and therefore moved his capital northwest. In 1599, Akbar shifted his capital back to Agra from where he reigned until his death.

Akbar adopted two distinct but effective approaches in administering a large territory and incorporating various ethnic groups into the service of his realm. In 1580 he obtained local revenue statistics for the previous decade in order to understand details of productivity and price fluctuation of different crops. Aided by Todar Mal, a hindu scholar, Akbar issued a revenue schedule that optimised the revenue needs of the state with the ability of the peasantry to pay.

Revenue demands, fixed according to local conventions of cultivation and quality of soil, ranged from one-third to one-half of the crop and were paid in cash. Akbar relied heavily on land-holding zamindars to act as revenue-collectors. They used their considerable local knowledge and influence to collect revenue and to transfer it to the treasury, keeping a portion in return for services rendered. Within his administrative system, the warrior aristocracy (mansabdars) held ranks (mansabs) expressed in numbers of troops, and indicating pay, armed contingents, and obligations. The warrior aristocracy was generally paid from revenues of nonhereditary and transferable jagirs (revenue villages).

An astute ruler who genuinely appreciated the challenges of administering so vast an empire, Akbar introduced a policy of reconciliation and assimilation of Hindus (including Jodhabai, later renamed Mariam-uz-Zamani begum, the Hindu mother of his son and heir, Jahangir), who represented the majority of the population. He recruited and rewarded Hindu chiefs with the highest ranks in government; encouraged intermarriages between Mughal and Rajput aristocracy; allowed new temples to be built; personally participated in celebrating Hindu festivals such as Deepavali, or Diwali, the festival of lights; and abolished the jizya (poll tax) imposed on non-Muslims. Akbar came up with his own theory of "rulership as a divine illumination," enshrined in his new religion Din-i-Ilahi (Divine Faith), incorporating the principle of acceptance of all religions and sects. He encouraged widow re-marriage, discouraged child marriage, outlawed the practice of sati, and persuaded Delhi merchants to set up special market days for women, who otherwise were secluded at home.

By the end of Akbar's reign, the Mughal Empire extended throughout north India even south of the Narmada river. Notable exceptions were Gondwana in central India, which paid tribute to the Mughals, Assam in the northeast, and large parts of the Deccan. The area south of the Godavari river remained entirely out of the ambit of the mughals. In 1600, Akbar's Mughal empire had a revenue of £17.5 million. By comparison, in 1800, the entire treasury of Great Britain totalled £16 million.

Akbar's empire supported vibrant intellectual and cultural life. The large imperial library included books in Hindi, Persian, Greek, Kashmiri, English, and Arabic, such as the Shahnameh, Bhagavata Purana and the Bible. Akbar regularly sponsored debates and dialogues among religious and intellectual figures with differing views, and he welcomed Jesuit missionaries from Goa to his court. Akbar directed the creation of the Hamzanama, an artistic masterpiece that included 1400 large paintings.

REIGNS OF JAHANGIR AND SHAH JAHAN

Mughal rule under Jahangir (1605–27) and Shah Jahan (1628–58) was noted for political stability, brisk economic activity, beautiful paintings, and monumental buildings. Jahangir married a Persian princess whom he renamed Nur Jahan (Light of the World), who emerged as the most powerful individual in the court besides the emperor. As a result, Persian poets, artists, scholars, and officers—including her own family members—lured by the Mughal court's brilliance and luxury, found asylum in India. The number of unproductive officers mushroomed, as did corruption, while the excessive Persian representation upset the delicate balance of impartiality at the court. Jahangir liked Hindu festivals but promoted mass conversion to Islam; he persecuted the followers of Jainism and even executed Guru Arjun Dev, the fifth saint-teacher of the Sikhs in 1606 for refusing to make changes to the Guru Granth Sahib (the Sikh holy book). The execution was not entirely for religious reasons; Guru Arjun Dev Ji supported Prince Khusro, another contestant to the Mughul throne in the civil war that developed after Akbar's death. Noor Jahan's abortive efforts to secure the throne for the prince of her choice led Shah Jahan to rebel against Jahangir in 1622. In that same year, the Persians took over Kandahar in southern Afghanistan, an event that struck a serious blow to Mughal prestige.

Between 1636 and 1646, Shah Jahan sent Mughal armies to conquer the Deccan and the lands to the northwest of the empire, beyond the

Khyber Pass. Even though they aptly demonstrated Mughal military strength, these campaigns drained the imperial treasury.

As the state became a huge military machine, causing the nobles and their contingents to multiply almost fourfold, the demands for revenue from the peasantry were greatly increased. Political unification and maintenance of law and order over wide areas encouraged the emergence of large centers of commerce and crafts—such as Lahore, Delhi, Agra, and Ahmadabad—linked by roads and waterways to distant places and ports.

The world-famous Taj Mahal was built in Agra during Shah Jahan's reign as a tomb for his beloved wife, Mumtaz Mahal. It symbolizes both Mughal artistic achievement and excessive financial expenditures at a time when resources were shrinking. The economic positions of peasants and artisans did not improve because the administration failed to produce any lasting change in the existing social structure. There was no incentive for the revenue officials, whose concerns were primarily personal or familial gain, to generate resources independent of what was received from the Hindu zamindars and village leaders, who, due to self-interest and local dominance, did not hand over the entirety of the tax revenues to the imperial treasury. In their ever-greater dependence on land revenue, the Mughals unwittingly nurtured forces that eventually led to the break-up of their empire.

REIGN OF AURANGZEB AND DECLINE OF EMPIRE

The last of the great Mughals was Aurangzeb. During his fifty-year reign, the empire reached its greatest physical size but also showed unmistakable signs of decline. The bureaucracy had grown corrupt; the huge army used outdated weaponry and tactics. Aurangzeb restored Mughal military dominance and expanded power southward, at least for a while. Aurangzeb was involved in a series of protracted wars: against the Pathans in Afghanistan, the sultans of Bijapur and Golkonda in the Deccan, the Marathas in Maharashtra and the Ahoms in Assam. Peasant uprisings and revolts by local leaders became all too common, as did the conniving of the nobles to preserve their own status at the expense of a steadily weakening empire.

The increasing association of his government with Islam further drove a wedge between the ruler and his Hindu subjects. Contenders for the Mughal throne were many, and the reigns of Aurangzeb's successors were short-lived and filled with strife. The Mughal Empire experienced dramatic reverses as regional nawabs or governors broke away and founded independent kingdoms. In the war of 27 years from 1680 to 1707, the Mughals suffered several heavy defeats at the hands of the Marathas. They had to make peace with the Maratha armies, and Persian and Afghan armies invaded Delhi, carrying away many treasures, including the Peacock Throne in 1739.

Successors - "the lesser Mughals"
- Bahadur Shah I (Shah Alam I), b. October 14, 1643 at Burhanpur, ruler from 1707-1712, d. February 1712 in Lahore.
- Jahandar Shah, b. 1664, ruler from 1712-1713, d. February 11, 1713 in Delhi.
- Furrukhsiyar (b.1683, r.1713-1719, d.1719 at Delhi).
- Rafi Ul-Darjat, ruler 1719, d. 1719 in Delhi.
- Rafi Ud-Daulat (Shah Jahan II), ruler 1719, d. 1719 in Delhi.
- Nikusiyar, ruler 1719, d. 1719 in Delhi.
- Mohammed Ibrahim, ruler 1720, d. 1720 in Delhi.
- Mohammed Shah, b. 1702, ruler from 1719-1720, 1720-1748, d. April 26, 1748 in Delhi.
- Ahmad Shah Bahadur, b. 1725, ruler from 1748-1754, d. January 1775 in Delhi.
- Alamgir II, b. 1699, ruler from 1754-1759, d. 1759.
- Shah Jahan III, ruler 1760?
- Shah Alam II, b. 1728, ruler from 1759-1806, d. 1806.
- Akbar Shah II, b. 1760, ruler from 1806-1837, d. 1837.

Bahadur Shah II aka Bahadur Shah Zafar, b. 1775 in Delhi, ruler from 1837-1857, d. 1862 in exile in Rangoon, Burma. Present-day descendents: A few descendants of the last Mughal Emperor, Bahadur Shah Zafar, are known to be living in Delhi, Kolkata, and Hyderabad. The majority of direct descendants still carry the clan name Temur with four major branches today: Shokohane-Temur (Shokoh), Shahane-Temur (Shah), Bakshane-Temur (Baksh) and Salatine-Temur (Sultan). There is also a line of direct descendants who carry the name "Mirza", living in Delhi, Pakistan and England.

STEEL AND CROWTHER'S JOURNEY OF 1615-16 FROM MOGHUL INDIA THROUGH PERSIA

This description of the journey of Richard Steel and John Crowther

(Crowder) was published in England soon after it took place, in Samuel Purchas' collection of travel accounts entitled *Haklyutus Posthumus or Purchas His Pilgrimes* (in the 1905-1907 re-edition, vol. IV). Purchas saw himself as continuing the work of Richard Haklyut, the pioneering English publisher of travel accounts in the late sixteenth century, one of whose goals was to give English travelers their place in the sun and to use the often inspiring tales of foreign enterprise as a stimulus to English overseas expansion.

This was the era of the activity of important English joint stock companies, among them the East India Company which was chartered at the end of 1600 with a monopoly for English trade that might be established in the East Indies. Despite the company's privileges, various other Englishmen were undertaking their own ventures, attempting to secure privileges for English trade in the East. Steel was one of these. On his way back through Persia, he encountered one of the two most famous such entrepreneur-adventurers, Richard Sherley, who was continuing his older brother Anthony's visionary and to a considerable degree self-serving undertakings in the service of Shah Abbas of Persia.

At the moment that Steel and Crowther set out from Moghul India for Persia, what had been the dominant position of the Portuguese in the Indian Ocean was coming to an end. The English and especially the Dutch were about to take over control of the Indian Ocean sea routes; within a few years of Steel's return home, in 1622, a combined force of the English fleet and Persian army took Hormuz from the Portuguese, thus ending their control of the entrance to the Persian Gulf and the important trade route through it.

Of interest in Steel's account is his evidence concerning the effect of the disruption of the Portuguese sea trade on the overland routes. The Portuguese no longer were obtaining goods from the inland areas of the Moghul Empire, and the Asian merchants who might have used Portuguese shipping to get to the Middle East were returning to the traditional overland routes.

The account provides much other valuable information on the overland trade: a sense of the way in which the Moghul and Safavid states controlled and supported the trade, the difficulties of the journey, some of the important products, and the role of the Asian merchants and caravaneers in the enterprise. It is worth remembering that this journey took place during when the Safavid state was at its apogee under Shah Abbas I (1587-

1629) and when the Moghul Empire was ruled by Emperor Jahangir (1605-1627), the successor to the great Akbar and the father of Shah Jahan, who would build the Taj Mahal for his beloved wife and then be buried there alongside her.

The text here is taken from Robert Kerr, ed., *A General History and Collection of Voyages and Travels....*, Vol. IX (Edinburgh and London, 1824), pp. 206-219, who in turn copied it from Purchas. As Kerr's editorial notes indicate, it is difficult to identify many of the towns. Rather than edit out some of what may seem to be of little more use than a catalogue of names and distances, I have left the text intact, since it does then provide a means of measuring the length of time such journeys might take. Even the cataloguing of towns and caravanserais provides an impression of the density of habitation and the degree to which the needs of travelers along the roads were being met.

Having been detained at Agimere from February, Mr. Edwards received a letter on the 17th March, 1615, from the Great Mogul, of which be delivered a copy, together with his other letters, to, Richard Steel, promising to procure the king's firmaun for our safety and furtherance, and to send it after us to Agra, where he directed us to wait for its reception. We went that night two coss [about 1.5 miles in Hindustan and 2 miles in Rajput] to *Mandill*. We had four servants, two horses, and a camel. The 18th we went twelve coss to *Bander Sandree* [Bunder-Sanory], a small village. The 19th, ten coss to *Mosobade* [Morabad].

The 20th to *Pipelo* [Peped], thirteen coss. The 21st to a town called *Chadfool* [Gohd?], seven coss. The 22nd to *Lalscotte)* thirteen coss. The 23d to *Mogolserai*, twelve coss. The 24th to *Hindone*, fourteen coss. The 25th to *Bramobad*, twelve coss. The 26th to *Futtipoor*, twelve coss. This has been a fair city, which was built by Akbar, and. contains a goodly palace belonging to the king. It is walled round in a handsome manner, and has many spacious gardens and sumptuous pleasure houses; but is now falling to ruin, and much ground with in the walls is now sown with corn, the king having carried off much of the best stone to his new city of Agra. The 27th we went twelve coss to Agra. In the English house there, we found one Richard Barber, an apothecary, who came over with Sir Robert Shirley, and had been sent here by Mr. Kerridge to take care of Nicholas Whithington.

Within two days journey of Agra, we passed by the country and city of Biana, where the finest indigo is made, the best being then worth thirty-six rupees the maund at Agra, but much cheaper in the country. Finding the promised firmaun came not, and the hot season of the year, fast approaching, we departed on the third of April, in the prosecution of our journey, leaving directions with Richard Barber to send it after us. We came that night to a serai called Boutta, six coss. The 4th to the town of *Matra*, fourteen coss, where we lay in a fair *serai*, and there we received the firmaun. The 5th we went twelve coss to a serai called *Chatta* [Chautra]. The 6th to a serai built by Azam Khan, nine coss.

The 7th to a serai built by Sheik Ferreede, called *Pulwali*, eleven coss. The 8th to a serai built by the same person, ten coss. The 9th to *Dillee* [Delhi], nine coss. This being a great and ancient city, formerly the seat of the kings where many of them are interred. At this time, many of the great men have their gardens and pleasure houses here, and are here buried, so that it is beautified with many fine buildings. The inhabitants, who are mostly Banians or Hindoos, are poor and beggarly, through the long absence of the court.

The 10th we went ten coss from Delhi to *Bunira*. The 11th to *Cullvower*, twelve coss. The 12th to *Pampette* [Paniput], twelve coss. This is a small handsome city, where they manufacture various sorts of girdles and sashes, and great quantities of cotton cloth, and have abundance of handicrafts. The 13th to *Carnaul*, twelve coss. The 14th to *Tanisera* [Tahnessir] fourteen coss.

The 15th, to *Shavade* [Shahabad], ten coss. The 16th to *Mogol-Sera*, or *Gaugur*, fifteen coss. The 17th to *Sinan* [Sirhind] fourteen coss, which is an ancient city, where they manufacture great store of cottons. The 18th to *Duratia*, fifteen coss. The 19th to *Pullower* [Bullolepoor], eleven coss. We this day passed in a boat over a great river called *Sietmege* [Sutuluge or Beyah-Kussoor], which is very broad, but full of shoals, and runs westward, to join the Sinde, or Indus. The 20th we came to a small town called *Nicodar*, eleven coss. The 21st, to *Sultanpoor*, an old town having a river which comes from the north, over which is a bridge of six arches~. At this place great store of cotton goods are made. Four coss beyond this place we passed another small river. The 22nd to *Chiurmul* [Gundwall], eleven coss. We were this day boated across a river as broad as the Thames at Gravesend, called *Vian*, which runs westwards to join the Sinde. On its banks Allom Khan, ambassador from the Great Mogul, to the king of Persia, had pitched his camp, which looked like a little city. The 23rd we went to *Khan Khanum Serai*, seventeen coss, and the 24th we reached Lahore, seven coss.

All the country between Agra and Lahore.is exceedingly well cultivated, being the best of India, and abounds in all things. It yields great store of powdered sugar [raw sugar], the best being worth two and one-half to two and three-fourths rupees the great *maund* of forty pounds. The whole road is planted on both ides with trees, most of which bear a species of mulberry. In the, night, this road is dangerously infested with thieves, but is quite secure in the day.

Every five or six coss, there are serais, built by the king or some great man, which add greatly to the beauty of the road, are very convenient for the accommodation to travellers, and serve to perpetuate the memory of their founders. In these the traveller may have a chamber for his own use, a place in which to tie up his horse, and can be furnished with provender; but in many of them very little accommodation can be by reason of the banians, as when once any person has taken up his lodging, no other may dispossess him. At daybreak the gates of these serais are opened, and then all the travellers prepare to depart; but no person is allowed to go away sooner, for fear of robbers. This made the journey very oppressive to us, as within two hours after the sun rose we were hardly able to endure the heat.

Lahore is a great and goodly city, being one of the fairest and ancientest in India. It stands on the river Indus or Sinde; and from this place came the most valuable of the Portuguese trade when they were at peace with the Moguls, as it formed the centre of all their traffic in Hindoostan. They here embarked their goods, which were carried down the river to Tatta, and were thence transported by sea to Ormus [Hormuz] and Persia; and such native merchants as chose to that way between India and Persia, paid them freight. They had also a great trade up this river, in pepper and other spices, with which they furnished that part of India. At this time, the merchants of India assemble at Lahore, where they invest a great part of their money in commodities, and, joining in caravans, they pass over the mountains of Candahar [Kandahar] into Persia; by which way it is computed there now pass yearly twelve or fourteen thousand camel loads, whereas formerly there did not go in this way above three thousand, all the rest going by way of Ormus. These merchants are put to great expence between Lahore and Ispahan, besides being exposed to great cold in winter and fervent heat in summer, and to bad and dangerous roads, usually spending six or seven months in the journey, and they estimate the charges of each camel-load at 120 or 130 rupees.

In this way Persia is furnished with spiceries, which are brought all the way from Masulipatam by land. We remained in Lahore from the 24th of April to the 18th of May, refreshing both ourselves and our horses, and providing servants an a necessaries for the journey. We also procured here recommendatory letters from an ambassador to the king of Persia.

We left Lahore on the 13th May, proposing to overtake a caravan which set out two months before, and went that day eleven coss to a small town named *Chacksunder*. The 14th to *Non-serai*, fifteen c.

The 15th to *Mutteray*, eight c. The 16th to *Quemal khan*, nineteen c. The 17th, to *Herpae*, sixteen c. The 18th to *Alicasava*, twelve c. The 19th *Trumba*, twelve c. and this way we overtook a small caravan that had left Lahore eight days before us. The 20th to *Sedousehall*, fourteen c. The 21st to *Callixechebaut*, fifteen c. The 22d to *Multan*, twelve c.

This is a great and ancient city, having the river Indus at the distance of three coss. All caravans must remain here ten or twelve days, before leave can be procured from the governor to proceed, on purpose that the city may benefit by their stay. It yields white plain cotton cloth and diaper. We remained five days, and were then glad to get leave to depart, by means of a present.

We passed the river on the 28th, and went twenty c. to a small village named *Pettoalle*. The 29th we another great river by a boat, and came that same night to a small river called *Lacca*, where we found the caravan we wished to overtake. We presented the caravan *basha* with a mirror and knife, when he directed us to pitch our tent near his own, that we might be more immediately under his protection.

This caravan had been here ten days, and remained till the 2nd of June, waiting, for an escort of cavalry to convoy them to *Chatcza* [Chatzan], a small fort in the mountains, having received information that a former caravan had been injured by the mountaineers. The 2nd June we resumed our journey, and travelled twelve c. entering into the mountains, where we were much distressed for want of fresh water, what water we met with being brackish. The 3rd and 4th we travelled all night, climbing high mountains, and following watercourses with various turnings and windings, insomuch that in travelling twelve coos our direct course did not exceed six c. The 5th, we again followed the bed of a watercourse or river, full of large pebbles, travelling eight c.. The 6th we rested.

The 7th we went four c. still along the watercourse, the 8th eight c. The 9th twelve c. and the 10th three c. when we came to *Chatcza* [Chatzan], a small fort with mud walls, in closed with a ditch, where the Mogul keeps a garrision of eighty or 100 horse, to scour the road from thieves, yet these are as great thieves as any, where they find an opportunity. The captain of this castle exacted two *abacees* for each camel in the caravan, though nothing was legally due, as he and his troops have their pay from the king. In the whole of our way, from the river Lacca to Chatzan, we found no sustenance for man or beast, except in some places a little grass, so that we had to make provision at Lacca, hiring a bullock to carry barley for our horses. The *Agwans* or *Afgans*, as the people of the mountains are called, came down to us every day at ou'r resting place, rather to look out what they might steal, than to buy as they pretended.

Having made provision for three days at Chatzan, we went thence on the 12th June, and travelled fourteen c. The 13th ten c. The 14th ten c. This day, the mountaineers brought down to us sheep, goats, meal, butter, and barley, in abundance, sufficient both for us and our cattle, all of which they sold at reasonable prices; and from this time forwards, they did the same every day, sometimes also bringing felts and striped carpets for sale.

The 15th we went six c., the 16th four c., the 17th ten c., the 18th nine c., the 19th nine c. when we came to a small town of the Afgans called *Duckee* [Dooky], where the Mogul keeps a garrison in a small square mud fort, the walls of which ar of a good height. This fort is a mile from the town.

We stopt here three days, as the caravan could not agree with the captain of the fort, who demanded a duty on every camel, and at last an *abacee* and a half was paid for each camel. The 23rd we went six c., the 24th we passed a place called *Secotah*, or the three castles, because of three villages standing near each othei on the side of a hill, forming a triangle. We this day went eight c. The 25th we rested, on account of bad weather. The 26th we went ten c. The 27th fourteen c. This day we paased through the *durues* or gates of the mountains, being narrow straits, with very high rocks on both sides, whence with stones a few men might stop the passage of a multitude, and where many caravans have been accordingly cut off. We this night, where we lodged, suffered much insolence from the Afgans; and next day, as we passed a small village called *Coasta*, they exacted from us two and one half *abacees* for each camel. The 28th we went five c., the 29th, passing a village called *Abdun*, eight c., the 30th six c. The 1st July in seven c. we came to a place called *Pesinga* [Pusheng, or Kooshinge] where there is a small fort like that at *Dooky*, in which is a for securing the way. At this place the captain exacted half an *abacee* for each camel. The 3rd we left the caravan and went forwards six c. The 4th we passed over a mighty mountain and descended into the plains beyond, having travelled that day, fourteen c. The 5th we went twenty c. and were much distressed to get grain for our cattle. The, 6th, in like distress both for them and ourselves, we went twelve c. and on the 7th, after eight c., we got to.the city of Candahar.

These mountains of' Candakar are inhabited by a fierce people, called *Agwans* or *Potans* [Afgans or Patans] who are very strong of body, somewhat fairer than the natives of Hindoostan, and are much addicted to robbery, insomuch that they often cut off whole caravans. At present they have become more civil, partly from fear of the Mogul, and partly from experiencing the advantages of trade, by selling their grain, sheep, and goats, of which they have great store, and by purchasing coarse cotton goods and other necesaries. Still, however, if they find any one straggling or lagging behind, they are very apt to make them slaves, selling, them into the mountains, and houghing them to prevent their running away, after which they are set to grind grain in hand-mills or to other servile employments.

The chief city, called likewise Candahar, is very ancient, and was in old times inhabited by Banians. At this place. the governor of the whole country resides, who has a garrison of twelve or fifteen thousand horse, maintained there by the Great Mogul, in regard of the neighbourhood of the Persians towards the north.

To the west, the city is environment by steep and craggy rocks, and to the south and east by a strong wall. In consequence of the frequent passage of caravans it has been considerably increased of late, so that the suburbs are larger than the city. Within the last two years in consequence of the Persian trade by way of Ormus being stopped, through war with the Portuguese, all the caravans between Persia and India must necessarily pass through this place; and here they hire camels to go into India, and at their return for Persia have to do the same. They cnnnot return without leave of the governor, who causes them to stop a month here or at the least fifteen or twenty days; owing to which it is inhabited by many lewd people, as all such places of resort commonly are.

Victuals for man and beast are to be had in great abundance at Candahar, yet are very dear owing to the great concourse of trade, occasioned by the meeting at this place of many merchants of India, Persia, and Turkey, who often conclude their exchanges of commodities here. At this place the caravans going for India usually unite together, for greater strength and security in passing through the mountains of Candahar; and those that come here from India generally break into smaller companies, because in many parts, of the route through Persia, a greater number would not find provisions, as all Persia, from hence to Ispahan, is extremely barren, so that sometimes not a.green thing is to be seen in two or three days travel; and even water is scarce, and that which is to be got is often brackish, or stinking and abominable.

We remained at this city for fourteen days, partly to procure company. for our farther journey, and partly for, refreshment after the fatigues and heats of our late journey, especially on account of John Crowther, who was so weak that he at one time doubted being able to proceed any farther.

We joined ourselves' to three Armenians and a dozen Persian merchants, along with whom we left the city of Candahar on the 23rd July, and went ten c. to a village called *Seriabe*. The 24th we came in twelve c. to *Deabage*, a small *dea* or village. The 25h in eight c. to *Cashecunna*, a small castle in which the Mogul has a garrison, being the utmost boundary of his dominions westwards, and confining with Persia.

The 26th we travelled seventeen c. and lodged in the open fields by the side of a river. The 27th, after four c. we came to a castle called *Greece*, the first belonging to the king of Persia. Here we delivered to the governor the letter we had got from the Persian ambassador at Lahore, and presented him a mirror and three knives. He would take nothing for our camels, while the others had to pay five *abacees* for each camel. He promised to give us a safe conduct under an escort of horse to the next governor, but we saw none; neither were we sorry for the omission, for he was little better than a rebel, and all his people were thieves.

The 28th we departed at night, going two *parasangs* [one is 2.78 English miles] and lodged at a *dea* or village called *Malgee*. A *farcing* or parasang is equal to two Indian cosses and a half. The 29th we went ten p. and lodged in the open fields, where we could get nothing but water. The 30th we went five p. to a small castle nanied *Gazikhan*. The 31st other five p. to an old ruined fort, where we could get nothing but water, and that was stinking. The 1st August we proceeded other five p. to an old fort called *Dilaram*, where we paid an *abacee* and a half for each camel. We staid here one day to rest our cattle, which was termed making *mochoane;* and on the 3rd we went seven p. to an old castle called *Bacon*. The 4th four p. and lodged in the open fields, where we found nothing but water. The 5th four p. and the 6th five p. to *Farra*.

Farra is a small town, surrounded by a high wall of bricks dried in the sun, as are all the castles and most of the buildings in this country, and is of a square form, about a mile in circuit. It has a handsome bazar or market-place, vaulted over head to keep out the rain, and in which all kinds of necessaries and commodities are sold. It is situated in a fertile soil, having plenty of water, without which nothing can be raised in this country; and it is wonderful to see with what labour and ingenious industry they bring water to every spot of good ground, which is but seldom to be found here, often carrying it three or four miles in trenches under ground.

At this town, all merchants going into Persia must remain for seven, eight, or ten days; and here the king's treasurer sees all their packs weighed, estimating the value of their commodities at so much the maund, as he thinks fit, and exacts a duty of three per cent ad valorem on that estimate. On their way into Persia, merchants are used with much favour, lest they should make complaints to the king, who will have merchants kindly treated; but on their return into India, they are treated with extreme rigour, being searched to the very skin for money, as it is death to transport any gold or silver coin from Persia, except that of the reiging king. They likewise look narrowly for horses and slaves, neither of. which are allowed to be taken out of the country.

We remained here two days waiting for certain Armenians, with whom we travelled the rest of the journey, leaving our former companions. The 9th of Augudst we went only one parasang to a river. The 10th we travelled seven p. and lodged in the open fields. The 11th, four p. to a small village, where we had plenty of provisions. The 12th, four p.. where we had to dig for water.

The 13th, eight p. and the 14th five p. to.a village named*Draw* [Durra], where we remained a day, as it is the custom of those who travel with camels to rest once in four or five days. The 16th, we adanced three p. The 17th, four p. The 18th, five p. to *Zaide-basha* [Sarbishe] where abundance of carpets are to be had.

The 19th we came to a village named *Mude* [Moti], where also are carpets. The 20th, five p. to *Birchen* [Berdjan], where are manufactured great quantities of fine felts, and carpets of camels hair, which are sold at the rates of from two to five *abacees* the *maund*. At this place we rested a day. The 22nd, we went to *Dea-zaide* [Descaden] where all the inhabitants pretend to be very religious, and sell their carpets, of which they have great abundance at a cheap rate. The 23rd, three p. The 24th, five p. to

Choore [Cors or Corra], an old ruined town. The *25th*, three p. The 26th, seven p. when we had brackish stinking water. The 27th we came to *Dehuge* [Teuke], where is a considerable stream of hot water, which becomes cool and pleasant after standing some time in any vessel. The 28th we went seven p. to *Dea-cuma*.

The 29th we went five p. to *Tobaz* [Tobas Kileke] where we had to pay half an abacee for each camel. At this place all caravans take four or five days rest, the better to enable them to pass the adjoining salt desert, which extends four long days journey, and in which many miscarry. We found here a small caravan of an hundred camels, which set off the next day after our arrival. Here, and in the former village, there is great store of dates; and 3000 maunds of the finest silk in Persia are made here yearly, and carried to *Yades* [Yezd], a fair city, where likewise they make much raw silk, and where it is manufactured into taffaties, satins, and damasks. The king does not allow the exportation of raw silk, especially into Turkey; but the Portuguese used to carry it to Portugal. *Yades* [Yezd] is about twelve days journey from Ispahan, and is twelve p. out of the way from the Indian route to the capital.

The 30th of August we advanced nine p. into the desert, and lay on the ground, having to send our beasts three miles out of the way for water, which was very salt. The 31st, after travelling ten p. we came to water which was not at all brackish. The 1st September we went five p. and had to send two miles for water. The 2nd we went nine p. to a small castle, where we procured a small quantity of provisions. The 3rd, five p. and lay in the fields, having to send far for water. The 4th, ten p. to *Seagan*. The 5th, four p.

The 6th, ten p. to a castle called *Irabad* [Hirabad], where we paid half an *abacee* for each camel. The 7th, six p. The 8th, eight p. to *Ardecan*, where we rested till the 10th, when we went four p. to *Sellef* The 11th, three p. to a small castle named *Agea Gaurume*. The 12th, nine p. to a spring in the fields. The 15th, three p. to *Beavas*. The 14th, four p. to *Goolabad*, whence Richard Steel rode on to Ispahan, without waiting for the caravan. The 15th we came to *Morea Shahabad* five p. The 16th, to *Coopa*, five p. The 17th, to *Dea Sabs* five p. The 18th, four p. and lay in the fields. And on the 19th, after three p. we came to *Ispahan*.

Richard Steel reached this city on the 15th at noon, and found Sir Robert Shirley already provided with his dispatches from the king of Persia as ambassador to the king of Spain. Sir Robert, attended by his lady, a bare-footed friar as his chaplain, together with fifty-five Portuguese prisoners, and his own followers, were preparing in all haste to go to Ormus, and embark thence for Lisbon. The purpose is, that seeing the Portuguese not able to stand, the Spaniards may be brought in. Six friars remain as hostages for his safe return to Ispahan, as otherwise the king has vowed to cut them all in pieces, which he is likely enough to do, having put his own son to death, and committed a thousand other severities. On his arrival at Ispahan, Richard Steel delivered his letters to Sir Robert, who durst hardly read them, except now and then, as by stealth fearing lest the Portuguese should know of them. He afterwards said it was now too late to engage in the business of our nation, and seemed much dissatisfied with the company, and with the merchants and mariners who brought him out.

But at length he said he was a true-hearted Englishman, and promised to effect our desires. On the 19th, the friars being absent, he carried both of us to the master of the ceremonies, or *Maimondare* and took us along with him to the Grand Vizier, *Sarek Hogea*, who immediately called his scribes or secretaries, and made draughts of what we desired: namely, three *firmauns*, one of which John Crowther has to carry to Surat; one for Richard Steel to carry to England, and the third to be sent to the governor of *Jasques*, all sealed with the great seal of the king. The same day that these firmauns were procured, being the last of September, Sir Robert Shirley set out for Shiras in great pomp, and very honourably attended.

"Firmaun or command given unto all our subjects, from the highest to the lowest, and directed to the *Souf-basha,* or constable of our country, kindly to receive and entertain the English Franks or nation, when any of their ships may arrive at Jasques, or any other of the ports in our kingdom, to conduct them and their merchandize to what place or places they may desire, and to see them safely defended upon our coasts from any other Franks whomsoever. This I will and command you to do, as you shall answer in the contrary. Given at our royal city, this 12th of *Ramassan,* in the year of our *Tareag,* 1024 [October, 1615]."

The chief commodities of Persia are raw silks, of which it yields, according to the king's books, 7700 batmans yearly. Rhubarb grows in Chorassan, where also worm-seed grows. Carpets of all sorts, some of silk and gold, silk and silver, half silk, half cotton, &c. The silver monies of Persia are the *abacee, mahamoody, shahee,* and *biftee,* the rest being of copper, like the *tangas* and *pisos* of India. The *abacee* weighs two *meticals,* the *mahmoody* is half an abacee, and the *shahee* is half a *mahamoody.* In the dollar or rial of eight there are thirteen shahees. In a shahee there are two *biftees* and a half, or ten *cashbegs*, one *biftee* being four *cashbegs*, or two *tangs*. The weights differ in different places; two *mahans* of Tauris being only one of' Ispahan, and so of the *batman*. The measure of length, for silks and other stuffs, is the same with the pike of Aleppo, which we judge to be twenty-seven English inches.

John Crowther returned into India, and Richard Steel went to England by way of Turkey, by the following route. Leaving Ispahan on the 2d December, 1615, he went five p. to a serail. The 3rd, eight p. to another serail. The 4th, six p. to a village. The 5th seven p. to *Dreag*. The 6th, seven p. to a serail. The 7th, eight p. to *Golpigan* [Chulpaigan]. The 8th, seven p. to *Curouan*. The 9th, seven p. to *Showgot*. The 10th, six p. to *Saro*[Sari]. The 11th, eight p. to *Dissabad*. The 12th, twelve p. to a fair town called *Tossarkhan*, where he rested some days, because the country was covered deep with snow. The 15th, *six p.'* to *Kindaner*. The 16th, eight p. to *Sano*. The 17th to *Shar nuovo*, where I was stopped by the *daiga*; but on shewing him letters from the vizier, he bade me depart in the name of God and of Ali. The 18th we passed a bridge where all travellers have to give an account of themselves, and to pay a tax of two *shakees* for each camel. The 19th we came to *Kassam-Khan*, the last place under the Persian government, and made a present to the governor that might give me a guard to protect me from the Turkomans, which he not only did, but gave me a licence to procure provisions free at his villages without payment, which I yet did not avail myself of.

The 21st of December I began to pass over a range of high mountains which separate the two empires of Persia and Turkey, which are very dangerous; and, on the 22nd, at the end of eight p. I arrived at a village. The 23rd, after travelling seven p. I lay under a rock.. The 4th I came to *Mando*, eight p. a town belonging to the Turks. The 25th, eight p. to *Emomester*. The 26th, eight p. to *Boroh*, passed over a river in a boat, and came, that night to Bagdat. I was here strictly examined and searched for letters which I hid under my saddle; but observing one trying there also, I gave him a sign on which he desisted, and followed me to my lodging for his expected reward I fared better than an old Spaniard, only a fortnight before, who was imprisoned in chains in the castle, and his letters read by a Maltese renegado. I found here a Portuguese, who had arrived from Ormus only two days before me. The pacha made us wait here twenty days for a sabandar of his.

The 16th of January, 1616, we passed the river Tigris and lay on the skirt of the desert. The 17th we travelled five *agatzas* being leagues or parasangs. The 18th we came to the Euphrates at *Tulquy*, where merchandize disembarked for Bagdat, after paying a duty of five per cent. passes to the Tigris, and thence to the Persian gulf. After a tedious journey, partly by the river Euphrates, and partly through the desert, and then by sea, he arrived, at Marseilles, in France, on the 15th April, and on the 10th May at Dover.

CONTRIBUTION OF MUGHALS TO THE SUBCONTINENT

The first Mughal emperor Babur wrote in his diary Tuzk Babri: "Hindustan is a country which has few pleasures to recommend it.... Indians have no idea of the charms of friendly society, of frankly mixing together, or of familiar intercourse.... They have no horses, no good grapes, or musk melons, no good fruits, no ice or cold water, no good food or bread in their bazaars, no bath or colleges, no candles, no torches, not a candle stick."

The Mughals were superior to their Indian counterparts in war but also considered themselves so culturally. They had taste for the fine things in life - for beautifully designed artifacts and the enjoyment and appreciation of cultural activities. However, the Hindus of India provided the Mughals with a richer philosophy and the plentiful spices and vegetarian options which were incorporated into modern Indian life. While the Mughals' superior position may have been appreciated, in reality, they probably borrowed as much as they gave. However, it could not be doubted that they introduced many changes to Indian society and culture, including:

- Centralised government which brought together many smaller kingdoms
- Delegated government with respect for human rights
- Persian art and culture amalgamated with native Indian art and culture
- Started new trade routes to Arab and Turk lands
- Mughalai cuisine
- Urdu and Hindi languages were formed for common Muslims and Hindus respectively
- Periods of great religious tolerance
- A style of architecture

- Landscape gardening
- A system of education that took account of pupils' needs and culture.

PERSIANS IN THE MUGHAL EMPIRE

Persians were the second largest nobility of the Mughal Empire of South Asia. Throughout the history of the Delhi Sultanate and its successor the Mughal Empire, Persian technocrats, bureaucrats, soldiers, traders, scientists, architects, teachers, poets, artists, theologians and Sufis migrated and settled in South Asia.

The name *Mughal* is derived from the original homelands of the Timurids, the Central Asian (Turkestan) steppes once conquered by Genghis Khan and hence known as *Moghulistan*, "Land of Mongols". Although early Mughals spoke the Chagatai language and maintained some Turko-Mongol practices, they became essentially Persianized and transferred the Persian literary and high culture to South Asia, thus forming the base for the Indo-Persian culture and the Spread of Islam in South Asia.

Humayun refuge in Persia

Mughal Emperor Humayun was defeated by Sher Shah Suri in 1540 and fled to the refuge of the Safavid Empire in Iran, marching with 40 men and his wife. Shah Tahmaspwelcomed the Mughal, and treated him as a royal visitor. Here Humayun went sightseeing and was amazed at the Persian artwork and architecture he saw: much of this was the work of the Timurid Sultan Husayn Bayqarah and his ancestor, princess Gauhar Shad, thus he was able to admire the work of his relatives and ancestors at first hand. He was introduced to the work of the Persian miniaturists, and Kamaleddin Behzad had two of his pupils join Humayun in his court. Humayun was amazed at their work and asked if they would work for him if he were to regain the sovereignty of Hindustan and they agreed.

Shah Tahmasp provided financial aid and 12,000 choice cavalry to regain his Empire. Persians nobles and soldiers joined Humayun in reconquest of South Asia. Thousands of Persians continued to migrate every year and were given high civil and military positions in the Mughal Empire. The large influx of Persians of different ranks and backgrounds into the Mughal service changed the nucleus of the Mughal nobility. The Turkic Turani nobility tended to fade away from the political scene and the Persian nobles improved their position. During 1545-1555 A.D. a number of Persians who came in Humayun's service were appointed to important central offices, such as diwan, wazir, and mir-saman (In charge of Imperial Palace).

Ma'asir al-Umara

Ma'asir al-Umara was written by Shah Nawaz Khan and his son, Abdul Hai Khan in 1780. This book contains the biographies of 738 Mughal nobles of which at least 198 or 26.8 per cent were Persians

Reasons for Immigration

Most of the Persians migrated to South Asia to prosper and obtain high positions in Mughal Empire. Many were Sunni Persians who felt discriminated in Shia Safavid Empire and migrated to mostly Sunni Mughal Empire.

There were also rebels and nobles who lost royal favour and migrated to Mughal Empire. The Mughals also preferred to employ foreign Muslim officials that had little or no local interests and thus were loyal to the Mughal emperor.

Mughal Emperor Akbar

The Mughals had a multi-racial and multi-religious ruling class in which non-Indians occupied a very major place. Commenting on the mansabdars listed in the Ain-i-Akbari, Moreland writes that just under 70 percent of the nobles whose origin is known were foreigners, mostly Persians, belonging to families which had either come to South Asia with Emperor Humayun or had arrived at the court after the accession of Emperor Akbar.

Shia Muslim Dynasties in South Asia

The Shia Muslims, especially Ithna ashariyya school, has deep rooted influence in present and history of South Asia from North to South with various Shia Muslim dynasties ruling South Asian provinces from time to time. Most of these kingdoms were established by Persian Shias.

Few prominent ones of the Indian Shia Muslim dynasties are as follows:
- Bahmani Sultanate (1347–1527 AD): The Bahmani Sultanate also called the *Bahmanid Empire* or *Bahmani Kingdom* was a Muslim state

of the Deccan in southern India and one of the great medieval Indian kingdoms. Bahmanid Sultanate was the first independent Islamic and Shi'ite Kingdom in South India.

- Sharqi Dynasty (1394 CE to 1479 CE): The Sharqi sultanate was an independent medieval Shia Muslim dynasty of North India, one of the many kingdoms that came up following the disintegration of the Delhi Sultanate. Between 1394 CE to 1479 CE, Sharqi dynasty ruled from Jaunpur in the present day state of Uttar Pradesh.
- Berar Sultanate (1490–1572 AD): On the establishment of the Bahmani Sultanate in the Deccan (1348), Berar Sultanate was constituted one of the five provinces into which their kingdom was divided, being governed by great nobles, with a separate army. The perils of this system becoming apparent, the province was divided (1478 or 1479) into two separate provinces, named after their capitals Gawil and Mahur.
- Bidar Sultanate (1489–1619 AD): Bidar Sultanate was one of the Deccan sultanates of late medieval India. Its founder, Qasim Barid was a Turk, domiciled in Georgia controlled by Persia. He joined the service of the Bahmani sultan Muhammad Shah III. He started his career as a *Sar-Naubat* but later became the *Mir-Jumla* (prime minister) of the Bahmani sultanate.
- Qutb Shahi dynasty (1518–1687 AD): The Qutb Shahi dynasty was a Turkic dynasty (whose members were also called the Qutub Shahis). They were the ruling family of the kingdom of Golconda in southern India. They were Shia Muslims and belonged to Kara Koyunlu of Persia.
- Adil Shahi dynasty (1527–1686 AD): The Adil Shahi dynasty ruled the Sultanate of Bijapur in the Western area of the Deccan region of Southern India from 1490 to 1686. Bijapur had been a province of the Bahmani Sultanate (1347–1518), before its political decline in the last quarter of the 15th century and eventual break-up in 1518. The Bijapur Sultanate was absorbed into the Mughal Empire on 12 September 1686, after its conquest by the Emperor Aurangzeb.
- Nawab of Awadh (1722–1858 AD): Of all the Muslim states and dependencies of the Mughal empire, Awadh had the newest royal family, the Nawabs of Awadh. They were descended from a Persian adventurer called Sa'adat Khan, originally from Khurasan in Persia.
- Najafi Nawabs of Bengal (1757–1880): The Persian Najafi Dynasty

of Nawabs of Bengal were Sayyids and were descendants of Prophet Muhammad through Al Imam Hasan ibn Ali, ruling from 1757 until 1880.
- Nawab of Rampur: Rampur, former princely state of British India. Previously ruled by Persian Shiite Muslim Nawabs of Rampur, it was incorporated into the state of Uttar Pradesh in 1949.

Awadh State

The most important Shia state in South Asia was established by Persian originally from Khurasan in Persia around 1722 AD with Faizabad as its capital and Sadat Ali Khan as its first Nawab. Awadh or Avadh is also known in various British historical texts as Oudh.

Qizilbash

The Qizilbash soldiers and officials settled in modern Pakistan during Mughal Emperor Humayun's return from exile in Safavid Persia and restoration of Mughal Empire. Emperor Humayun lost his South Asian territories to the Pashtun noble, Sher Shah Suri, and, with Persian aid, regained them 15 years later in 1555 AD. Humayun's return from Persia, accompanied by a large retinue of Persian noblemen and soldiers, signalled an important change in Mughal court culture, as the Central Asian origins of the dynasty were largely overshadowed by the influences of Persian art, architecture, language and literature.

CONDUCT OF A BATTLE IN MUGHALS

An open country was one of the first necessities for a successful action by a Moghul army, for without this their cavalry could not deploy freely. Even ground covered with thick scrub was unfavourable, while hills and ravines still more hampered their movements. In a mountainous region they were at a terrible disadvantage.

Their mail-clad horsemen were quite unequal to guerilla warfare. In their palmiest days they found themselves unable to reach the Pathans amidst their rocks. In their decadence they were helpless as children against the nimble Marathas.

Usually one, if not both, the armies made ready for battle by drawing out the guns in a long line and protecting them by earth works, the guns being also connected together by chains or hide-straps, to prevent the horsemen of the other side from riding through the line and cutting down the gunners.

If the guns were not too numerous, it was often the practice to post them behind the clay walls of the houses in some village. or to take up a commanding position on the top of an old brick-kiln ; or a temporary entrenchment might be formed out of the earthen bank and ditch which usually surround a grove of mango trees. A discharge of rockets from the artillery position generally began the action. Then the guns were brought into play. The fire never became very rapid. In the middle of the 18th century their firing once in a quarter of an hour. In 1721 the usual rate of fire of the heavy guns was one shot every three hours (one pas). Haidar Quli Khan's men cooled their guns, loaded them, and fired them at intervals of three-quarters of an hour. In Babar's time the rate of firing must have been very slow. In his battle near Kanauj Ustad Quli Khan (mir atash) made very good use. The first day he discharged eight projectiles, the second he shot sixteen, and so continued for three or four days.

Owing to the slowness of the draught oxen, who were unable to keep up with an advancing line, the artilleryseldom took any further part in the battle, once the cavalry advance had passed beyond the entrenched position which had been taken up at the outset. From the same cause, it seldom happened that in case of a retreat or defeat the guns could be saved. They had to be spiked and left behind or as Blacker puts it.

While the artillery duel went on, the rest of the army was drawn up at some distance behind the guns in the order of battle with standards displayed, drums beating, and horns blowing. As the army took up its position for battle, the long brass horns sounded and heralds made proclamation. Shouts and battle cries, coupled with abusive or taunting language, were copiously resorted it. Such cries were Allahu akbar ! (God is great) and Din! Din! (The faith! The faith!). Akbar used the cry of Ya Muin! (O Helper!).The most common cry in later times was Din! Din! Muliammad! Mahratta war cry was "Gopal ! Gopal! or Har Har, Mahadeo". These are the names of Hindu gods.

Cavalry charges - When the guns were supposed to have done their work and had sufficiently demoralized the opposing army, successive charges were delivered from first one wing, then the other. The horsemen began with matchlock fire and a discharge of arrows, finally coming to close quarters and hand to hand fighting with sword, mace, or spear. In this the matchlock played a conspicuous part. In the south of India it was the practice to make the first attack against the rear of an army.

Caltrops khasak is the word for a caltrop thrown down to impede the movements of cavalry.

As to the distinctive difference between Moghul cavalry and that of European armies in their methods of fighting. First of all, to show how formidable such solid but irregular bodies of cavalry. Yet a few European squadrons could ride them down and disperse them. There was a want of sympathy between the parts, and this prevented one part depending upon the assistance of another. Owing to its size, an army of Moghul horse could, for the moment, meet the attack of a small compact body by a portion only of its total strength, and since as against disciplined cavalry an equal front of an irregular body of troops can never stand the shock of an attack, the Moghuls were bound to give way. The whole being thus broken up into parts, the parts avoided exposure to the brunt of the action. The part actually attacked fled, but the parts not menaced did not combine to fall on the rear of the pursuers. On the other hand, the disciplined troops divided, reassembled, charged and halted on a single trumpet-call, and threatened each single part in turn. But if the drilled cavalry tried skirmishing, it was soon found that the Moghul horse, apparently so despicable, were most formidable in detail. In single combat a European seldom equalled the address of a native horseman.

The objective was the elephant of the opposite leader, and round it the fiercest of the battle raged. The centre was the ultimate object of attack and every effort was made to get closer and closer to it. As a rule, a battle in India was a series of isolated skirmishes, the contending bodies holding themselves at first at some distance from each other, and ending in close individual fighting. Numbers always decided the day, that the smaller invariably gave way before the larger force. Accident as frequently as not was decisive, while treacherous desertion or half-hearted support was a frequent occurrence.

The most decisive point of a battle was, however, the death or disappearance of the leader. If he was known to have been killed, or could not be seen on his elephant, the troops desisted at once, and the greater part forthwith sought their own safety in flight. In order to be conspicuous, the leader rode on an elephant, preceded by others bearing displayed standards. Later times Indian generals have abandoned the custom and now appear on horseback, nay have learned to discipline their troops and to have an artillery well served. The troops were very subject to panic and sudden flight. Many battles were lost by the event above referred to, the death or disappearance of the leader.

Untimely plundering - There was also an undisciplined eagerness to break off and begin plundering before the day was really decided. This habit often ended disastrously for those who had too easily assumed themselves to be the victors.

Single combat - Some times emperors of High rank officers challenged for single combat. For example Akbar challenged his opponent, Daud Lodi, to a fight in single combat. It does not appear that any of these duels actually took place. Challenges to single combat seem to have been not unusual between men of lower rank. Individual horsemen would ride up within speaking distance and, with contemptuous abuse of a mode of warfare excluding individual prowess, would give a general challenge to single combat.

The Utara Dismounting or fighting on foot, was a peculiarity of Indian horsemen of which they were very proud. It was specially affected among Indian Mahomedans by the Barhah Sayyads. It is a custom of the Hindu tribes. it was an old-established custom amongst their tribes . The Moghul horseman had to serve sometimes as infantry. It was a special feature of Rajput tactics.

This dismounting was resorted to at the crisis of a battle. When the horsemen alighted, they bound themselves together by the skirts of their long coats. There are many references to this mode of fighting in the descriptions of battles in the early part of the 18th century. The Persians in the Indian service scoffed at this habit, and attributed it not to valour but to defective horsemanship. This manoeuvre of utdra has the appearance of bravery and they boast of it. Some times men binding themselves together when fighting.

Some other technical terms of fighting There are several words and phrases which often occur in accounts of battles, and seem to have, in that connection, a more or less technical meaning. They are Harakat-i-mazbush- This means literally the expiring throes of a slaughtered animal, but seems used to express a feeble and hesitating attack, which is never carried home. The men made a feeble purposeless onslaught and were slain not by their own swords, but by those of their opponents.

Qazaqi - This is a military incursion, guerilla warfare, free-booting, brigandage. It may be a loose attack in open order, followed by retreat as soon as the attack has been delivered. It is used to surrounding and overpowering any body of men.

Talaqi-i-fariqain - It denotes that the two armies are in touch and within striking distance of each other. Siyah namudan - the first faint signs of an enemy's appearance in the distance. Hallah - An on-rush or charge.

Yurish - An on-rush or charge. Haiat-i-majmui - some sort of combined advance. Chapkunchi - a reconnaissance. Sipahi-i'falez - a defeated, non-resisting body of troops.

Defeat - In case of a reverse the heavy guns were generally abandoned, as they could not be removed. We are told that in such cases they were spiked and rendered useless. Generally, on the retreat of an Indian army, so great was the dispersion that some days elapsed before the direction of flight taken by the principal body could be ascertained.

There were no dispositions taken to cover its escape, no stratagems to mask its route, cover its baggage, gain an advance, lay an ambuscade, or mislead a pursuer. All impediments to flight were successively abandoned, and a retreat became a sauve qui pent. This result is attributable partly to the want of discipline and to defective leadership, which leaves every individual to rely more on himself than on his commander.

Juhar - This well-known Hindu practice of killing women and children to prevent their falling into the enemy's hand. Sometimes Mughals also followed this.

Proclamation of Victory - When the day was won, the victor ordered his drums to strike up and his horns to blow, both to announce the victory to his own side and to produce further dis heartenment among his opponents. Sometimes, to re-animate the drooping energies of his men, a general would order his drums to beat as for a victory, in the hope that they would be cheated into the belief that the day was going favourably for them, and thus inspirited, might turn an imagined into a real success.

Pillars of heads - It was the custom for a subordinate commander to accompany his despatch announcing any success with as many heads of the slain as could be collected. This was a survival of the Central Asian practice of erecting a pillar or pyramid formed of the heads of the dead enemy.

Stratagems, Losses

Reports of Battles - Somewhat in the same way that after a battle a modern general sends off a despatch to his superiors, a Moghul commander prepared and submitted a report to the emperor. Often he also drew up a separate description of the fight for distribution to his friends and equals.

These latter papers were styled a roll. If the emperor was especially satisfied with any general, he gave orders that the victory should be recorded in the imperial diary of proceedings, equivalent to our gazette.

Stratagems of War - Deceit and stratagem did not play a leading part in Moghul warfare. This may be so, still they were not unknown. Some men sed to join enemy force. In battle they desert enemy line and attack them. Ambush was not an uncommon stratagem. Matchlockmen were hidden in high crops, or on the edge of a ravine, at a spot where the opposite leaders would most probably pass. At the proper moment a volley would be discharged, and occasionally with deadly effect. An ambush was not unfrequently supplemented by pretended flight, so arranged as to draw the pursuers on and bring them under fire.

Some times they place a large body of army with enemies uniforms and symbols to cheat enemies. If enemy think that it was his allied force. Then he entered into the enemy plan. They may killed or made prisoner. When a leader took to flight on his elephant, it was not unusual for him to change places with the driver in order to escape molestation in case of pursuit and capture. Night surprises were also a form of stratagem not unfrequently employed.

Statistics of Losses - To obtain any idea of the numbers of killed or wounded is exccedingly difficult, historians either omitting to mention them, or if they do so, contradicting each other irreconcilably.

After a battle no attempts were made to ascertain the losses or count the slain. Any statements are mere guesses. They are much exaggerated for the defeated, and much diminished for the victorious army.

From these causes such statements are quite worthless, and can form no basis for the calculation of percentages, or suchlike strict arithmetical treatment. Incidentally, we learn from passing allusions the severity of the losses in a battle, or the number of the slain in some special group of those who were present. The battles in India were much less bloody than in Europe.

Slain and wounded - Plundering of the slain and wounded seems to have been universal. The camp followers were those chiefly concerned, but the fighting men were not above lending a hand. It was a legitimate source of income. The dead bodies left on a field of battle do not seem to have been usually buried, they were left to lie as they fell.

But sometimes their being collected in great pits, which were styled ganj-i-shahid, or martyr store-houses. The wounded seem to have been left mostly to their fate. There was no organization for their succour, nor any attempt to heal their wounds. This was left to their relations or friends.

Forts and Strongholds

As early as Alexander's time the Indians possessed walled and fortified towns. The practice of building such strong places was never abandoned, and by the sixteenth century, when the Moghul rule began, petty forts held by chiefs of Hindu clans or by grantees from Mahomedan sovereigns, were scattered thickly over the country. The Mahratta territory possessed so many fortressess.

In the plains of the Ganges and Indus, these forts were usually placed on an artificial mound, the earth for which was taken from the foot of the site, thus forming on one or more sides a large pond or marsh, which protected the fort from a sudden attack. As a rule these forts consisted of four high walls, enclosing a rectangular space.

They were provided with a bastion or tower at each corner. They had a fortified gate on one side, the entrance lane turning several times at right angles before arriving at the interior of the place. This narrow tortuous entrance lane was generally enfiladed with guns and loop-holed on every side. The gateways the strongest part of the Indian forts.

The outer walls were generally of clay and very thick. They were loop-holed for musketry, round earthen-ware pipes being inserted in the walls for this purpose. If the owner were lucky enough to have any wallpieces, they would be mounted on the flat roofs of the houses built against the inside of the wall.

These outer walls might be from twenty to thirty feet in height. Such a stronghold was safe against any small force, and with the means then in use, could hardly be reduced except by starvation. At the more important places they added one and sometimes two ditches, together with outworks, so as to render regular approaches necessary. In hilly country and in the Dakhin the fortresses were of much more elaborate construction.

Bound Hedge - As an additional protection, such places were often surrounded by a thick plantation of thorny trees or an impenetrable screen of bambus. Some of the latter were of great depth enemy troops came across bambu hedges which a cannonball was unable to penetrate. Quick-handed diggers and axemen were collected to cut this down and uproot these. it was a usual custom in Bundelkhand to protect a fort by a wide belt of thorny jungle. these jungles as retarding his operations considerably.

Going to an entirely different part of India, we find that the town adjoining the fortress of Ahmadnagar in the Dakliin had inside a low wall an immense prickly-pear hedge about twenty feet high. No human being could pass it without cutting it down, a work of the utmost difficulty, as it presented on every side the strongest and most pointed thorns imaginable. Being full of sap, fire would not act upon it, and an assailant while employed in clearing it, would be exposed to the enemy's matchlocks from behind it; thus it was stronger than any abbatis or other barrier. Good instance of the adoption of these protective belts of jungle in the case of Bobbili, 1.40 miles N. E. of Vizagapatnam, which was attacked by Bussy in 1757. Hill Forts- In the parts of India where detached eminences, often of great extent, are found, these were commonly selected for the sites of fortresses. The most celebrated of these in Northern India were the two forts of Ruhtas, one in the Panjab, the other in Bahar, Kalinjar in Bundelkhand, Chitor in Mewar. Further south there were Asirgarh in Khandesh, Daulatabad near Aurangabad, and many others equally celebrated. Forts on the tops of hills were extremely numerous in the Deccan. In that part of the country there was generally a walled town at the foot of the hills, and the fort itself was provided with two or more enceintes. In the Dakhin stone walls were common, that material being abundant. Many of these hill forts, if properly defended, were absolutely impregnable, unless by the tedious process of strict blockade. On the contrary, he thought the fortresses in the plains exceedingly weak.

Places of Refuge - Most of the petty semi-independent princes were careful to provide themselves with some fort or place of safety, generally situated in a country difficult of access and at some distance from their capital. Here their reserves of treasure and munitions of war were stored and carefully guarded. Ranthambhur used to furnish such a store-house for the rajahs of Jaipur.

Walled Towns - In the western half of Northern India, walled towns were frequent. All the principal places being provided with a high brick wall. In that part of the country, even the smallest village was capable of some defence, the flat-roofed, clay-built huts being huddled very close together, and the only entry being through a few narrow, tortuous paths between the houses. Some of the largest towns had walls as well as fortresses, as for instance Lahore and Delhi. At these places the fortress was built in one corner of the town, a continuation of the town wall forming its outer side. Such strongholds were palace as well as fortress, and covered

Rise of Mughal Empire

a considerable extent of ground. Other towns, such as Agrah and Allahabad, although they possessed first-classfortresses, had no wall round the town itself. In their case, the fortress stood apart from the rest of the town.

Descriptions of small Forts -

- Forts in Audh - The low bank of earth was the outer parapet of the fort of Amethi (insouth-east Audh), with a very deep ditch of irregular profile separating it from the level of the field. It wassome time ere we made out the entry. The gateway was approached by a dam across a ditch full of water, which was dominated by a bastion with the embrasures directed upon the dam. A sort of causeway at the other bank led us to a high gateway in a mud curtain, which was also flanked by a musketry fire and by a few embrasures. The lines of all the works were exceedingly irregular. The gates were of wood, studded and clamped with iron.
- Bundelkhand ordinary native fort - These forts are in general of mud, but from six to twelvefeet at the bottom of the wall are often of masonry. They are surrounded by a deep ditch, and the defences consist of small round-towers connected by curtains. Some of them have two or three lines of these walls and towers within each other. On the glacis are generally large excavations for grain; but this, of course, is only in dry situations. The mud walls receive the shot without being shattered, and they are in consequence very difficult to breach.
- General description of the small forts in the Dakhin - Imagine a mound of earth of about one hundred and fifty yards diameter and about sixty or seventy feet high. Then the sides of this are scarped off by labour, and the prominent parts shaped into flanking towers. Let the whole be reveted and surmounted by a parapet, and then only an entrance will be wanted. A gateway pierced in the revetement of a reentering angle, something lower than the interior of the fort, will form the inner communication, and on each side will be projected a tower to flank it and to plunge a fire into the next (gateway?). This will be found in a lower wall, the extremities of which will terminate in the revetement of the place, inclosing a small space ; and it will be likewise flanked by projecting towers, independent of the defences being loop-holed. These works, it is evident, may be frequently repeated; and the form of the traverses as well as the relative position of the gates continually varied;but

the general practice avoids placing two successive gates exactly opposite, and the outer aperture is invariably on lower ground than that next within, to favour the ascent. On some occasions so much earth may be scarped off as to form a high glacis, which makes the space left between it and the wall actually a ditch; but in very few cases is a ditch actually excavated round a garhi.

Imperial Fortresses - In the official manuals we have several lists of these places. The greater number of these forts were in the Dakhin, and in the better days of the Moghul period, the charge of them was committed to imperial officers called qilahdars, who were appointed direct from the capital, and were quite independent of the governor of the province. This arrangement was rendered necessary from the importance of these strongholds, both as a means of retaining hold of the country, and owing to their employment as great store-houses and arsenals. Moreover, if left under the control of a governor, he might be tempted to make a try for independence, when the possession of one of these fortresses would contribute largely to his chances of success.

Sieges

In India the art of fortification remained in the same state as it was in Europe before the introduction of the regular systems. The Indians placed their reliance more on a strong profile than on a judicious plan. They never realised the importance of the maxim that every work of a fortress should be flanked by some other. Nothing proved more forcibly their ignorance of the attack and defence of fortified places than their manifest superiority when acting on the defensive. A native army scarcely ever succeeded in taking a place which attempted resistance. It was generally reduced to terms through the distress caused by the force lying around it. On the contrary, some very vigorous defences had been made, prolonged by determined defence of the breach and by bold sallies to the trenches. Mining had found its way to some but not to all parts of India.

Strong places were most commonly reduced by strict investment and starving out. There were few captures by a coup de main (sar-i-suwari), the walls were not often breached, and rarely escaladed. Treachery within the walls was as frequent a cause of surrender as any other thing. In sitting down before a fortress, a Moghul army tried to surround it completely so as to prevent any ingress or egress. Earth works (murchal) were thrown up, in which the siege guns were placed. The system of digging approaches

Rise of Mughal Empire

and laying mines (naqb) was known and practised, at any rate in Northern India.

There was also a plan, to which recourse was sometimes had, of building high towers with the branches of trees, and when these were of a height to command the interior of the place, guns were mounted on them. These were called siba. Scaling ladders were not unknown, and were occasionally brought into use. Elephants were frequently brought up to batter in the wooden gates of a fort.

The gates always covered by some work, could not be broken in except by grenades or by pushing against them elephants, protected by iron, or by setting fire to them. It was as a protection against elephants that the gates were studded with iron spikes; to meet which it was the practice to furnish the elephant with an iron frontlet. Often the gateway was bricked up when a siege was imminent, and this device rendered it impossible to blow it in. when one of their armies sits down before a place, the object appears rather to be to harass the besieged and weary them out by a strict blockade, than to effect an entrance by breaching the walls: for although guns are used, they are placed at such a distance from the town, out of musket shot, and not always in battery, that their effect is uncertain, and even this desultory fire is only kept up at intervals during the day; for at night, to guard against the consequences of a sally, the guns are always withdrawn to the camp; and this ridiculous process is continued till the besieged are tired out, and a compromise is entered into.

The investment of an eastern fortress did not in general consist of anything beyond a blockade. The surrender of these forts has been caused more by treachery and scarcity than by any other means. This take a long years. The food of the Indians being almost entirely rice which is the least perishable of any article of subsistence, the defence of such places may be the longer protracted.

Though the natives did not understand the advantage of a glacis, still they saw the necessity of covering the foot of the wall from the enemy's fire when exposed to it, and formed a defence similar to a fausse-braye, which they call rainee. They are very partial to loopholes to fire through, Each of these narrow and confined [entrance] lanes is generally enfiladed with guns and loopholed on every side, so that should the enemy force the outer gate, they find themselves exposed to a continuation of fresh dangers from an invisible garrison at every turn.

The Indians, in the defence of their forts, behave with the greatest gallantry and courage, and in this differ from the Europeans, who often fancy that, when a practicable breach is made in their walls, surrender becomes justifiable. But here all feel desirous of fighting man to man, and look upon the contest in the breach as the fittest occasion for meeting their enemies with sword and dagger. They use large heavy wall pieces called gingalls. They send a ball of two or more ounces to a very considerable distance. Having no shells or handgrenades, they cast bags of gunpowder into the ditch, which exploding by fire thrown on them, scorch the assailants and at times they have recourse to thick earthen-ware pots with fuses and full of powder, the pieces of which wound dreadfully. They have been known to line the sides of the ditch with straw thatches, and by throwing other lighted thatch on their enemies, envelop them in flames.

Approach by Sap and Mine

The word used for the galleries of approach seems to have been sabat. sabat is a covered passage connecting two houses. The ordinary Hindi word for a mine is surang and surang urana is to spring a mine. This mode of attack was known and practised. For instance Sher Shah (1545-6) at the siege of Kalinjar advanced galleries (sabat) to the foot of the wall, and then prepared naqb, which appears to mean here mines, and not the mere digging through of a wall. Again at a siege of Budaon in 1555-6 the besiegers resorted to mining, and the commander of the garrison thwarted them by counter-mining, having detected the direction of their approach by putting his ear to the ground and listening. Some times besiegers mine under the walls. many Europeans are employed as sappers in Mughal Army.

Sabat - It is a trench or approach made in besieging a fortress. The sabat were constructed in the following manner. "The zigzags, commencing at gunshot distance from the fort, consist of a double wall, and by means of blinds or stuffed gabions covered with leather, the besiegers continue their approaches till they arrive near to the walls of the place to be attacked. A body of carpenters, stone-cutters, blacksmiths, excavators, earthworkers, and hovelmen were set to work to construct sabat These men laboured at making sabat and digging mines (naqb).

Sabat is the name for two walls which are made at the distance of a musketshot. Under the shelter of planks and baskets which are held together by skins, the said walls are carried close to the fort. Then the matchlock men and the mine-diggers (naqqab) come in safety, through the wide way between those walls, to the foot of the fort, and there they dig a mine and fill it with gunpowder. When the fort has been breached, the rest of the array reaches the spot by way of the sabat, and effects an entry into the fort. It was a trench begun at some distance from a fortress, deep and wide enough to conceal the workers, the excavated earth being thrown up on each side to increase the protection. In rocky soil it may have been necessary to form the protecting wall of material, such as planks, trees, or earth, brought from elsewhere. But in most instances the obvious and easy method was to dig a trench in the ground, and use the earth from it to heighten the sides. But a sabat was not a tower or erection, built up from the surface of the ground. Apparently open trenches were resorted to by the Mahrattahs so far back as 1670 at the siege of Karnala. They advanced by throwing up breastworks of earth.

Sandbags - In order to facilitate an attack, the ditch of a fort was at times filled up with sacks filled with earth.

Movable shields - Some time besiegers use movable wooden screens, or mantlets, mounted on ordinary cart-wheels. These they brought close to the walls, and from their shelter showered bullets and arrows on the besieged.. Mantlets in general come under Light Artillery.

Shatur - It was made of the trunks of trees, something connected with a siege. This is a shelther under which to approach the walls, something like the Roman vinea, a roof of planks and wicker work supported on poles eight feet long, and carried by the men as they advanced.

Malchar - The malchar was something in the nature of an approach by trenches.

Temporary wall - Another device was to surround a fortress with a temporary wall, leaving a few openings at which strong guards were posted, and no one was allowed to enter or come out without a pass. The materials employed were trunks of trees and clay.

Towers (Siba)

A building of high wooden towers, on which guns were mounted, the inside of the fortified place being thereby commanded, so as to make it untenable. At a distance of two arrows flight, batteries were erected of a size sufficient to allow of the guns being worked. They were about three cubits (42 feet) in height and in shape like bastions. A constant fire was kept up on both sides. Whenever a gunner shewed his head above the top of the earthwork, he would be fired at by one of the enemy concealed behind the battlements. In the same way a head showing above the wall was immediately fired at. The enemies answered shot for shot, and the imperialists were unable to move out to an attack in the open.

Some times the besiegers threw up chob-sibae, and drove subterannean passages towards each corner of the fort. These are the mounds of earth raised on the trunks of trees and placed from distance to distance round the fort.Some erect independent structures, and not part of a fortress.

Some times They filled up a house with earth, and on this as a base they raised a square mound, which commanded the gate and every part within the fort. Some times A vast mound of earth was raised to a level with the wall and the artillery mounted on it. Some times they constructed of the trunks of trees in successive layers, crossing each other and compacted by earth rammed between the intervals. The contrivances in the rear for raising the guns were removed when the erection was complete.

Storming-With the inefficient artillery of those days, a breach was very rarely effected, and we hear of very fewforts being actually stormed. Entrance was oftener secured through breaking in the gate, and for this purpose elephants were employed.

Scaling ladders - The name for scaling ladders was narduhan, Steingass, 1395. Babar mentions them more than once. From time to time they were used. They also used in later times. For instance, at the end of 1719, when Girdhar Bahadur was besieged in Allahabad fort by Haidar Quli Khan and other imperial officers, a general attack in two directions was ordered. One of these was headed by Sher Afgan Khan, Daud Khan, an officer under Muhammad Khan, Bangash, and others. They drove the besieged back to the very foot of the wall, then Daud Khan, Bangash, brought up the scaling ladders, hoping to make an entry, but after much struggle and effort, he was obliged to abandon the attempt.

Modes of repelling assault Burning oil, Powder Bags etc. - They has been made to the throwing down from the walls of bags of gunpowder and burning thatch. Huqqah-i-atash used for a similar purpose. At the siege of Chitor the Rajputs brought sacks of cotton cloth and fascines steeped in oil, which they endeavoured to set fire to while the breach was being stormed.

As to the throwing of skins full of gunpowder with a match attached. The defenders of a fort in the Dakhin in the fourth year of Shahjahan, From inside the fort they threw rockets and bullets and grenades and stones and lighted powder-skins. Some times huqqah or hand-grenade and the handi or firepot.

The people on the walls continually threw down upon their heads ponderous pieces of amber and flaming packs of cotton previously dipped in oil, followed by pots filled with gunpowder and other combustibles, the explosion of which had a terrible effect. Stones - Where the fort was on an eminence and stones were available, these latter were stored, and rolled down the hill upon any besieger. Sometimes defenders defend fort simply by(the garrison) rolling down stones and large masses of granite on the assailants.

Evacuation after a repulsed Assault - During siege they would silently evacuate the place they had defended so well. Naturally Europeans wondered and sought for a cause. The object did not seem to be to divert the attacking force from some enterprize of greater danger to the general cause. The effort was nearly always isolated and desperate. Why not abandon the place at once, or ask for terms? It seemed that it must be a point of honour with them to try their strength, and having proved their valour, they then withdrew.

Reduction by Starvation Many instances of this cause of surrender might be adduced. This was, for example, the principal reason of the surrender of Agrah in, when Nekusiyar, after laying claim to the throne, was invested in that fort by Husain Ali Khan. "After a month, provisions began to be scarce. Many of those who had joined from the country round began to desert, getting over the walls at night, only to be seized by the Nawab's sentries. These fugitives informed Husain Ali Khan of the disheartened and suffering condition of the garrison. All the good grain had been used up, and nothing was left but inferior pulses, and even these had been stored over seven years and smelt so strong, that even the fourfooted beasts would not eat them with avidity. Attempts were made to bring in small supplies of flour, which were dragged up by ropes let down from the battlements. Some of the artillery of the besieging force took part in this traffic. After this was found out, the strictness of watch was redoubled, anything moving in the river at night was fired upon, and expert swimmers were kept ready to pursue and seize any one who attempted to escape by way of the river. Negotiations commenced, and the fort was surrendered on the 12th Aug. 1719, after an investment of nearly three months.

2

The Founder of Mughal Empire: Babur

Mughal Emperor Babur, was the founder of Mughal Dynasty (Mughal Empire) in India. He was born in 1488 in a family of the Chaghtai Turks. On his father's side he was connected with Tamerlane and on his mother's side he could trace his origin from Chinghiz Khan. He lost his father when he was only eleven years old. From his father he inherited Farghana, a small principality of Turkestan.

In 1497, he conquered Samarkand, but he was unable to retain his kingdom for long. He, however, would not give it up as lost forever. He reconquered it only to lose it again. Baffled in his attempt to recover it, he turned his attention eastward and made himself king of Kabul in 1504. In 1522, he added Kandahar to his newly won kingdom.

He thereupon led several expeditions against the neighboring posts on Indian frontier. Soon after he received an invitation from Daulat Khan Lodi and Rana Sangram Singh to come and help them in a war against Ibrahim Lodi, the reigning Sultan of Delhi. To the adventurous nature of Babur, no invitation could be more tempting. He responded at once and came at the head of a well-equipped army. In the battle of Panipat (1526 A.D.) he defeated the last of the Delhi Sultans. He followed up his success by occupying Delhi and Agra.

But Babur now stood face to face with Rana Sanga. The Rana invited Babur in the hope that like Tamerlane his successor would retire after collecting spoils. But Babar had no intention of leaving India. Thus Sanga's dream of founding a neo-Hindu Empire on the ruins of Sultanate had little chance, of being fulfilled. A trial of strength between Babur and Sanga thus became inevitable. The encounter took place on the field of Khanua where Babur's military superiority won the day. On the field of Khanua was decided the fate of India. Babur occupied Chanderi and strengthened his position further by defeating his Afghan rivals in the Battle of Ghagra. In 1530, the founder of the Mughal Empire died.

Babur was an interesting and colourful personality. Beginning life as a soldier of fortune, he ended as the founder of one of the greatest empires of the cast. He was a tactful general, shrewd judge of man, and an enterprising and bold personality. To his military talents he combined the polished manners of a cultured gentleman. He possessed a fine literary taste and composed exquisite poems in Persian language. He was also conversant with a very elegant prose style, as revealed in his memoirs.

Historical Background of Babur

Babur was born on February 23 [February 14] 1483 in the town of Andijan, in the Fergana Valley in contemporary Uzbekistan. He was the eldest son of Omar Sheykh Mirza, ruler of the Fergana Valley, the son of Ab? Saa?d Mirza (and grandson of Miran Shah, who was himself son of Timur) and his wife Qutlugh Nigar Khanum, daughter of Yunus Khan, the ruler of Moghulistan (and great-great grandson of Tughlugh Timur, the son of Esen Buqa II, who was the great-great-great grandson of Chaghatai Khan, the second born son of Genghis Khan) Although Babur hailed from the Barlas tribe which was of Mongol origin, his tribe had embraced Turkic and Persian culture, converted to Islam and resided in Turkestan and Khorasan. His mother tongue was the Chaghatai language (known to Babur as Turki, "Turkic") and he was equally at home in Persian, the lingua franca of the Timurid elite. Hence Babur, though nominally a Mongol (or Moghul in Persian language), drew much of his support from the local Turkic and Iranian peoples of Central Asia, and his army was diverse in its ethnic makeup, including Tajiks (Sarts as called by Babur), Pashtuns (Afghans), Arabs, as well as Barlas and Chaghatayid Turco-Mongols from Central Asia.

Babur's army also included Qizilbash fighters, a militant religious order of Shi'a Sufis from Safavid Persia who later became one of the most influential groups in the Mughal court. Babur is said to have been extremely strong and physically fit. He could allegedly carry two men, one on each of his shoulders, and then climb slopes on the run, just for exercise.

Legend holds that Babur swam across every major river he encountered, including twice across the Ganges River in North India. His passions could be equally strong. In his first marriage he was "bashful" towards isha Sultan Begum, later losing his affection for her. Babur also had a great passion to kill people, cut heads of people and create pillars out of cut head. He claimed to have created several such pillars in his autobiography. Though religion had a central place in his life, Babur also approvingly quoted a line of poetry by one of his contemporaries: "I am drunk, officer.

Punish me when I am sobre." Babur related that one of his uncles "was addicted to vice and debauchery. He kept a lot of catamites. In his realm, wherever there was a comely, beardless youth, he did everything he could to turn him into one. During his time this vice was so widespread, that to keep catamites was considered a virtue." He gave up drinking alcohol only two years before his death for health reasons, and demanded that his court do the same. But he did not stop chewing narcotic preparations, and did not lose his sense of irony. He wrote: Everyone regrets drinking and swears an oath [of abstinence]; I swore the oath and regret that.

CONQUEST OF THE LODI EMPIRE

Writing in retrospect, Babur suggested his failure in attaining Samarkand was the greatest gift Allah bestowed him. Babur had now resigned all hopes of recovering Fergana, and although he dreaded an invasion from the Uzbeks to his West, his attention increasingly turned towards India and its lands in the east, especially the rich lands of the Delhi Sultanate.

Babur claimed to be the true and rightful Monarch of the lands of the Lodi dynasty. He believed himself the rightful heir to the throne of Timur, and it was Timur who had originally left Khizr Khan in charge of his vassal in the Punjab, who became the leader, or Sultan, of the Delhi Sultanate, founding the Sayyid dynasty. The Sayyid dynasty, however, had been ousted by Ibrahim Lodi, a Ghilzai Afghan, and Babur wanted it returned to the Timurids.

Indeed, while actively building up the troop numbers for an invasion of the Punjab he sent a request to Ibrahim; "I sent him a goshawk and asked for the countries which from old had depended on the Turk," the 'countries' referred to were the lands of the Delhi Sultanate. Following the unsurprising reluctance of Ibrahim to accept the terms of this "offer," and though in no hurry to launch an actual invasion, Babur made several

The Founder of Mughal Empire: Babur

preliminary incursions and also seized Kandahar - a strategic city if he was to fight off attacks on Kabul from the west while he was occupied in India - from the Arghunids. The siege of Kandahar, however, lasted far longer than anticipated, and it was only almost three years later that Kandahar and its Citadel (backed by enormous natural features) were taken, and that minor assaults in India recommenced. During this series of skirmishes and battles an opportunity for a more extended expedition presented itself.

Upon entering the Punjab plains, Babur's chief allies, namely Langar Khan Niazi advised Babur to engage the powerful Janjua Rajputs to join his conquest. The tribe's rebellious stance to the throne of Delhi was well known. Upon meeting their chiefs, Malik Hast (Asad) and Raja Sanghar Khan, Babur made mention of the Janjua's popularity as traditional rulers of their kingdom and their ancestral support for his patriarch Amir Timur during his conquest of Hind.

Babur aided them in defeating their enemies, the Gakhars in 1521, thus cementing their alliance. Babur employed them as Generals in his campaign for Delhi, the conquer of Rana Sanga and the conquest of India.

The section of Babur's memoirs covering the period between 1508 and 1519 is missing. During these years Shah Ismail I suffered a large defeat when his large cavalry-based army was obliterated at the Battle of Chaldiran by the Ottoman Empire's new weapon, the matchlock musket. Both Shah Ismail and Babur, it appears, were swift in acquiring this new technology for themselves. Somewhere during these years Babur introduced matchlocks into his army, and allowed an Ottoman, Ustad Ali, to train his troops, who were then known as Matchlockmen, in their use.

Babur's memoirs give accounts of battles where the opposition forces mocked his troops, never having seen a gun before, because of the noise they made and the way no arrows, spears, etc. appeared to come from the weapon when fired. These guns allowed small armies to make large gains on enemy territory. Small parties of skirmishers who had been dispatched simply to test enemy positions and tactics, were making inroads into India. Babur, however, had survived two revolts, one in Kandahar and another in Kabul, and was careful to pacify the local population after victories, following local traditions and aiding widows and orphans.

Who was Ibrahim Lodi?

Ibrahim Lodi was the last Sultan of Delhi Sultanate. He was defeated and killed in the First Battle of Panipat fought with Mughal Emperor Babur in 1526. He ascended the throne of Delhi in 1517 A.D., after the death of his father Sikandar Lodi.

Soon after his accession to the throne he had to march against his own younger brother who at the instigation of some nobles set himself as an independent king at Jaunpur. The headstrong Sultan could never tolerate such a thing, so he at once marched against his brother and after facing a good deal of trouble he was able to crush his rebellion.

The ill-fated prince was caught and beheaded by the Sultan's order. Then followed a reign of terror and the different nobles began to be insulted by him one by one.

The situation took such a serious turn that under the leadership of Azam Humayun and his son Islam Khan, who were deprived of their high posts and thereafter disgraced, there was raised a standard of revolt against the Sultan which caused him much trouble. Thousands of people perished in this desperate fight between the royalists and the rebels. At last the Sultan was victorious and most of the leaders of rebels were slain.

Now Ibrahim Lodi turned against all his relatives and chiefs alike. He lost his faith in them and began to punish both his friends and foes alike. As a result of these repressive and blind measures he turned all the Lodi, Luhani, Formuli and other powerful nobles into his worst enemies.

In Oudh, Jaunpur and Bihar, Darya Khan Luhani declared himself independent and in the Punjab, Daulat Khan Lodi asserted his independence when he came to know that his son Dilawar Khan was greatly insulted by the Sultan. Similarly Alam Khan, the Sultan's uncle, ran to the Punjab for his life. It was under these circumstances that Alam Khan and Daulat Khan Lodi invited Babur, the ruler of Kabul, to invade India.

BABUR IN INDIA

By the early 16th century the Muslim sultans of Delhi (an Afghan dynasty known as Lodi) are much weakened by threats from rebel Muslim principalities and from a Hindu coalition of Rajput rulers. When Babur leads an army through the mountain passes, from his stronghold at Kabul, he at first meets little opposition in the plains of north India. The decisive battle against Ibrahim, the Lodi sultan, comes on the plain of Panipat in April 1526.

The Founder of Mughal Empire: Babur

Babur is heavily outnumbered (with perhaps 25,000 troops in the field against 100,000 men and 1000 elephants), but his tactics win the day. Babur digs into a prepared position, copied (he says) from the Turks - from whom the use of guns has spread to the Persians and now to Babur. As yet the Indians of Delhi have no artillery or muskets. Babur has only a few, but he uses them to great advantage. He collects 700 carts to form a barricade (a device pioneered by the Hussites of Bohemia a century earlier). Sheltered behind the carts, Babur's gunners can go through the laborious business of firing their matchlocks - but only at an enemy charging their position. It takes Babur some days to tempt the Indians into doing this.

When they do so, they succumb to slow gunfire from the front and to a hail of arrows from Babur's cavalry charging on each flank. Victory at Panipat brings Babur the cities of Delhi and Agra, with much booty in treasure and jewels. But he faces a stronger challenge from the confederation of Rajputs who had themselves been on the verge of attacking Ibrahim Lodi. The armies meet at Khanua in March 1527 and again, using similar tactics, Babur wins. For the next three years Babur roams around with his army, extending his territory to cover most of north India - and all the while recording in his diary his fascination with this exotic world which he has conquered.

1ST BATTLE OF PANIPAT

Babur made four probing raids before the Battle of Panipat. Meanwhile some other disgruntled Afghan nobles invited Babur to invade India. Possibly Rana Sangram Singh of Mewar too had asked Babur to attack Ibrahim Lodi against whom he had a long-standing grudge. All of them hoped that Babur would leave India after defeating Ibrahim Lodi and plundering the country. But Babur had other intentions. He wanted to be the Padshah of India. With this purpose he proceeded towards India in November 1525.

First battle of Panipat took place between Babur and Sultan Ibrahim Lodi. It was fought in the year 1526 A.D. at Panipat, few miles away from Delhi. Babur's forces consisted of fifteen thousand men and had only fifteen to twenty pieces of field artillery. Lodi had one lakh men along with hundred war elephants. However Babur scored over Lodi because he had guns which he used to scare the elephants away. The scared elephants trampled Lodi's own men. For about a week, both the armies faced each other and engaged in skirmishes. The real battle started on the morning of 21 April 1526 A.D. and by noon it was over.

Ibrahim Lodi lay dead on the field and his army was destroyed. Ibrahim Lodi was abandoned by his vassals and generals. It marked the reign of the Mughals in India. The artillery, the Tulghuma method of warfare and superior generalship of Babur, on the one hand, and the weaknesses of Ibrahim Lodi, on the other hand, were responsible for the success of Babur in this battle. Babur was experienced and a more capable commander than Ibrahim whom he described in his Memoirs as "an inexperienced young man careless in his movements, who marched without order, halted or retired without method, and engaged without foresight." Babur had fine artillery, a more effective mobile cavalry and he used better war-tactics while Ibrahim had no artillery and fought in a traditional way depending on his war-elephants which having no experience of facing fire-arms and destroyed their own army in panic. Ibrahim's army was not well-organised. He had lost the sympathy of the Afghan-nobility as well as the loyalty of his subjects. Mostly his army consisted of hastily collected mercenary soldiers. Therefore, though the Afghans fought bravely, they proved no match to the well-trained army of Babur. The first battle of Panipat was significant in a way because it was one of the earliest battles which involved the use of gunpowder firearms and field artillery. The results of the battle of Panipat sealed the fate of Lodi dynasty in India. It was wiped out of Indian politics. The power of the Afghans was weakened in India though not completely destroyed. Babur soon occupied Delhi and Agra and thus laid down the foundation of the rule of the Mughal dynasty in India though he had yet to fight more battles to safeguard his claim over his Indian possessions.

CAUSES AND SUCCESS OF BABUR

Babur was successful in capturing Bhira (1519-1520), Sialkot (1520) and Lahore (1524) in Punjab. Finally, Ibrahim Lodi and Babur's forces met at Panipat in 1526. Babur's Soldiers were less in number but the organization of his army was superior. Ibrahim Lodi was defeated in the battle of Panipat. Success at the Battle of Panipat was a great achievement of Babur's military tactics. Babur had an active army of only 12000 soldiers while Ibrahim's army had an estimated strength of 100,000 soldiers.

When face to face in the battle field Babur's tactics were unique. He effectively applied the Rumi (Ottoman) method of warfare. He encircled

Ibrahim's army from two flanks. In the centre his cavalry mounted attack with arrows and gun fires by expert ottoman gunners. The trenches and barricades provided adequate defence against march of the enemy. The Afghan army of Ibrahim Lodi suffered heavy causalities. Ibrahim Lodi died in the battle field. Babur was thus able to take control of Delhi and Agra and got the rich treasure of Lodis. This money was distributed among Babur's commanders and soldiers.

BATTLE OF CHANDERI

They also reported that large masses of wood were being gathered and assembled and great fires blazing behind the main fort walls. Babar's troops meanwhile had in one night secretly cut a road through though the hill, which is now the road through the Kati Ghati (rock cut gate) in order to carry his cannons to high ground along a ridge near the fort. There he placed his cannons pointing at the fort. This spot was later named the Babar Kattan. Morning came and no word was received from Medini Rai. Babar took this as an acceptance of the terms of war and prepared his troops for battle. He sent lookouts to assess the situation. As the lookouts peered over the outer fort walls they were amazed to see the dead bodies of 100s of Medini Rai's troops. They had all taken swords to each other in mutual suicide by thrusting their weapons into each other. There were 1000s of dead Chanderi troops everywhere.

The lookouts reported back to Babar. And Babar writes in his memoirs that he then took the fort walls of Chanderi without ever having to sound his battle kettle drums. Babar's army virtually walked into the main fort. Now during the night the court of Medini Rai had decided that they could not surrender as this would mean that all of the woman would fall into the hands of the Muslim Mughal ruler. They feared the first choice also as they felt they would not be able to leave unmolested and the woman would again fall into Mughal hands. They also feared the third choice as they were unprepared for battle and if they lost the woman of the court would again be the spoils of warfare. So they made a fourth choice, they would take their fate into their own hands. In the night giant masses of wood were made into crematory piles and by different accounts between 600 to 1500 woman of the court including the queen committed jauhar, either throwing themselves into the fire or having themselves ritually killed and then cremated. They did this in order to protect their caste and honour. This act was one of the largest Jauhar rituals ever preformed in Indian history. Also as per Babur's account, that day 3000 of Medini Rai's troops preformed mass warrior suicide. Other accounts states that up to 6000 of Rai's troops died that day. It was an awful scene of death and sacrifice that met Babur as he entered the main fort. Then he writes that at this time there appeared the last of Medini Rai's troops numbering about 300 who were wielding their swords and met Babur's troops at full charge. Babur reports that their temperament was so fierce it threw his troops back and a frightening battle ensued with his army defeating Rai's. Babur had won Chanderi fort, it was the 28th of January 1528.

Babur's own account of the battle for Chanderi can be read in his memoirs. Babur appointed Ahmad Shah Khilji as administrator/ruler of Chanderi on payment of tax equaling 50 lakh in promise. Babur died in 1530 A.D. and his son Humayun became Emperor. Then the Malwa Sultan, Mallu Khan captured Chanderi, so Humayun sent his brother's, Askari Bagh and Hindal Mirza to recapture the town. After Humayun there were many rulers in Chanderi, one of them was Sher Shah Suri who ruled till 1546. And he was succeeded by Akbar. During Emperor Akbar's rule his historian Abu Fazal wrote about Chanderi. He states that Chanderi is a town worth visiting. That there are 14,000 stone built houses, 61 palaces, 384 bazaars, 350 camel caravan serai, 1200 mosques, 1200 step wells, 6659 cavalry, 5970 horse infantry, and 90 elephants. Abu Fazal also noted that the state of Chanderi's yearly income was 3,10,37,783 rupees. In 1605 the Mughal court handed over the rule of Chanderi to the Bundela Kings who ruled over Chanderi until 1858.Chanderi, the City of Weavers is the working title of the independent film and video documentary directed by Byron Aihara on the hand weavers of Chanderi, India, who make the world renowned Chanderi sari.

Lavish Lifestyle and Final Major Battle

Late in 1528 Babur celebrated a great festival, or *tamasha*. All nobles from the different regions of his empire were gathered, along with any noble who claimed descent from Timur or Genghis Khan. This was a celebration of his Khanal, Chingissid lineage, and when guests were sat in a semi-circle the farthest from Babur (who was, naturally, at the centre) was seated over 100 metres from him.

The huge banquet involved giving presents and watching animal fights, wrestling, dancing and acrobatics. Guests presented Babur with tribute of gold and silver, and were in turn presented with sword-belts and cloaks of honour (*khalats*). The guests even included Uzbegs (who under Shaybani Khan had ousted the Timurids from Central Asia and were now the occupiers of Samarkand) and a group of peasants from Transoxiana who were now being rewarded for befriending and aiding Babur before he was a leader.

After the festival, many of the other gifts given to Babur were sent to Kabul, "to adorn the ladies" of his family. Babur was far too generous concerning wealth, and by the time of his death the empire's coffers were almost empty; troops were even ordered to return a third of their income back to the treasury.

He was known to cough up blood, had numerous boils on his person, suffered from Sciatica and also bled fluid from his ears. He was a heavy drinker and took hashish, perhaps as a means of alleviating the various illnesses he suffered from. These substances were strictly forbidden by the orthodox doctrines of Islam, although in the *Baburnama* Babur does write without censure of relatives in Ferghana who indulged in strong liquor. Nevertheless, Babur, who had fought as a warrior for Islam, was now indulging in the forbidden (*Haraam*). The evening before the battle of Khanwua, he smashed his drinking cups vowing never to drink again-a vow he kept.

On May 6, 1529, Babur defeated Mahmud Lodi, Ibrahim's brother, who led an army of those disaffected with his rule, at the Battle of Ghaghra, thus crushing the last remnant of Lodi resistance in North India.

BATTLE OF GHAGHRA

The Rajputs were thus disposed of but Babur had still to deal with the Afghan rulers of Bihar and Bengal. In 1529 Babur defeated the combined Afghan forces at the Battle of Ghagra (May, 1529).

The Battle of Ghaghra, fought in 1529 and was the last major battle for the conquest of India by the Mughal Empire. It followed the first Battle of Panipat in 1526 and the Battle of Khanwa in 1527. The forces of now Emperor Zahir ud-Din Muhammad Babur of the emerging Mughal Empire were joined by Indian allies in battle against the Eastern Afghan Confederates under Sultan Mahmud Lodi and Sultanate of Bengal under Sultan Nusrat Shah.

Background

Sultan Mahmud Lodi, who aspired to the throne of Delhi and who had been declared the rightful heir to the Delhi Sultanate by the Western

Afghan Confederates and aided by the Rajput Confederates, was put to flight after the defeat at the Battle of Khanwa in 1527. He took refuge in Gujarat. After trying to get in touch with his kinsmen in the east he managed to join them. He at the head of the Eastern Afghan Confederates took Bihar. On the death of Sultan Muhammad Shah Lohani the Pathan king of Bihar of the new dynasty, an event which occurred some time after Babur's expedition to Chanderi, he was succeeded by his son Sultan Jalal ud-Din Lohani a minor, that the chief management of affairs at least in Bihar then devolved on that prince's mother Dudu and on Farid Khan better known as Sher Shah Suri who had already risen into distinction; that the country was distracted by the rival claims of the Lohani nobles related to the young King, of Baban and Bayezid whose influence was very extensive, of Sher Shah Suri and of other chiefs, and that these factions added to the effects of the discomfiture which the Pathans received in the preceding campaigns from the armies of Babur at length induced the young prince to take refuge in the territories of the Sultan of Bengal.

In this state of things the Afghans of Jaunpur and indeed of India in general, in order to avert the total ruin of their affairs and to unite all interests as far as was practicable resolved to call in Sultan Mahmud Lodi who had already with the support of Rana Sanga made an effort to mount the throne of Delhi.

When defeated in that attempt he had retired to Gujarat whence he afterwards proceeded to Pana in Bundelkhand where he remained waiting for some favourable change of affairs and now accepted the invitation to ascend the throne of Bihar and Jaunpur. He was speedily joined by his countrymen from every quarter and seems to have taken possession of nearly the whole of Bihar without opposition. What excites most surprise is the secrecy and success with which intrigues and movements so extensive appear to have been conducted a fact to be explained perhaps by the deep interest which every Pathan felt in the national success and the fidelity which tribesmen show to their chiefs and to each other. The very day after receiving this news Babur returned to Agra where he intimated to his council his resolution immediately to assume the command of the eastern army and accordingly taking with him such troops as were at hand he set out on February 2, 1529 and crossing the Doab reached the right bank of the Ganges at Dakdaki on February 27, 1529. Here he was met by his son Humayun, General Askari and several generals who came from the other side.

He arranged with them that while his army marched down the right bank of the river theirs should march down the left and should always encamp over against his. The information which he here received was but little satisfactory.

He found that the Pathans who were straining every nerve to recover their military and political ascendancy had gathered round Sultan Mahmud Lodi to the number of a 100,000 men that the Sultan had detached Baban and Sheikh Bayezid with a large force to Sirwar while he himself with Fateh Khan Shirwani the minister of Sultan Jalal ud-Din Lodi and of Sultan Ibrahim Lodi in succession by whom Mahmud had been joined and who had now deserted Babur as he had done his first master kept along the Bihar bank of the Ganges and was marching on Chunar that Sher Shah Suri, whom Babur had distinguished by marks of his favour having given him several perganas and entrusted him with a command, had joined the insurgents, had crossed the Ganges and occupied Benares from which the officers of Sultan Jalal ud-Din Sherki a descendant of the older dynasty of the country who held the city under Babur's authority had fled on his approach.

There were therefore at this time three competitors for the Eastern or Sherki kingdom

- Sultan Jalal ud-Din Sherki the representative of the older kings who ruled the country before it was conquered by Sultan Sikander Lodi. He had lately submitted to Babur and sought his protection. His claims had become rather obsolete but seemed to have been revived at this period, and acknowledged by Babur, evidently to serve an immediate purpose.
- Sultan Jalal ud-Din Khan Lohani whose father and grandfather had headed the revolt against Sultan Ibrahim Lodi. He was supported by many Afghan nobles in Bihar but had lately been forced to seek refuge with the Sultan of Bengal his ally.
- Sultan Mahmud Lodi the brother of the late Sultan Ibrahim Lodi and the representative of the Lodi dynasty of Delhi whom the great body of the Pathans had now united to support in his claims not on Bihar merely but on Delhi itself.

Babur informed of the real state of affairs continued his march down the banks of the Ganges. In passing Karra he was magnificently entertained by Sultan Jalal ud-Din Sherki the prince whose pretensions he favoured and on whom he bestowed the nominal command of a division of his army. When he had made a march or two below that city the effects of his activity became visible. He learned that Sultan Mahmud Lodi who had recently advanced to Chunar and even made an assault upon it had no sooner received certain information of the Emperor's approach than filled with consternation he raised the siege and retreated in confusion and that Sher Shah Suri had in like manner abandoned Benares and recrossed the river with such precipitation that two of his boats were lost in the passage. The imperial army having reached Allahabad where the Ganges and Yamuna rivers unite, their streams began on March 10, 1529 to cross the latter river to Priag whence Babur proceeded by Chunar, Benares and Ghazipur hastening to attack Sultan Mahmud who had now taken a position behind the Son River. At Ghazipur, Mahmud Khan Lohani an Afghan of influence came and submitted to him and while yet near the same place Sultan Jalal ud-Din Khan Lohani the expelled prince and still one of the competitors for the throne of Bihar, Sher Shah Suri the future sovereign of Delhi and other Afghans of influence sent to tender their submission. This amounted to a breaking up of the Lohani dynasty of Bihar leaving only Sultan Mahmud Lodi and his adherents to be combated.

Babur now proceeded to cross the Kermnas and encamped beyond Chousa (that was to become celebrated by the calamity of his son) and Baksara or Buxar. Marching thence he found that Sultan Mahmud whose army had been daily suffering from defection and who had been lying not far off attended by only 2000 men had retired with precipitation on the approach of an advanced party of the imperial army had been pursued and several of his men slain. He also now took refuge with the army of Bengal which had crossed the Ganges probably in the intention of co operating with him. Babur proceeded to the district of Ari in Bihar lying between the Ganges and the Son River at their confluence where he invested Muhammad Zaman Mirza with the government of Bihar and fixed the revenue to be paid out of that province.

The Emperor had now arrived opposite to where the Ghaghara River (also called Gogra in some texts) joins the Ganges from the north east and where apparently the kingdom of Bengal commenced on the left bank of that river. Here he learned that Sultan Mahmud Lodi was in the Bengal camp at the junction of the two rivers with a body of Afghans and that when he and his followers wished to remove their families and baggage they were not permitted by the Bengalis probably wishing to retain them as hostages Sultan Jalal ud-Din Khan Lohani his rival who had lately sent

The Founder of Mughal Empire: Babur

his submission to Babur was in like manner hindered from departing in consequence of which he had come to blows with the Bengalis had effected a passage over the Ganges into Bihar with his followers and was on his march to join the imperial army. The Emperor therefore who considered that the position of the army of Bengal and the conduct of its leaders had violated their neutrality prepared to call them to account. Nusrat Shah, the Sultan of Bengal had recovered some of his lost territories from the Pathans after the collapse of the Delhi Sultanate.

Battle

Babur found the army of Kherid, as the Bengal army was called, lying between what is at present the territory of Saran. It was encamped near the junction of the Ganges and the Ghaghara River so as to be able to defend both the course of the Ghaghara River and the left bank of the Ganges after the union of the two rivers. He discovered too that the Bengali generals had collected about a 100-150 vessels on their side of the stream by means of which they were able at once to hinder the passage of an enemy and to facilitate their own.

Such an army he could not safely leave behind especially as the troops of Baban and Bayezid had also taken refuge upon and in strength occupied the upper course of the Ghaghra River. He was indeed at peace with Bengal but the shelter afforded to his flying enemy the position of the Kherid army and the equivocal conduct of its leaders made it indispensable that he should have a categorical declaration as to the disposition and intention of the Bengali government.

He therefore dispatched an envoy to Nusrat Shah the Sultan of Bengal. Babur was now joined by Sultan Junaid Birlas from Jaunpur with about 20,000 men. The tardy arrival of these troops subjected their commander to a temporary disgrace. Not having received a satisfactory answer to his demands, the Emperor resolved to compel the army beyond the Ghaghra River to quit its strong position. He made the necessary arrangements for the intended attack. He formed his army into six divisions Four of these consisting of Askari's army which was already on the left bank of the Ganges and of Sultan Junaid's which had recently joined on the same side were ordered to be prepared to cross the Ghaghra River either in boats at Haldi or by fording still farther up that river. Askari was the youngest son of Babur. The other two divisions were still on the right bank of the Ganges. One of these under the Emperor's personal direction was to effect the passage of that river and then to cover the operations of Ustad Ali Kuli his chief engineer and commander of the Artillery who was directed to plant a battery on the banks of the Siru or Ghaghra River above its union with the Ganges directly opposite to the Bengali camp which it would be able to cannonade and afterwards to cover the passage of the Emperor's division when it crossed the Ghaghra River to attack the enemy.

Mustafa Rumi another engineer who had a party of musketeers and artillery supported by Muhammad Zaman Mirza and the sixth division was to open a cannonade on the flank of the enemy's camp from the Bihar bank of the Ganges below the junction of the rivers. The main body of the army which was that under Askari after passing the Ghaghra River at Haldi was ordered to march down upon the enemy so as to draw them from their camp and induce them to march up that river and by this diversion to keep them occupied until the two divisions of Babur and Muhammad Zaman under cover of the fire of the artillery and matchlock men could be transported across. The whole army was accordingly put in motion Askari's four divisions marched for Haldi.

The batteries both on the Ghaghara River and Ganges were constructed and commenced their fire. The Bengali army behaved with great bravery and pushed parties across to attack the Emperor's troops both above and below the junction of the rivers. At length after various movements Babur received notice that Askari had effected a passage over the Ghaghra River at the Haldi Ghat and was now ready for action and that he had been strengthened by the defection of Shah Muhammad Maaruf an Afghan nobleman of the highest rank and consequence who had deserted the confederacy with his followers and now joined his camp. The general attack was therefore fixed for next morning but in the meantime there was some fighting between the vessels in the river. On the morning of May 6, 1529 as soon as Askari's army was known to be in motion the Bengali troops moved up to meet him whereupon Babur ordered both his division and that of Muhammad Zaman to cross over without delay.

This was affected bravely though not without sharp resistance. The troops got across some in boats, some by swimming, some floating on reeds. They were met with equal gallantry on landing but kept together formed and made repeated vigourous charges. As Askari advanced downwards the enemy finding themselves surrounded and driven in on three sides finally quit the field in confusion.

Aftermath

This victory was decisive in its consequences. Numbers of the Afghans who till now had been refractory having lost all hope of re establishing an Afghan government in the East submitted and Sultan Jalal ud-Din Khan Lohani the late King of Bihar whose escape from the Bengali camp has been mentioned arrived with many of his principal Amirs and acknowledged Babur. Other chiefs imitating their example petitioned to be received into the Emperor's service. 7000-8000 Lohani Afghans had already joined him and were now rewarded and employed.

The feuds between the Lohani and Lodi factions in the Eastern provinces were fatal to the Pathan national interest. As for the Sultan of Bengal Nusrat Shah, he hastily accepted peace proposals, previously communicated to him via the envoy Babur had sent before the battle. This would be Baburs' last major engagement. He continued to consolidate his power and establish administrative infrastructure in his new Empire distributing jagirs (Estates) to loyal nobles and allies. He died at the age of 47 on December 26, 1530 of an unknown illness and was succeeded by his eldest son, Humayun.

AS A LOVER OF ART

Babur had a great love for fine arts and architecture. There was unprecedented growth of fine arts during the very short period of Babur's Rule. He patronized the art of painting. He had to taste for music also. He got constructed many beautiful buildings in Gwalior, Daulpur and Agra.

Narrating his contribution in the field of architecture he has said in his Tuzuk-i-Baburi, "680 labourers used to work everyday on my buildings at Agra while 1941 stone cutters worked everyday on my buildings at Sikri. Bian, Daulpur, Gwalior and Kol (Aligarh)." It is said that he had invited master architects from Constantinople to plan an execute his building projects.

Estimating the personality of Babur, Lanepoole says, "Babur is perhaps the most captivating personality in the Oriental history." Though Babur cannot be said to be the Real Founder of the Mughal Dynasty in India yet he holds a high place in the Indian History. No one can deny the fact that he laid the Foundation of the Mughal Rule in India through his conquests.

BATTLE OF KHANWA

The victory at Panipat, however, did not make Babur's position secure. He had yet to defeat Rana Sangram Singh (or Rana Sanga) of Mewar, and the Afghan chiefs of Eastern India. Rana Sanga, who also had asked Babur to invade India, thought that after plundering Babur would go back to Kabul. But Babur's decision to stay in India spurred the Rana to action. Some Afghan chiefs also joined him. When Babur was informed of the Rana's war-like preparations, he adopted a policy of conciliation toward the petty Afghan Chiefs and declared war against Rana Sanga. The two armies met at Khanwa on March 17, 1527. The Rajputs fought with their traditional bravery but they could not withstand the deadly artillery fire. In this hotly contested fight the Rajputs suffered disastrous defeat with heavy loss of life. Rana Sangha escaped and died broken-hearted. With his death the dream of a Rajputs empire received a serious setback. In celebration of this victory Babur assumed the title of Ghazi.

The Battle of Khanwa also spelled as Khanua in some texts, was the second in a series of three major battles, victories in which gave Zahir ud-Din Babur overlordship over North India. The Battle of Panipat was the first of the series, the Battle of Ghaghra was the last. This battle was fought near the village of Khanwa, about 60 km west of Agra on March 17, 1527. Babur defeated a formidable army raised by Rana Sanga of Mewar in this ten hour battle and firmly established his rule over northern India. Babur's grandson Akbar the Great established the city and fort of Fatehpur Sikri in honour of his grandfather's victory in this battle.

Background

Maharana Sangram Singh better known as Rana Sanga was the ruler of Mewar, a region lying within the present-day Indian state of Rajasthan, between 1509 and 1527. He was a scion of the Sisodia clan of Suryavanshi Rajputs.

He defended his kingdom bravely from repeated invasions from the Muslim rulers of Delhi, Gujarat and Malwa. He was one of the most powerful of the Hindu kings of that time. Above all, his continued expansion helped him unite the Rajputs under one confederacy. This war was not the first event that introduced the two formidable commanders Rana Sanga and Babur. Before Emperor Babur had set out from Kabul, his new dominion, on his last Indian expedition he had received from the Rana an embassy conveying expressions of regard and it seems to have been

The Founder of Mughal Empire: Babur

arranged that while Babur attacked Sultan Ibrahim Lodi by marching upon Delhi, Rana Sanga was to attack him on the side of Agra.

Babur on his part complains that while he advanced and occupied these two capitals the Rana did not make a single movement. On the other hand the Rana complained of broken faith and in particular claimed Kalpi, Dholpur and Biana as his by agreement all of which had been occupied by Babur. And as Agra itself had till recent times been considered as only a dependency of Biana that city might also have been understood to accompany it.

Successes of the mighty power of the Rana might seem to justify at once his hopes of seating himself on the vacant throne of the Lodi's and his more glorious ambition of expelling both the Afghan and the Turkic-Mongol invaders from India and restoring her own Hindu race of kings and her native institutions. In the meanwhile however he acknowledged Sultan Mahmud Lodi the son of Sultan Sikandar Lodi who had been set up by the Western Afghan Confederates as the legal successor of Sultan Ibrahim Lodi. The preparations made by Rana Sanga evidently with the intention of marching towards Biana had induced Babur not only to collect a strong force near Agra for the purpose of repelling his attack but hastily to recall Humayun from Jaunpur.

Soon after Rana Sanga was joined by Raja Hasan Khan Meo of Meo Rajputs who are Muslims of Indian descent, and ethnic cousins of the Jat and Gujjar castes. Raja Hasan Khan was ruler of Mewat a region lying south of Delhi, spread across south Haryana and northeast Rajasthan. This news was particularly unwelcome to the Emperor Babur. The Khan was a chief of great power and influence. At the Battle of Panipat his son Naher Khan had been made prisoner and he had ever since kept up a friendly correspondence with the Emperor and a negotiation for his release. Babur hoping that if he set the son at liberty he would attach the father by the strongest ties of gratitude invested Naher Khan with a dress of honour and sent him back to his father. But though the son had made the fairest promises no sooner did the old man hear that he was out of Babur's hands and on his way to join him than without even waiting to see him he marched from Alwar his capital and joined the Rana Sanga.

Initial Skirmishes

On February 11, 1527, the Emperor Babur marched out of Agra to proceed against Rana Sanga but halted a few days near the city to collect and review his troops, and to get in order his train of artillery, the baggage and camp followers. As in this warfare he had little reliance on the Afghan chiefs or his Indian allies who had joined him, he sent several of them to strengthen his various garrisons.

He then marched westward to Medhakur where he had previously caused wells to be dug and thence next day to Fatehpur Sikri which from its having plenty of water he considered as a good situation for a camp but being apprehensive that the Rana who was now near at hand might attempt to occupy the ground before his arrival he marched out with his troops in order of battle ready to attack the enemy should they appear and took possession of the place which had been chosen for his encampment close by a tank.

He was now joined by Mahdi Khwaja and the troops from Bayana which he had called in. They had had some sharp encounters with the Rajputs in which they had been severely handled and taught to respect their new enemy. A party from the garrison had some days before incautiously advanced too far from the fort when the Rajputs in great force fell upon them and drove them in.

All the troops that had been engaged in this affair united in bestowing unbounded praise on the gallantry and prowess of the enemy. Indeed the Chagatai Turkic-Mongols found that they had now to contend with a foe more formidable than either the Afghans of India or any of the natives of India to whom they had yet been opposed. The Rajputs energetic chivalrous fond of battle and bloodshed animated by a strong national spirit and led on by a hero were ready to meet face to face the boldest veterans of the camp and were at all times prepared to lay down their life for their honour. A small party being sent out to get notice of their motions discovered that they were encamped at Bisawer.

Emperor Babur was accustomed to commit to his principal Baigs in turn the charge of the advance and pickets. When it was Mir Abdal Aziz's, day that rash and impetuous youth pushed on seven or eight miles from Fatehpur Sikri. The Rajputs hearing of this incautious forward movement dispatched to meet him a body of 4000-5000 horsemen who without hesitation charged the instant they came up.

His force did not exceed a 1000-1500. Many of his men were killed others taken prisoners and carried off the field on the very first onset. The moment the news of what was going on reached the camp, Mohib Ali Khalifa Emperor Babur's Grand Vizier's son and his followers were

The Founder of Mughal Empire: Babur

pushed forward to their assistance and there being no room for delay, numbers of separate horsemen, as fast as they were equipped, were sent off at the best of their speed while a regular detachment under Muhammed Ali moved forward to support them Mohib Ali who arrived first found every thing in disorder.

Mir Abdal Aziz's horse tail standard taken and many excellent officers slain. Not only was he unable to turn the tide of success but was himself unhorsed though finally brought off by a desperate charge of his followers. The Emperor's troops were then pursued for about two miles and it was only the arrival of the regular detachment under Muhammad Ali that checked the enemy. Meanwhile when the alarm reached the camp the whole troops were called out and marshaled in battle order to meet the hostile army which was thought to be approaching. But after the imperial line had advanced a mile or two with all its artillery it was found that the enemy satisfied with their success had returned to their camp. These repeated successes of the Rajputs, the unexpected valor and good conduct they displayed and their numbers for they are said to have amounted to a 120,000 horsemen along with their Mewat allies would have been one of the largest armies Babur had ever had to face, even in modern times such a huge army would have disheartened any battle hardened soldier. Babur began to see the discouragement of his troops.

Every precaution was now taken to strengthen his position and to give his troops time to recover their spirit. At this critical juncture he received a small yet welcome reinforcement of 500 men from Kabul. Babur decided to divert the attention of the enemy towards Mewat by sending some troops there, to ravage the territory. But the diversion did not answer his expectations.

Babur Rallies his Troops

Babur was now in some measure cooped up in his camp while the enemy was in possession of the open country. The uneasiness which he in consequence experienced in this state of inaction appears very naturally to have excited feelings of religious compunction in his mind. When he reviewed his past life he keenly felt that he had long and openly violated one of the strictest injunctions of his faith by the use of wine. Like other habitual offenders he had all along firmly resolved to give up the evil custom at some future time but that time had been constantly deferred. He now resolved to perform his vows. Babur said;

- Having sent for the gold and silver goblets and cups with all the other vessels used at drinking parties I directed them to be broken up and renounced the use of wine purifying my mind. The fragments of the goblets and other gold and silver drinking vessels I directed to be divided among derwishes and the poor. The first person who followed me in my repentance was Asas who also accompanied me in my resolution of ceasing to cut the beard and of allowing it to grow.

This was a visible sign commonly adopted by such as were under the influence of a vow. Many nobles and others to the number of 300 followed the example of their sovereign. Salt was thrown into the ample store of wine just arrived from Ghazni all the rest found in the camp was poured upon the ground and a well was ordered to be dug and an almshouse built on the spot to commemorate this great religious event of repentance. As a boon to his Muslim followers and subjects he gave up the Temgha or stamp tax in all his dominions so far as concerned Muslims and published a firman (royal edict) to that effect on February 26.

The dejection and alarm of Babur's troops had at this time reached their extreme point. The contagion had infected even his highest officers. He excepts only Mir Ali Khalifa his Grand Vizier who he says all along behaved admirably. Babur whose bold and elastic mind never gave admittance to despair but even in the lowest depths of danger turned to any gleam of hope saw that matters were fast advancing to a crisis and that some stirring and energetic measures were indispensably required. He determined to make a bold exertion to infuse a portion of his own heroic ardor into the drooping spirits of his followers and for that purpose he addressed himself to the religious feelings so powerful with all Muslims but especially with such as are engaged in a Jihad against infidels.

He thus made the most famous and most important speech of his life;

- Noblemen and soldiers! Every man that comes into the world is subject to dissolution When we are passed away and gone, Allah survives One and Unchangeable. Whoever sits down to the feast of life must, before it is over, drink of the cup of death. He who arrives at the inn of mortality, the world must one day without fail take his departure from that mansion of sorrow. How much better then is it to die with honour than to live with infamy

Babur's Advance

With his troops now in high spirits Babur decided to advance from the entrenchments in which the army had so long been cooped up. It was on March 12, 1527 that Babur drew forward his guns and a kind of defensive cover that moved on wheels and which served as a breastwork supporting them by his matchlock men and all his army. He himself galloped along the line animating his troops and officers and giving them instructions how to conduct themselves in every emergency that could occur. The army having advanced a mile or two halted to encamp. As soon as the Rajputs heard that they were in motion several bodies of them galloped close up to the guns.

Babur not intending to engage in a general action that day quietly finished his entrenchments and ditches and then sent out a few horsemen to skirmish with them and try the temper of his men.

They took several prisoners and returned with a number of heads elevated on their spears or dangling from their saddle bows which had a wonderful effect in restoring the confidence of the troops. He now threw up other trenches in a position about a mile or two farther in advance near the spot which he had pitched upon as favourable for a general engagement and when they were finished advanced to occupy them dragging forward his guns. His people having reached their ground were still busy in pitching their tents when news was brought that the enemy was in sight. All were instantly ordered to their posts. Babur mounted and drew up his troops riding cheerfully along the ranks and confidently assuring them of victory.

Battle Positions of Babur

The center Babur took to himself assisted by Chin Taimur Sultan the right wing he committed to Humayun who had under him Kasim Hussein Sultan, Hindu Baig and Khusroe Kokultash the left wing he entrusted to Syed Mehdi Khwaja with Muhammad Sultan Mirza, Abdal Aziz and Muhammad Ali.

He appointed strong reserves to carry out rescue efforts wherever required. On the right and left placed two flanking columns chiefly composed of Mughal troops who formed what is called the Tulughma and were on a signal given to wheel round on the enemy's flank and rear in the heat of battle. This arrangement he had learned to his cost in his early wars with the Uzbeks and he had practiced it in his later wars with brilliant success. His Indian allied troops appear to have been stationed chiefly in the left. His artillery under Ustad Ali Kuli was placed in the center in front connected by chains and protected by the moveable defences or breastworks which he had constructed, behind which were placed matchlock men and in their rear a body of chosen troops ready either to repel any attack from behind or themselves to rush forward and charge the enemy whenever the chains that connected the guns were dropped to permit their passage. The army abounded with veteran commanders who had learned the art of war under the Emperor himself.

Battle Positions of Rana Sanga

In the Rajput army the commanders under Rana Sanga were generally great chieftains who from their territorial possessions could bring a large force into the field. Thus Silhadi a Tomar Rajput chieftain of northeast Malwa the Chief of Bhilsa is rated at 30,000 Purabiya Soldiers; Hasan Khan of Mewat 12,000; Raul Uday Singh Nagari of Dongerpur 10,000; Medini Rao the Chief of Chanderi 10,000. The first and last of these had acted an important part in the history of Malwa.

Sultan Mahmud Lodi a son of Sultan Sikander Lodi of Delhi who was acknowledged by the Afghans of the Delhi kingdom and by the Rana as the successor of his brother Ibrahim Lodi though he possessed no territory yet had with him a body of 10,000 adventurers who hoped to be liberally rewarded should fortune raise him to the throne. There were other chiefs who could command each from 4000-7000 men and all were animated by the most exalted hopes and by hatred of the common enemy. They also possessed 500 war elephants and included 7 Rajas, 9 Raos and 104 Rawals and Rawats (lesser chieftains). A more gallant army could not be put into the field.

The Battle

Khanwa is about 60 km west of Agra. Here the epic battle between the Muslim Mughals and the Hindu Rajputs would play out. The battle began about 9:30 in the morning by a desperate charge made by the Rajputs on Babur's right. Bodies of the reserve were pushed on to its assistance and Mustafa Rumi who commanded one portion of the artillery on the right of the center opened a fire upon the assailants. Still new bodies of the enemy poured on undauntedly and new detachments from the reserve were sent to resist them. The battle was no less desperate on the left to which also it was found necessary to dispatch repeated parties from the reserve. When the battle had lasted several hours and still continued to rage, Babur sent orders to the flanking columns to wheel round and charge and he soon after ordered the guns to advance and by a simultaneous movement the household troops and cavalry stationed behind the cannon were ordered to gallop out on right and left of the matchlockmen in the center who also moved forward and continued their fire hastening to fling themselves with all their fury on the enemy's center.

When this was observed in the wings they also advanced. These unexpected movements made at the same moment threw the enemy into confusion. Mughal cannon fire caused the elephants in the Rajput army to stampede. Mughal cavalry archers made repeated flanking charges from the left and right of their fortified position. These mounted archers inflicted maximum losses on Rajput ranks, as the latter were not accustomed to these tactics, their center was shaken, the men who were displaced by the attack made in flank on the wings and rear were forced upon the center and crowded together. Still the gallant Rajputs were not appalled. They made repeated desperate attacks on the Emperor's center in hopes of recovering the day but were bravely and steadily received by the Mughals and swept away in great numbers. Towards evening the Rajput defeat was complete and the slaughter was consequently dreadful. The fate of the battle was decided. Nothing remained for the Rajputs to do but to force their way through the bodies of their kinsmen and enemy that were now in their rear and to affect a retreat. Emperor Babur pursued them as far as their camp which was about three or four miles from his own. On reaching it he halted but detached a strong body of horse with orders to pursue the broken troops of the Rajput Confederates without halting to cut up all they met and to prevent them from re assembling. But Rana Sanga escaped. Babur later mentions his regret in not going with the detachment in pursuing the broken Rajput troops because of Rana Sanga's escape.

Aftermath of Battle

No victory could be more complete. The enemy were quite broken and dispersed. The whole fields around were strewed with the dead as well as the roads to Bayana and Alwar. Among the slain were Hasan Khan who fell by a matchlock shot, Raul Uday Singh of Dongerpur, Rai Chanderbhan Chauhan, Manikchand Chauhan (later awarded Kotharia jagir posthumously) and many other chiefs of note. Clearly Babur's superior leadership and modern technology won the day. Babur henceforth assumed the proud title of Ghazi (Victorious Veteran of Jihad).

As for Sultan Mahmud Lodi, he also fled eastwards and would again pose a challenge to Babur two years later at the Battle of Ghaghra. Since the time Babur had left Agra for this battle, insurrection and revolt appeared on every hand. The towns and forts of which with so much labour he had gained possession were fast changing masters. Raberi and Chandwar on the Yamuna River; Koel in the Doab and Sambhal beyond the Ganges all of them near Agra had been retaken by the Afghans. His troops had been obliged to abandon Kanauj. Gwalior was blockaded by the Rajputs of the vicinity Alim Khan Jilal Khan Jighat of Kalpi who was sent to relieve it instead of executing his orders had marched off to his own country. Many Hindu chiefs deserted the cause of Babur. Indeed the previous conquests and recent success of Rana Sanga a Hindu had inspired all his countrymen with hopes that a change of dynasty was about to take place and they hailed with joy the prospect of a native government.

But after the battle of Khanwa, Babur sent forces to chastise the insurgents and quickly retook lost territories. Being now disengaged of his most formidable enemies he was enabled to send a force to recover Chandwar and Raberi places not far distant from Agra of which the insurgents had made themselves masters during his operations against Rana Sanga. The consternation occasioned by his success was such that this object was affected with little difficulty and even Etawah lower down the Yamuna which had never yet submitted to his power, was surrendered by Kutb Khan. Rana Sanga died shortly after this battle in 1527 at Baswa on Mewar's northern border.

THE FAMILY TREE OF BABAR

Although Babar hailed from the Barlas tribe which was of Mongol origin, his tribe had embraced Turkic and Persian culture, converted to Islam and resided in Turkestan and Khorasan. His mother tongue was the Chaghatai language (known to Babar as Turkî, "Turkic") and he was equally at home in Persian, the lingua franca of the Timurid elite.

Hence Babar, though nominally a Mongol (or Mughal in Persian language), drew much of his support from the local Turkic and Iranian people of Central Asia, and his army was diverse in its ethnic makeup. It included Persians (known to Babar as "Sarts" and "Tajiks"), ethnic Afghans, Arabs, as well as Barlas and Chaghatayid Turco-Mongols from Central Asia. Babar's army also included Qizilbâsh fighters, a militant religious order of Shi'a Sufis from Safavid Persia who later became one of the most influential groups in the Mughal court.

The Founder of Mughal Empire: Babur

Babar claimed in his memoir to be strong and physically fit; claiming to have swam across every major river he encountered, including twice across the Ganges River in North India. His passions could be equally strong. In his first marriage he was "bashful" towards Aisha Sultan Begum, later losing his affection for her. Babar also had a great passion to kill people, cut heads off people and create pillars out of the cut off heads. He claimed to have created several such pillars in his autobiography.

Though religion had a central place in his life, Babar also approvingly quoted a line of poetry by one of his contemporaries: "I am drunk, officer. Punish me when I am sober". He quit drinking alcohol before the Battle of Khanwa, only two years before his death for health reasons, and demanded that his court do the same. But he did not stop chewing narcotic preparations, and did not lose his sense of irony. He wrote, "Everyone regrets drinking and swears an oath (of abstinence); I swore the oath and regret that."

Babar's early relations with the Ottomans were very troubling because the Ottoman Sultan Selim I provided his arch rival Ubaydullah Khan with powerful matchlocks and cannons. In the year 1507, when ordered to accept Selim I as his rightful suzerain Babar refused, and gathered Qizilbash servicemen in order to counter the forces of Ubaydullah Khan during the Battle of Ghazdewan. In the year 1513, Ottoman Sultan Selim I reconciled with Babar (probably fearing that he would join the Safavids), dispatched Ustad Ali Quli the artilleryman and Mustafa Rumi the Matchlock marksman and many other Ottoman Turks, in order to assist Babar in his conquests. Thenceforth this particular assistance proved to be the basis of future Mughal-Ottoman relations.

In 1495, at twelve years of age, Babar succeeded his father as ruler of Farghana, in present-day Uzbekistan. His uncles were relentless in their attempts to dislodge him from this position as well as many of his other territorial possessions to come. Thus, Babar spent a large portion of his life without shelter and in exile, aided by friends and peasants. In 1497, he besieged the city of Samarkand for seven months before eventually gaining control of it. Meanwhile, a rebellion amongst nobles back home approximately 350 kilometres (220 miles) away robbed him of Farghana. As he was marching to recover it, Babar's troops deserted in Samarkand, leaving him with neither Samarkand nor Fergana.

In 1501, he laid restriction on Samarkand once more, but was soon after defeated by his most challenging rival, Muhammad Shaybani, khan of the Uzbeks. Samarkand, his lifelong obsession, was lost again. Escaping with a small band of followers from Fergana, for three years Babar concentrated on building up a strong army, recruiting widely amongst the Tajiks of Badakhshan in particular. In 1504, he was able to cross the snowy Hindu Kush mountains and captured Kabul from the Arghunids, who were forced to retreat to Kandahar. With this move, he gained a wealthy new kingdom and re-established his fortunes and assumed the title of Padshah. In the following year, Babar united with Sultan Husayn Mirza Bayqarah of Herat, a fellow Timurid and distant relative, against the usurper Muhammad Shaybani. However, the death of Sultan Husayn Mirza in 1506 delayed that venture. Babar instead stayed at Herat, spending just two months there before being forced to leave due to diminishing resources. Nevertheless, he marvelled at the intellectual abundance in Herat, which he stated was "filled with learned and matched men.", and became acquainted with the work of the Uzbek poet Mir Ali Shir Nava'i, who encouraged the use of Chagatai as a literary language. Nava'i's proficiency with the language, which he is credited with founding, may have influenced Babar in his decision to use it for his memoirs.

A brewing rebellion finally induced him to return to Kabul from Herat, Khorasan. He prevailed on that occasion, but two years later a revolt among some of his leading generals drove him out of Kabul. Escaping with very few companions, Babar soon returned to the city, capturing Kabul again and regaining the allegiance of the rebels. Meanwhile, Muhammad Shaybani was defeated and killed by Ismail I, Shah of Shia Safavid Persia, in 1510, and Babar used this opportunity to attempt to reconquer his ancestral Timurid territories. Over the following few years, Babar and Shah Ismail would form a partnership in an attempt to take over parts of Central Asia. In return for Ismail's assistance, Babar permitted the Safavids to act as a suzerain over him and his followers. Conversely, Shah Ismail reunited Babar with his sister Khânzâda, who had been imprisoned by and forced to marry the recently deceased Shaybani.

Writing in retrospect, Babar suggested his failure in attaining Samarkand was the greatest gift Allah bestowed him. Babar had now resigned all hopes of recovering Fergana, and although he dreaded an invasion from the Uzbeks to his West, his attention increasingly turned towards India and its lands in the east, especially the rich lands of the Delhi Sultanate.

Mustafa Rumi, leading Babar's forces armed with early Matchlocks. Babar claimed to be the true and rightful Monarch of the lands of the

Lodi dynasty. He believed himself the rightful heir to the throne of Timur, and it was Timur who had originally left Khizr Khan in charge of his vassal in the Punjab, who became the leader, or Sultan, of the Delhi Sultanate, founding the Sayyid dynasty. The Sayyid dynasty, however, had been ousted by Ibrahim Lodi, a Ghilzai Afghan, and Babar wanted it returned to the Timurids. Indeed, while actively building up the troop numbers for an invasion of the Punjab he sent a request to Ibrahim; "I sent him a goshawk and asked for the countries which from old had depended on the Turk," the 'countries' referred to were the lands of the Delhi Sultanate.

Following the unsurprising aversion of Ibrahim to accept the terms of this "offer," and though in no hurry to launch an actual invasion, Babar made several preliminary incursions and also seized Kandahar — a strategic city if he was to fight off attacks on Kabul from the west while he was occupied in India – from the Arghunids. The siege of Kandahar, however, lasted far longer than anticipated, and it was only almost three years later that Kandahar and its Castles were taken, and that minor assaults in India recommenced. During this series of skirmishes and battles an opportunity for a more extended expedition presented itself.

Upon entering the Punjab plains, Babar's chief allies, namely Langar Khan Niazi advised Babar to engage the powerful and famous Muslim, Janjua Rajputs to join his conquest. The tribe's rebellious stance to the throne of Delhi was well known. Upon meeting their chiefs, Asad Malik Hast and Raja Sanghar Ali Khan, Babar made mention of the Janjua's popularity as traditional rulers of their kingdom and their ancestral support for his patriarch Timur during his conquest of the Tughluq dynasty. Babar aided them in defeating their enemies, the Gakhars in 1521, thus gaining their alliance. Babar then won their support and service during the Battle of Panipat and later on during the Battle of Khanwa. By that time the Lodi empire was also significantly weakened in Punjab-Rajasthan areas because of strong resistance from Rajputs especially Rana Sanga.

The section of Babar's memoirs covering the period between 1508 and 1519 is missing. During these years Shah Ismail I suffered a large defeat when his large cavalry-based army was eradicated at the Battle of Chaldiran by the Ottoman Empire's new weapon, the matchlock musket. Both Shah Ismail and Babar, it appears, were swift in acquiring this new technology for themselves. Somewhere during these years Babar introduced matchlocks into his army, and allowed an Ottoman, Ustad Ali, to train his troops, who were then known as Matchlockmen, in their use. Babar's memoirs give accounts of battles where the opposition forces mocked his troops, never having seen a gun before, because of the noise they made and the way no arrows, spears, etc. appeared to come from the weapon when fired.

These guns allowed small armies to make large gains on enemy territory. Small parties of skirmishers who had been dispatched simply to test enemy positions and tactics, were making inroads into India. Babar, however, had survived two revolts, one in Kandahar and another in Kabul, and was careful to pacify the local population after victories, following local traditions and aiding widows and orphans.

MILITARY CAREER OF BABUR

In 1495, At only twelve years of age, Babur obtained his first power position, succeeding his father as ruler of Farghana, in present-day Uzbekistan. His uncles were relentless in their attempts to dislodge him from this position as well as many of his other territorial possessions to come. Thus, Babur spent a large portion of his life shelterless and in exile, aided only by friends and peasants. In 1497, Babur attacked the Uzbek city of Samarkand and after seven months succeeded in capturing the city. Meanwhile, a rebellion amongst nobles back home approximately 350 kilometers (200 miles) away robbed him of Farghana. As he was marching to recover it, Babur's troops deserted in Samarkand, leaving him with neither Samarkand nor Fergana. By 1501, he was ready again to regain control of Samarkand, but was shortly thereafter defeated by his most formidable enemy, Muhammad Shaybani, khan of the Uzbeks. Samarkand, his lifelong obsession, was lost again. Escaping with a small band of followers from Fergana, for three years Babur concentrated on building up a strong army, recruiting widely amongst the Tajiks of Badakhshan in particular. In 1504, he was able to cross the snowy Hindu Kush mountains and capture Kabul from the Arghunids, who were forced to retreat to Kandahar. With this move, he gained a wealthy new kingdom and re-established his fortunes and assumed the title of Padshah. In the following year, Babur united with Husayn Bayqarah of Herat, a fellow Timurid and distant relative, against the usurper Muhammad Shaybani.

However, the death of Husayn Bayqarah in 1506 delayed that venture. Babur instead occupied his allies' city of Herat, spending just two months there before being forced to leave due to diminishing resources. Nevertheless, he marvelled at the intellectual abundance in Herat, which he stated was "filled with learned and matched men.", and became

The Founder of Mughal Empire: Babur

acquainted with the work of the Uzbek poet Mir Ali Shir Nava'i, who encouraged the use of Chagatai as a literary language. Nava'i's proficiency with the language, which he is credited with founding, may have influenced Babur in his decision to use it for his memoirs, Baburnama. A brewing rebellion finally induced him to return to Kabul from Herat, Khorasan. He prevailed on that occasion, but two years later a revolt among some of his leading generals drove him out of Kabul.

Escaping with very few companions, Babur soon returned to the city, capturing Kabul again and regaining the allegiance of the rebels. Muhammad Shaybani was defeated and killed by Ismail I, Shah of Shia Safavid Persia, in 1510, and Babur used this opportunity to attempt to reconquer his ancestral Timurid territories.

Over the following few years, Babur and Shah Ismail would form a partnership in an attempt to take over parts of Central Asia. In return for Ismail's assistance, Babur permitted the Safavids to act as a suzerain over him and his followers.

Conversely, Shah Ismail reunited Babur with his sister Khanzada, who had been imprisoned by and forced to marry the recently deceased Shaybani. Persia had become the bastion of Shia Islam under Shah Ismail, who claimed descent from Imam Musa al-kazim, the seventh Shia Imam. Coins were to be struck in Ismail's name, and the Khutba at the Mosque was also to be read in his name.

In effect, Babur was supposed to be holding Samarkand as a vassal territory for the Persian Shah, though in Kabul, coins and the Khutba would remain in Babur's name. With this assistance, Babur marched on Bukhara, where his army were apparently treated as liberators, Babur having greater legitimacy as a Timurid, unlike the Uzbegs. Towns and villages are said to have emptied in order to greet him, and aid and feed his army. At this point, Babur dismissed his Persian aide, believing them no longer needed. In October 1511 Babur made a triumphant re-entry into Samarkand, ending a ten year absence. Bazaars were draped in gold, and again villages and towns emptied to greet the liberator.

ADMINISTRATION OF BABUR

Mughal Emperor, Babur was successful as a soldier and conqueror. But the administration of Babur was less structured. Babur had created a system of administration that could function very well in the time of war only.

The old administrative machinery of the Sultanate of Delhi had crumbled as the result of the Mughal attack, but Babur could not give a good system of administration to the land. He divided the territory among his chiefs Military and officials and entrusted to them the work of administration. Military governorship were thus set up.

Babur's empire was rather a stack of little states under one price than one uniformly governed kingdom. Many of the hill and frontier districts yielded a little more than nominal submission. Each local governor had his own system of administration and enjoyed power of life and death over the people with his contingent of troops whenever he was summoned to do so, and to remit annual revenues to the central treasury. Otherwise he was independent. Babur did not take steps to establish a common revenue system for the empire. No attempt was made to survey the land and fix a uniform demand on the basis of the actual produce of the soil. Judicial administration was also haphazard. Thus, there was little uniformity in the political situation of the different parts of this vast empire.

Financial Administration of Babur was also weak. He did not realize that the success of administration depended upon sound finance, and squandered away the immense wealth that he had the good luck to acquire in the treasuries of Delhi and Agra.

Later on, when Babur realized that the day-to-day administration could not be carried on without money, he was obliged to impose additional taxes in order to obtain necessary equipment for the army and to pay the salaries of the troops and the civil establishment. Next, he was compelled to have the recourse to imposing a heavy fee on all office-holders. Every official was required to pay a certain fixed sum to the royal treasury. This produced disastrous results. Offices began to be purchased by money and merit ceased to be the criterion for government appointments. Notwithstanding these measure, financial stringency continued and his son and successor, Humayun had to suffer from the effects of financial breakdown.

He bequeathed to his son a monarchy which could be held together only by the continuance of war conditions, which in times of peace was weak and structure less.

LAST DAYS

After Babar fell seriously ill, Humayun was told of a plot by the senior nobles of Babur's court to bypass the leader's sons and appoint Mahdi

Khwaja, Babur's sister's husband, as his successor. He rushed to Agra and arrived there to see his father was well enough again, although Mahdi Khwaja had lost all hope of becoming ruler after arrogantly exceeding his authority during Babur's illness. Upon his arrival in Agra it was Humayun himself who fell ill, and was close to dying.

Babar is said to have circled the sick-bed, crying to God to take his life and not his son's. The traditions that follow this tell that Babur soon fell ill with a fever and Humayun began to get better again. This is not accurate, as there are months separating the recovery of Humayun and the death of Babur, and Babur's final illness was rather sudden. His last words apparently being to his son, Humayun, "Do nothing against your brothers, even though they may deserve it."

He died at the age of 47 on January 5 [O.S. 26 December 1530] 1531, and was succeeded by his eldest son, Humayun. Though he wished to be buried in his favourite garden in Kabul, a city he had always loved, he was first buried in a Mausoleum in the capital city of Agra. Roughly nine years later his wishes were fulfilled by Sher Shah Suri and Babur was buried in a beautiful garden Bagh-e Babur in Kabul, now in Afghanistan. The inscription on his tomb reads (in Persian):

If there is a paradise on earth, it is this, it is this, it is this! Babar's legacy was a mixed one. He is considered a national hero in Uzbekistan and Kyrgyzstan, and is held in high esteem in Afghanistan where he is buried. However, the Sikh Guru, Nanak, wrote a series of complaints against Babur in the Guru Granth Sahib, claiming Babur "terrified Hindustan" and was a "messenger of death." He also claimed that women with braided hair "were shaved with scissors, and their throats were choked with dust" and that "the order was given to the soldiers, who dishonored them, and carried them away." Soldier of fortune as he was, Babur was not the less a man of fine literary taste and critical perception. His autobiography is known as Tuzk-e-Babri (also Baburnama, Memoirs of Babur) originally written in Turki, is an example of his literary capacity.

DEATH AND LEGACY OF BABUR

After Babar fell seriously ill, Humayun was told of a plot by the senior nobles of Babur's court to bypass the leader's sons and appoint Mahdi Khwaja, Babur's sister's husband, as his successor. He rushed to Agra and arrived there to see his father was well enough again, although Mahdi Khwaja had lost all hope of becoming ruler after arrogantly exceeding his authority during Babur's illness. Upon his arrival in Agra it was Humayun himself who fell ill, and was close to dying. Babar is said to have circled the sick-bed, crying to God to take his life and not his son's.

The traditions that follow this tell that Babur soon fell ill with a fever and Humayun began to get better again. His last words apparently being to his son, Humayun, "Do nothing against your brothers, even though they may deserve it." He died at the age of 47 on January 5 [26 December 1530] 1531, and was succeeded by his eldest son, Humayun. Though he wished to be buried in his favourite garden in Kabul, a city he had always loved, he was first buried in a Mausoleum in the capital city of Agra. Roughly nine years later his wishes were fulfilled by Sher Shah Suri and Babur was buried in Bagh-e Babur (Babur Gardens) in Kabul, Afghanistan. The inscription on his tomb reads (in Persian):

- If there is a paradise on earth, it is this, it is this, it is this!
- Babur is considered a national hero in Uzbekistan and Kyrgyzstan, and is held in high esteem in Afghanistan where he is buried. In October 2005 the Pakistan military developed the Babur (cruise missile), named in honour of him.

3

The Reign of Humayun

Babur's eldest son and successor, Humayun, was 22 years old when his father passed away. Humayun lacked the experience and the tough fiber necessary to consolidate a new dynasty. Thus, the first decade of his rule brought a steady erosion of Mughal authority in northern India. In particular, Humayun had to deal with the determined hostility of the Afghans who were still allied with the dispossessed Lodi regime.

Humayun was defeated and dislodged by insurrections of nobles from the old Lodi regime. In 1540, the Mughal domain came under the control of one of those nobles, Farid Khan Sur, who assumed the regional name of Shir Shah Sur. Humayun would spend the next 15 years in exile in Sind, Iran, and then Afghanistan. During this exile, Humayun's Persian wife, Hamida Begum, a native of Turbat-I Shaykh Jam in Khurasan, gave birth to the future emperor Akbar.

According to Blair and Bloom, Shir Shah Sur was one of the finest rulers India had ever known. He introduced important fiscal and monetary reforms which were incorporated into the Mughal system of administration.

Hambly writes that Shir Shah's Delhi, once again the capital of a great empire, was bounded on the east by the Jumna and extended northwards as far as Kotla Firuz Shah. Its southern limit, Hambly continues, must have been the enormous citadel known as the Purana Qala beyond which gardens stretched as far as the Nizamuddin area, the traditional burial-ground of Muslim nobility. Shir Shah Sur, with his imperial vision and ability to translate that vision into constructive action, rates a place in the front ranks of India's statesmen.

After Shir Shah's death, the kingdom survived for about nine years in the hands of his son, Islam Shah. But Islam Shah's unconciliatory nature alienated many Afghan chieftains. Eventually, the squabbling for succession among Shir Shah's followers allowed Humayun and the Mughals to return to power in 1555. Iran's Shah Tahmasb (1524-76) had provided Humayun with the necessary troops to recapture Kandahar and then Kabul. But less than a year after regaining power, Humayun died unexpectedly at the age of 48 when he fell down the steps of his library in his haste to obey the muezzin's call to prayer.

Humayun's most noted achievement was in the sphere of painting. His devotion to the early Safavid School, developed during his stay in Iran, led him to recruit Persian painters of merit to accompany him back to India. These artists, wrties Hambly, laid the foundation of the Mughal style which emerged from its Persian chrysalis as an indigenous achievement in which Indian elements blended harmoniously with the traditions of Iran and Central Asia.

Humayun constructed a citadel at Delhi. Named Din-Panah (Refuge of Religion), this structure is thought to have been destroyed during the reign of Shir Shah Sur. The most celebrated building associated with Humayun is his tomb at Delhi, write Blair and Bloom. Humayun's mausoleum is a devotion of Hamida Begum, his widow, who supervised its construction during the reign of their son Akbar.

According to Blair and Bloom, Humayun's tomb marked the beginnings of a major development in the history of Indo-Islamic architecture. The tomb is set to the east of the shrine of Nizam al-Din Awliya (one of India's most revered Sufi saints) and in the center of a large garden that is 348 meters square. The garden is divided into 36 squares by cross-axially arranged water channels and pathways. Blair and Bloom write that the flat surfaces, the restrained combination of red stone and white marble in the flat panels, and the massive size of the tomb create an impression of sobriety.

On the interior of the tomb, continue Blair and Bloom, the central space contains Humayun's cenotaph; two stories of octagonal chambers containing cenotaphs for various members of Humayun's family fill the corners. Blair and Bloom add that this type of plan, often called hasht bihisht (Eight Paradise), is known to have been used in Timurid Iran. Contemporary historians believe the tomb was designed by Mirak Mirza Ghiyath, an architect of Iranian descent who had worked in Heart, Bukhara, and India before undertaking this project, note Blair and Bloom.

The Reign of Humayun

Humayun's tomb fits into the Iranian tradition of imperial mausoleums -- a tradition that can be seen, for example, in Uljayatu's tomb at Sultaniyya and Timur's at Samarqand. Brend writes that it is obvious that the taste for Timurid architecture in the mid-16th century shows the Mughals attempt to connect their line in India with their forebears in Iran through the use of forms identified with the Timurid.

PERSONAL TRAITS

Humayun was portrayed in the biography Humayun-nama written by his sister Gulbadan Begum, as being extraordinarily lenient, constantly forgiving acts which were deliberately aimed at angering him.

In one instance the biography records that his youngest brother Hindal killed Humayun's most trusted advisor, an old Sheikh, and then marched an army out of Agra. Humayun, rather than seek retribution, went straight to his mother's home where Gulbadan Begum was, bearing no grudge against his younger brother, and insisted he return home.

His many documented acts of mercy may have stemmed largely from weakness, but he does seem to have been a gentle and humane man by the standards of the day. He lacked his father's craftiness and athleticism. Though he could be a formidable warrior when he chose to be, he was more laid back and indolent.

He was also deeply superstitious, and fascinated by Astrology and the Occult. Upon his accession as Padishah (Emperor), he began to re-organise the administration upon mystically determined principles. The public offices were divided into four distinct groups, for the four elements. The department of Earth was to be in charge of Agriculture and the agricultural sciences, Fire was to be in charge of the Military, Water was the department of the Canals and waterways while Air seemed to have responsibility for everything else.

His daily routine was planned in accordance with the movements of the planets, so too was his wardrobe. He refused to enter a house with his left foot going forward, and if anyone else did they would be told to leave and re-enter. His servant, Jauhar, records in the Tadhkirat al-Waqiat that he was known to shoot arrows to the sky marked with either his own name, or that of the Shah of Persia and, depending on how they landed, interpreted this as an indication of which of them would grow more powerful. He was a heavy drinker, and also took pellets of Opium, after which he was known to recite poetry. He was, however, not enamoured of warfare, and after winning a battle would spend months at a time indulging himself within the walls of a captured city even as a larger war was taking place outside.

EARLY REIGN

Upon his succession to the throne, Humayun had two major rivals interested in acquiring his lands - Sultan Bahadur of Gujarat to the south west and Sher Shah Suri (Sher Khan) currently settled along the river Ganges in Bihar to the east. Humayun's first campaign was to confront Sher Khan Suri. Halfway through the counter offensive Humayun had to abandon it and concentrate on Gujarat, where a threat from Ahmed Shah had to be squelched. In this he succeeded and annexed Gujarat and Malwa. Champaner and the great fort of Mandu followed next.

During the first five years of Humayun's reign, these two rulers were quietly extending their rule, although Sultan Bahadur faced pressure in the east from sporadic conflicts with the Portuguese. While the Mughals had acquired firearms via the Ottoman Empire, Bahadur's Gujurat had acquired them through a series of contracts drawn up with the Portuguese, allowing the Portuguese to establish a strategic foothold in north western India. Humayun was made aware that the Sultan of Gujarat was planning an assault on the Mughal territories with Portuguese aid. Showing an unusual resolve, Humayun gathered an army and marched on Bahadur. His assault was spectacular and within a month he had captured the forts of Mandu and Champaner. However, instead of pressing his attack and going after the enemy, Humayun ceased the campaign and began to enjoy life in his new forts. Bahadur, meanwhile, escaped and took up refuge with the Portuguese.

SHER SHAH SURI

Shortly after Humayun had marched on Gujarat, Sher Shah saw an opportunity to wrest control of Agra from the Mughals. He began to gather his army together hoping for a rapid and decisive siege of the Mughal capital. Upon hearing this alarming news, Humayun quickly marched his troops back to Agra allowing Bahadur to easily regain control of the territories Humayun had recently taken. A few months later, however, Bahadur was dead, killed when a botched plan to kidnap the Portuguese viceroy ended in a fire-fight which the Sultan lost. Whilst

The Reign of Humayun

Humayun succeeded in protecting Agra from Sher Shah, the second city of the Empire, Gaur the capital of the vilayat of Bengal, was sacked.

Humayun's troops had been delayed while trying to take Chunar, a fort occupied by Sher Shah's son, in order to protect his troops from an attack from the rear. The stores of grain at Gauri, the largest in the empire, were emptied and Humayun arrived to see corpses littering the roads.

The vast wealth of Bengal was depleted and brought East giving Sher Shah a substantial war chest. Sher Shah withdrew to the east, but Humayun did not follow: instead he "shut himself up for a considerable time in his Harem, and indulged himself in every kind of luxury." Hindal, Humayun's 19-year old brother, had agreed to aid him in this battle and protect the rear from attack but abandoned his position and withdrew to Agra where he decreed himself acting emperor. When Humayun sent the grand Mufti, Sheikh Buhlul, to reason with him, the Sheikh was killed. Further provoking the rebellion, Hindal ordered that the Khutba or sermon in the main mosque at Agra be read in his name, a sign of assumption of sovereignty.

When Hindal withdrew from protecting the rear of Humayun's troops, Sher Shah's troop quickly reclaimed these positions, leaving Humayun surrounded. Humayun's other brother, Kamran, marched from his territories in the Punjab, ostensibly to aid Humayun. However, his return home had treacherous motives as he intended to stake a claim for Humayun's apparently collapsing empire. He brokered a deal with Hindal which provided that his brother would cease all acts of disloyalty in return for a share in the new empire which Kamran would create once Humayun was deposed. Sher Shah met Humayun in battle on the banks of the Ganges, near Benares, in Chausa. This was to become an entrenched battle in which both sides spent a lot of time digging themselves into positions.

The major part of the Mughal army, the artillery, was now immobile, and Humayun decided to engage in some diplomacy using Muhammad Aziz as ambassador. Humayun agreed to allow Sher Shah to rule over Bengal and Bihar, but only as provinces granted to him by his Emperor, Humayun, falling short of outright sovereignty. The two rulers also struck a bargain in order to save face: Humayun's troops would charge those of Sher Shah whose forces then retreat in feigned fear.

Thus honour would, supposedly, be satisfied. Once the Army of Humayun had made its charge and Sher Shah's troops made their agreed-upon retreat, the Mughal troops relaxed their defensive preparations and returned to their entrenchments without posting a proper guard. Observing the Mughals' vulnerability, Sher Shah reneged on his earlier agreement. That very night, his army approached the Mughal camp and finding the Mughal troops unprepared with a majority asleep, they advanced and killed most of them. The Emperor survived by swimming the Ganges using an air filled "water skin," and quietly returned to Agra.

In Agra

When Humayun returned to Agra, he found that all three of his brothers were present. Humayun once again not only pardoned his brothers for plotting against him, but even forgave Hindal for his outright betrayal. With his armies travelling at a leisurely pace, Sher Shah was gradually drawing closer and closer to Agra. This was a serious threat to the entire family, but Humayun and Kamran squabbled over how to proceed. Kamran withdrew after Humayun refused to make a quick attack on the approaching enemy, instead opting to build a larger army under his own name. When Kamran returned to Lahore, his troops followed him shortly afterwards, and Humayun, with his other brothers Askari and Hindal, marched to meet Sher Shah just 240 kilometres (150 miles) east of Agra at the Battle of Kanauj on 17 May 1540. The battle once again saw Humayun make some tactical errors, and his army was soundly defeated. He and his brothers quickly retreated back to Agra, humiliated and mocked along the way by peasants and villagers. They chose not to stay in Agra, and retreated to Lahore, though Sher Shah followed them, founding the short-lived Sur Dynasty of northern India with its capital at Delhi.

In Lahore

The four brothers were united in Lahore, but every day they were informed that Sher Shah was getting closer and closer. When he reached Sirhind, Humayun sent an ambassador carrying the message "I have left you the whole of Hindustan (*i.e.* the lands to the East of Punjab, comprising most of the Ganges Valley). Leave Lahore alone, and let Sirhind be a boundary between you and me." Sher Shah, however, replied "I have left you Kabul. You should go there." Kabul was the capital of the empire of Humayun's brother Kamran Mirza, who was far from willing to hand over any of his territories to his brother. Instead, Kamran approached Sher Shah, and proposed that he actually revolt against his brother and side with Sher Shah in return for most of the Punjab. Sher Shah dismissed his help, believing it not to be required, though word soon spread to Lahore about the treacherous proposal and Humayun was urged to make an example of Kamran and kill him. Humayun refused, citing the last words of his father, Babur "Do nothing against your brothers, even though they may deserve it."

Withdrawing further

Humayun decided that it would be wise to withdraw still further. He asked that his brothers join him as he fell back into Sindh. While the previously rebellious Hindal remained loyal, Kamran and Askari instead decided to head to the relative peace of Kabul. This was to be a definitive schism in the family. Humayun expected aid from the Amir of Sindh, whom he had appointed and who owed him his allegiance. While the Amir, Hussein, tolerated Humayun's presence, he knew that raising an army against Sher Shah would ultimately end in disaster, and he therefore politely refused all of Humayun's requests for military assistance. Whilst in Sindh, Humayun met and married Hamida (a young girl from village paat) - who was to become the mother of Akbar - on 21 August 1541. The date was selected after Humayun consulted his astrolabe to check the location of the planets. In May 1542, the Raja of Jodhpur, Rao Maldeo Rathore, issued a request to Humayun to form an alliance against Sher Shah and so Humayun and his army rode out through the desert to meet with the Prince.

As they made their way across the desert, the prince became aware of how feeble Humayun's army had now become. Furthermore, Sher Shah had offered him more favourable terms and so he sent word that he no longer wanted to see Humayun, who was now less than 80 km (50 miles) from the city. Thus, Humayun and his troops, and his heavily pregnant wife, had to retrace their steps through the desert at the hottest time of year. All the wells had been filled with sand by the nearby inhabitants after Humayun's troops had killed several cows (a sacred animal to the Hindus), leaving them with nothing but berries to eat. When Hamida's horse died no one would lend the Queen (who was now eight months pregnant) a horse, so Humayun did so himself, resulting in him riding a camel for six kilometeres (four miles), although Khaled Beg then offered him his mount. Humayun was later to describe this incident as the lowest point in his life.

He ordered Hindal to join his brothers in Kandahar. However, while Humayun was on his travels, Hussein, the Amir of Sindh, had killed Maldeo's father, prompting the Raja to change his mind about Humayun.

He decided to ride out to meet him in Umarkot, a small town by a desert oasis. Humayun was afforded full courtesies and was given new horses and weapons as the men formed an alliance against Sindh. Umarkot was to become the centre of operations for this battle, and it was here, on 23 November 1542 that the 15-year old Hamida, gave birth to her first child, a boy they called Jalaluddin (later Akbar), the heir-apparent to the 34-year old Humayun.

EARLY CONFLICTS OF HUMAYUN AND SHER SHAH SURI

The success of Sher Shah Suri (Sher Khan) was not to be an easy one. The Lion King, Sher Shah Suri was doing everything in his power to unite the Indian Afghans and to improve their material and moral conditions he had a hostile element within his own race to contend with.

The Indian Afgans were preparing for driving the Mughals out and regaining their supremacy in Hindustan.

Mahmud Lodi was planning an attack on the Mughals. Mahmud Lodi paid a visit to Sher Khan in the latter's jagir and persuaded him to cooperate with him and make united attack on the Mughal army of Humayun. Sher Khan gave his assent to the plan and became a member of this Afghan confederacy.

After many months of preparations a campaign was now organized. Under the lead of Mahmud Lodi, the Afghans occupied Banaras and marched on Jaunpur. The emboldened Afghans now marched upon Lucknow and captured it. The two armies faced each other at Daunrua in the Nawabganj tahsil of the present Barabanki district in Awadh and a well-contested battle was fought there in August 1532, in which the Afghans were badly defeated. Their leader, Mahmud Lodi, fled to Orissa and he spent the rest of his life there, dying in 1542. Sher Khan recovered South Bihar on the failure of the uprising and again became its ruler.

Humayun did not return to Agra immediately after his easy victory over Mahmud Lodi at Daunrua. He besieged the fortress of Chunargarh, which Sher Khan had obtained by his marriage with Lad Malika in 1530. But circumstances helped Sher Khan greatly to defy the Mughal army. Soon after he had laid siege, Humayun received the alarming news of the hostile movements of Bahadur Shah of Gujarat, who was preparing to have trial of strength with the Mughals. Under these circumstances, Humayun decided to make a hurried peace with Sher Shah Suri. He

The Reign of Humayun

agreed to allow Sher Khan to remain in possession of the fortress of Chunar on the latter's agreeing to place a contingent of 5,000 troops, commanded by his third son, Qutb Khan, for service in the Mughal army. These terms were acceptable to both and hence a peace was mad and in January 1533. Humayun returned to Agra in order to settle his scores with Bahadur Shah.

RETREAT TO KABUL

The war against Sindh had led to a stalemate, and so Hussein decided to bribe Humayun to leave the area. Humayun accepted and in return for 300 camels (mostly wild) and 2000 loads of grain, he set off to join his brothers in Kandahar, crossing the Indus River on 11 July 1543. In Kamran's territory, Hindal had been placed under house arrest in Kabul after refusing to have the Khutba recited in Kamran's name. His other brother Askari was now ordered to gather an army and march on Humayun. When Humayun received word of the approaching hostile army he decided against facing them, and instead sought refuge elsewhere. Akbar was left behind in camp close to Kandahar for, as it was December it would have been too cold and dangerous to include the 14-month old toddler in the forthcoming march through the dangerous and snowy mountains of the Hindu Kush. Askari found Akbar in the camp, and embraced him, and allowed his own wife to rear him. She apparently treated him as her own.

REFUGE IN PERSIA

Humayun fled to the refuge of the Safavid Empire in Iran, marching with 40 men and his wife and her companion through mountains and valleys. Amongst other trials the Imperial party were forced to live on horse meat boiled in the soldiers' helmets. These indignities continued during the month it took them to reach Herat, however after their arrival they were reintroduced to the finer things in life. Upon entering the city his army was greeted with an armed escort, and they were treated to lavish food and clothing.

They were given fine accommodations and the roads were cleared and cleaned before them. Shah Tahmasp, unlike Humayun's own family, actually welcomed the Mughal, and treated him as a royal visitor.

Here Humayun went sightseeing and was amazed at the Persian artwork and architecture he saw: much of this was the work of the

Timurid Sultan Husayn Bayqarah and his ancestor, princess Gauhar Shad, thus he was able to admire the work of his relatives and ancestors at first hand. He was introduced to the work of the Persian miniaturists, and Kamaleddin Behzad had two of his pupils join Humayun in his court. Humayun was amazed at their work and asked if they would work for him if he were to regain the sovereignty of Hindustan: they agreed. With so much going on Humayun did not even meet the Shah until July, some six months after his arrival in Persia.

After a lengthy journey from Herat the two met in Qazvin where a large feast and parties were held for the event. The meeting of the two monarchs is depicted in a famous wall-painting in the Chehel Sotoun (Forty Columns) palace in Esfahan.

The Shah urged that Humayun convert from Sunni to Shia Islam, and Humayun eventually and reluctantly accepted, in order to keep himself and several hundred followers alive. much to the disapproval of his biographer Jauhar. With this outward acceptance of Shi'ism the Shah was eventually prepared to offer Humayun more substantial support. When Humayun's brother, Kamran, offered to cede Kandahar to the Persians in exchange for Humayun, dead or alive, the Shah refused. Instead the Shah threw a party for Humayun, with 300 tents, an imperial Persian carpet, 12 musical bands and "meat of all kinds". Here the Shah announced that all this, and 12,000 choice cavalry were his to lead an attack on his brother Kamran. All that Shah asked for was that, if Humayun's forces were victorious, Kandahar would be his.

Reception of Humayun in Persia Account of the Safavis (or Sophis)

At the time when Humayun entered Persia the throne was occupied by Shah Tahmasp, the second of the Safavi (or Sophi) kings. His father was descended from a family of dervises, which had derived importance and influence from its sanctity, and was still principally supported by the enthusiasm of the nation for the Shia religion, which had been widely disseminated by the family, and formally established in Persia by Shah Ismael, the first king of the race. Though the Shias and Sunnis differ less than Catholics and Protestants, their mutual animosity is much more bitter; and the attachment of the Persians to their sect is national as well as religious; the Shia faith being professed in no great kingdom but theirs. Coming so early in the succession to its founder, Shah Tahmasp was not only a devout adherent but an ardent apostle of this new religion; and

Magnificence and hospitality of Shah Tahmasp

Humayun's reception was marked with every circumstance of hospitality and magnificence. The governor of every province received him with the highest honour, and the people of every city came in a body to meet him; he was lodged in the king's palaces, and entertained with regal splendour; but in the midst of this studied respect, he was treated with little delicacy, and all semblance of generosity disappeared as often as he disputed the will of the Persian monarch, or became in any way obnoxious to his pride or caprice.

His Arrogance and Caprice

Though welcomed from the moment of his arrival, he was not allowed to approach the capital; and many months elapsed before he was admitted to an interview with the king. During this interval, he sent his most confidential officer, Behram Khan, on a mission to Shah Tahmasp; and it was through a circumstance in the treatment of his envoy that he was first reminded how completely he was in the power of another.

Forces Humayun to Profess the Shia Religion

More effectually to unite his followers by some visible symbol, the first Safavi had made them wear a particular description of cap; from which the Persians took the name they now bear. This sectarian distinction was an object of as much aversion to the other Mahometans as a rosary and crucifix would have been to a Calvinist of the seventeenth century.

On one occasion of Behram's attendance at court, the king desired him to wear the cap; and on Behram's representing that he was the servant of another prince, and was not at liberty to act without orders, Tahmasp told him "he might do as he pleased," but gave evident signs of great displeasure; and, sending for some offenders, ordered them to be beheaded on the spot, with a view to strike a terror into the refractory ambassador.

Shah Tahmasp's meeting with Humayun was on terms of perfect equality, and in every way suitable to his own grandeur and the dignity of his guest. Yet the two kings were scarcely seated, when Tahmasp told the king of India that he must adopt the disputed cap; and Humayun, to whom the demand was not unexpected, at once consented with an appropriate compliment.

His assuming it was announced by a triumphal flourish from the king of Persia's band, and welcomed by a general salutation to both monarchs by the Persian courtiers. Some more private conversation probably passed on the subject of religion, in which Humayun was not so compliant; for next day, when Tahmasp was passing Humayun's palace on a journey, the latter prince went to the gate to salute him, but the Persian passed on without noticing him, and left Humayun mortified and humiliated. Some days after, when a large supply of firewood was sent to Humayun, it was accompanied by a message that it should serve for his funeral pile if he refused to embrace the Shia religion. To this the exiled prince replied with humility, but with firmness, and requested leave to proceed on his pilgrimage; but Tahmasp was inexorable, declaring that he was determined to extirpate the Sunnis, and that Humayun must adopt the religion of the country he had voluntarily entered, or take the consequences.

After all this intimidation, a cazi deputed by Shah Tahmasp to confer with him presented Humayun with three papers, and told him he might take his choice which he would sign. Humayun rejected them in succession, with indignation, and at one time started up to call his attendants. His anger was composed by the cazi, who conducted his negotiation with kindness as well as with address, and succeeded in convincing him that, although he might give up his own life for his religion, he had no right to sacrifice those of his adherents; and that his duty as well as his interest called on him to comply with a demand which he had no means of effectually resisting.

The memoir writer does not mention, and may not have known, the contents of the paper; and Abul Fazl, with courtly dexterity, passes over the whole subject of religion, and scarcely hints at a temporary misunderstanding between the kings; but it seems clear that it must have contained a profession of the Shia religion, and a promise to introduce it into India, as well as an engagement to cede the frontier province or kingdom of Candahar. This last article was carried into effect; and it was probably a sense of the impossibility of fulfilling the other that made Humayun so indifferent to a rupture with Persia, when the period of performance drew near. That Humayun himself professed to have been converted appears from a pilgrimage which he made to the tomb of Shekh Safi at Ardebil, a mark of respect not very consistent with the character of a professed Sunni.

The Reign of Humayun

After the contest about this paper, Humayun was neglected for two months; and when Tahmasp renewed his attentions, they were not unmixed with ebullitions of an overbearing temper on points unconnected with the favourite topic of religion. Tahmasp had heard from some of Humayun's enemies, that, during that monarch's prosperity, on some practice of divination to discover the destiny of reigning princes, he had placed the king of Persia in a class inferior to that in which he ranked himself. Tahmasp now took him to task for this assumption, and, on Humayun's endeavouring to explain his reasons, told him that it was through such arrogance that he came to be driven out of his kingdom by peasants, and to leave his women and his child in the hands of his enemies.

Nevertheless the public conduct of the king of Persia continued to be as cordial and as generous as ever. He gave great hunting and drinking parties in honour of Humayun; and, when the time of that prince's departure approached, he loaded him with attentions, and on one occasion laid his hand on his heart and entreated his guest to forgive him if he had ever failed in what was due to him. He then dismissed Humayun, with a promise that 12,000-horse should be ready to join him in Sistan. But the two kings were not destined to part without one more explosion of temper from the king of Persia. Instead of marching straight to the frontier, Humayun loitered about different places which he wished to visit, until he was overtaken by Tahmasp who was moving on some business through his dominions. He no sooner saw Humayun's tents than he exclaimed, "What! has he not yet left this country?" and sent a messenger to direct him to make a march of twelve farsakhs (upwards of forty miles) without a moment's delay.

Sends an Army to Restore Humayun

In Sistan, Humayun found 14,000 horse (instead of the 12,000 promised), under the command of the king's son, Morad Mirza. Carman was still in possession of Cabul. Candahar had been surprised by Hindal, but retaken; and that prince had been forgiven by his brother, and was now governor of Ghazni, the government of Candahar being intrusted to Mirza Asked. Camran had also taken Badakhshan from his relation, Soliman, who had been placed there by Baer: it comprehended the south of Bactria; the northern part of that province, including Balkh, was in the hands of the Uzbegs. Shir Shah was still alive, and there was little to be hoped from an invasion of Hindostan.

Humayun's own troops, while in Persia, only amounted to 700 men, and they were probably not more numerous when he marched with the Persian force against the fort of Bost, on the river Helmand. That place soon surrendered, and the force advanced unobstructed to Candahar (March, 1545).

The eagerness of the Persians, and their fear that Mirza Askeri might escape with his treasures, led them at first to a tumultuary attack, which was repelled by the garrison, and the siege was then opened in form. It lasted for more than five months, during which time Humayun sent Behram Khan to Cabul to endeavour to bring Camran to terms. His mission was unsuccessful; and as for a long time none of the chiefs or inhabitants of the country joined Humayun, the Persians began to be disheartened, and to talk of returning to their own country. At length things took a favourable turn: deserters of different ranks came in from Cabul; and the garrison of Candahar being reduced to distress for subsistence, many of the troops composing it escaped to their own homes, while others let themselves down from the walls and came over to the besiegers.

Mirza Askeri was now obliged to surrender; and, by the intervention of his aunt, the sister of Baber, he obtained a promise of pardon from his brother (September, 1545). But Humayun's heart seems to have been hardened by his long misfortunes and disappointments; and his proceedings, which formerly were chiefly to be blamed for weakness, began to assume a darker character. Askeri was compelled to make his appearance before the conqueror with his sword hung naked from his neck, and to display his submission in the most humiliating forms. When this was over, Humayun with seeming generosity placed him by his side, and showed him every mark of forgiveness and returning kindness. A great entertainment was given to celebrate the reconciliation; but when the festivity was at its height, and all fears and suspicions had been laid aside, some orders which Askeri had written to the Beloch chiefs for apprehending Humayun during his flight to Persia were produced; and, on pretext of this long past act of enmity, he was made prisoner, and kept in chains for nearly three years.

The fort and treasures were made over to the Persians, on which the greater part of their troops returned home; and the garrison which was left under Morad Mirza began, according to Abul Fazl, to oppress the inhabitants. Abul Fazl enters on a long apologetical narrative of the events that followed; which, for its own cant and hypocrisy, as well as the perfidy of the acts it defends, is not surpassed by any thing even in the Memoirs of But treacherously recovered by Humayun, after the departure of the

Persian army Tamerlane. The sum is, that the Persian prince having suddenly died, Humayun, still professing the most fervent attachment to Shah Tahmasp, obtained admission on friendly terms into the city, slaughtered many of the garrison, and made an extraordinary merit of allowing the rest to return to their own country.

It is probable that the sophistical pretexts of Abul Fazl are not chargeable to Humayun, who might plead that he was not bound to observe an engagement wrung from him by force. This argument, however, if admissible, as far as relates to his conversion, does not apply to the cession of Candahar. That was the price of the assistance of the king of Persia; and by availing himself of that assistance, after he was free from restraint, he ratified his engagement anew; and his infraction of it, especially with the concomitant circumstances, must leave him under the stigma of treachery, though not, perhaps, of ingratitude.

Taking of Cabul

After the occupation of Candahar, Humayun marched for Cabul, although the winter had already set in with extraordinary severity. As he advanced, he was joined by his brother Hindal; and afterwards by other deserters, in such numbers that, when he reached Cabul, Camran found it impossible to resist, and fled to Bakkar on the Indus, where he threw himself on the protection of Husen Arghun, prince of Sind. Humayun entered Cabul, and recovered his son Akber, now between two and three years of age.

Expedition to Badakhshan

After remaining for some months at Cabul, Humayun set out to recover Badakhshan, which was again in the hands of Mirza Soliman. Before his departure, he thought it prudent to put his cousin, Yadgar Mirza, who had just joined him, and was suspected of fresh intrigues, to death. What is remarkable in this event is, that the governor of Cabul flatly refused to carry the order into execution, and that Humayun directed another person to perform it without inflicting any punishment on the governor.

4

Akbar the Great

Akbar, also known as Akbar the Great, ascended the throne of Mughal Empire at the young age of 14 in 1556.

As we have already noted, the battle of Khanua (1527) did not result in the total eclipse of Rajput influence in the north. Rajputana still formed a powerful factor in the history of India. Gifted with the true insight of a statesman and liberal in outlook, Akbar realized the value of Rajput alliance in his task of building up an Empire in India for his dynasty, which was a foreign one, at the cost of the Afghans, who were the "children of the soil ". Thus he tried, as far as possible, to conciliate the Rajputs and ensure their active co-operation in almost all his activities. By his wise and liberal policy, he won the heart of most of them to such an extent that they rendered valuable services to his empire and even shed their blood for it. The Empire of Akbar was, in fact, the outcome of the co-ordination of Mughul prowess and diplomacy and Rajput valour and service.

In 1562, Raja Bihari Mall, of Amber (Jaipur), tendered his submission to Akbar and cemented his friendship with him by a marriage alliance. Bihari Mall, with his son, Bhagwan Das and grandson, Man Singh, proceeded to Agra. He was given a command of 5,000 and his son and grandson were also admitted to high rank in the army. Thus was opened the way through which the Mugbul Emperors were able to secure for four generations "the services of some of the greatest captains and diplomats that medieval India produced".

Its independence was, however, galling to Akbar, who cherished the ideal of an all-India empire, the economic interests of which also demanded

Akbar the Great

a control over Mewar, through which lay the high ways of commerce between the Ganges-Jumna Doab and the western coast. The ambitious design of Akbar was facilitated by the prevalence of internal discord in Mew&r, following the death of Ranga Bangs, and by the weakness of Udai Singh, the unworthy son of a noble sire. "Well had it been for Mewar," exclaims Tod, "had the annals of Mewar never recorded the name of Udai Singh in the catalogue of her princes." When Akbar besieged the fort of Chitor in October, 1567, Udai Singh fled to the hills, leaving his capital to its fate. But there were some brave followers of the Rana, notably JiLlr-ii and Patta, who offered a stubborn opposition to the imperialists for four months (20th October, 1567, to 23rd February, 1568) till Jaimall was killed by a musket-shot fired by Akber himself. Patts she fell dead later. The death of the leaden of the defence disheartened the besieged garrison, who rushed on their enemies sword in hand ' and fought bravely till they perished to a man. The Rajput women performed the rite of Jauhar. Akbar then stromed the fort of Chitor. According to Abul Fazl 30,000 persons were slain, but the figure seems to be Akbar's wrath fell also upon what Tod calls highly exaggerated. Thus be removed the huge kettledrums (eight or ten feet in diameter, the reverberation if which proclaimed for miles around the entrance and exit of the princes from the gates of Chitor) and also t he massive candelabra from the shrine of the Great Mother of Chitor, to Agra.

Struck with terror at the fall or Chitor, the other Rajput chiefs, who had so long defied Akbar, submitted to him. In February 1569, Rai Surjana Hara of Ranthambhor surrendered to Akbar the keys of his fortress and entered into the imperial service. raja Ramchand, the chief of Kalinjar in Bundelkhand, followed suit in the same year. The occupation of Kalinjar greatly strengthened Akbar's military position and marks important step in the progress of Mughul imperialism. In 1570 the rulers of Bikaner and Jaisalmer not only submitted to the Mughul Emperor but also gave their daughters in marriage to him.

Thus, one by one, the Rajput Chiefs acknowledged Mughul away, but Mewar still refused to own it. Udai Singh retained his independence though he had lost his ancestral capital. After his death on death on the 3rd March, 1572, at Gogunda true Patriot nineteen miles north-west of Udaipur Mewar found a true patriot and leader in his son Pratap, who, being in every respect faithful to the traditions of his country, offered uncompromising resistance to the invaders. The magnitude of his task can be well understood when we noted that without a capital, and with only slender resource he had to oppose the organized strength of the Mughul emperor, who was then " immeasurably the richest monarch on the face of the earth". Further, his fellow chiefs and neighbours and even his own brother, devoid of the high Rajput ideals of chivalry and independence, had allied themselves with the Mughals. But no obstacle was too alarming for this national hero of Rajputana, who was made of nobler stuff than his relatives. "The magnitude of the peril confirmed the fortitude of Pratap, who vowed in the words of the bard, 'to make his mother's milk resplendent', and he amply redeemed his pledge. "

The inevitable imperial invasion of his territory took place in April, 1576, under a body of troops commanded by Man Singh of Amber and Asaf Khan, and a furious battle was fought at the pass of Haldighat near Gogunda. Pratap was defeated, and barely escaped with his life, which was saved by the selfless devotion of the chief of Jhala, who drew upon himself the attack of his imperialists by declaring himself to be the Rana.

Mounted on his beloved horse "Chaitak", the Rana betook himself to the hills, and his strongholds were captured by his enemies one by one. But Pratap could not think of submission even in the midst of the direst adversity. Hunted from rock to rock by his implacable enemy, and "feeding his family from the fruits of his native hills", he continued the war with undaunted spirit and energy and had the satisfaction of recovering many of his strongholds before be died on the 19th January, 1597, at the age of fifty-seven.

The Rajput patriot was anxious for his motherland even at his last moment, for he had no faith in his son; and before he expired, he exacted, from his chiefs "a pledge that his country should not be abandoned to the Turks".

"Thus closed the life of a Rajput whose memory,"observes Tod, "is even now idolized by every Sisodia." Pratap's is indeed an inspiring personality in Indian history. The Rajputs have produced abler generals and more astute statesmen than Pratap, but not more brave and noble patriotic leaders than he. Pratap's son, Amar Singh, tried to carry out the behest of his father but was attacked by a Mughul army under Man Singh in 1599 and was defeated after a gallant resistance. Akbar could not undertake any other invasion of Mewar owing to illness.

After annexing Ranthambhor and Kalinjar in A.D. 1569, the Mughuls subjugated Gujarat. With rich and flourishing ports on its coasts, Gujarat had an attractive commercial position and a special economic advantage.

Its possession had therefore been coveted by the preceding rulers of Delhi, even by Humayun, whose occupation of it was, however, temporary. But Akbar must have realized the importance of occupying this province for the interests of his Empire, and the prevailing distracted condition of Gujarat under its nominal king, Muzaffar Shah III, gave him an excellent opportunity for it. As a matter of fact, his intervention being sought by Itimad Khan, the leader of a local faction, had some justification. In 1572 Akbar marched in person against Gujarat, defeated all opposition and pensioned off the puppet king. He captured Surat on the 26th February, 1573, after besieging it for a month and a half, and the Portuguese, who came in touch with him on this occasion, courted his friendship.

But no sooner had he reached his headquarters at Fatehpur Sikri than insurrections broke out in the newly conquered province, in which some of his own cousins took part. Highly enraged at this, Akbar marched hurriedly to Ahmadabad, having traversed six hundred miles in eleven days, and thoroughly vanquished the insurgents in a battle near Ahmadabad on the 2nd September, 1573. Gujarat thus came under Akbar's authority and became henceforth an integral part of his Empire. It turned out to be one of its profitable sources of income, chiefly through the reorganization of its finances and revenues by Todar Mal, whose work in that province was ably carried on by Shihab-ud-din Ahmad from 1577 to 1583 or 1584. "The conquest of Gujarat, " remarks Dr. Smith, "marks an important epoch in Akbar's history." Besides placing its resources at the disposal of the Empire, it secured for it free access to the sea and brought it in contact with the Portuguese, which in some ways influenced the history of India. But the Mughuls made no attempt to build up any sea-power and their shortsightedness in this direction helped the intrusion of the European traders.

The more important province of Bengal was next conquered by the Mughuls. The Sur kings made themselves independent in Bengal during the short and stormy reign of Muhammad 'Adil Shah and ruled it till 1564, when, taking advantage of the disorders following the murder of the reigning young king, Sulaiman Kararani, governor of South Bihar, extended his authority over Bengal also. Till his death in A.D. 1572, Sulaiman formally recognised the overlordship of Akbar and maintained friendly relations with him. He transferred his capital from Gaur to Tanda and annexed the Hindu kingdom of Orissa. But his son, Daud, who, according to the author of the Tabaqat, "knew nothing of the art of government", soon " forsook the prudent measures of his father ". He incurred the

Emperor's resentment not only by proclaiming his independence but also by attacking the outpost of Zamania on the eastern frontier of the Empire (situated in the Ghazipur district of U.P.).

In 1574 Akbar himself marched against the presumptuous governor of Bengal and expelled him from Patna and Hajipur during the rainy season. He returned to Fathpur Sikri, leaving Mun'im Khan in charge of the Bengal campaign. Daud retreated towards Orissa and was defeated by the Mughul troops at Tukaroi near the eastern bank of the Suvarnarekha on the 3rd March, 1575. But this battle had no decisive result owing to the ill-advised leniency of Mun'im Khan towards the vanquished foe, who was consequently able to strike once more to recover Bengal in October, 1575. This necessitated another campaign against Daud, who was finally defeated and killed in a battle, near Rajmahal, in July, 1576. Bengal henceforth became an integral part of the Mughul Empire. But the weak policy of the imperial governor, Muzaffar Khan Turbati, who was "harsh in his measures and offensive in his speech ", gave rise to fresh troubles in that province. Further, the authority of the Emperor continued to be long resisted there by some powerful Bengal chiefs, the most important of whom were Isa Khan of East Central Dacca and Mymensingh, Kedar Rai of Vikrampur, Kandarpanarayan of Chandradvipa (Bakarganj) and Pratapaditya of Jessore. Orissa was finally annexed to the Empire in 1592.

In the meanwhile, Akbar had to face a critical situation due to the sinister motives of his stepbrother, Mirza Muhammad Hakim who governed Kabul as an independent ruler for all practical purposes. In conspiracy with some nobles of the eastern provinces, and some discontented officers of the court, like Khwaja Mansur, the Diwan of the Empire, and others, he cherished the ambition of seizing the throne of Hindustan for himself and even invaded the Punjab. Considering it inadvisable to ignore any longer his intrigues and movements, Akbar marched from his capital on the 8th February, 1581, towards Afghanistan with about 50,000 cavalry, 500 elephants and a large number of infantry. Mirza Muhammad Hakim, on hearing of the Emperor's advance, fled from the Punjab to Kabul without offering any opposition to his brother.

The Emperor thereupon entered Kabul on the 9th August, 1581. Mirza Muhammad Hakim was defeated, but was restored to the government of his province on taking a vow of fidelity to the Emperor, who returned to Delhi early in December, 1581. The victory at Kabul brought immense relief to Akbar. It gave him, writes Smith, "an absolutely free hand for the rest of his life, and may be regarded as the climax of his career". Kabul was formally annexed to the Delhi empire after the death of Muhammad Hakim in July, 1585.

Mian Bahadur Shah, a ruler of Khandesh, refused to submit to the imperial authority. Akbar, relieved of the danger of Uzbeg invasion after the death of 'Abdullah Khan in 1598, marched to the south in July, 1599. He soon captured Burhanpur, the capital of Khandesh, and easily laid siege to the mighty fortress of Asirgarh, than which "it was impossible to conceive a stronger fortress, or one more amply supplied with artillery, warlike stores and provisions". The besieged garrison, though greatly weakened owing to the outbreak of a terrible pestilence which swept off many of them, defended the fortress for six months, when Akbar hastened to achieve his end by subtle means. Unwilling to prolong the siege as his son Salim had rebelled against him, the Emperor inveigled Milan Bahadur Shah into his camp to negotiate for a treaty, on promise of personal safety, but detained him there and forced him to write a letter to the garrison with instructions to surrender the fort. The garrison, however, still held out. Akbar next seduced the Khandesh officers by lavish distribution of money among them, and thus the gates of Asirgarh "were opened by golden keys". This was the last conquest of Akbar.

Having organized the newly-conquered territories into three subahs of Ahmadnagar, Berar and Khandesh, and appointed Prince Daniyal viceroy of Southern and Western India, that is to say, of the three Deccan subahs with Malwa and Gujarat, Akbar returned to Agra in May, 1601, to deal with the rebellious Salim. The Deccan campaigns of Akbar resulted in pushing the Mughul frontier from the Narmada, to the upper courses of the Krishna river (called here the Bhima,). But "the annexation was in form only. The new territory was too large to be effectively governed or even fully conquered. Everywhere, especially in the south and the west, local officers of the old dynasty refused to obey the conqueror, or began to set up puppet princes as a screen for their self-assertion. The Sultans of Bijapur and Golkunda seized the adjacent districts of their fallen neighbours".

AKBAR'S ADMINISTRATION

The principle and systems of Mughal administration was mainly the product of the genius of Akbar. His administrative system requires careful study as it continued to be the basis of the administrative system up to the time of the British rule.

The Mughal Emperors were despotic rulers in whose hands all civil and military powers of the state were concentrated. The emperor was the supreme commander of the imperial forces and fountain-head of justice; his word was law. But as it was not possible for any person to bear the whole burden, the emperor took advice and active assistance from his ministers. Of the ministers, four were important. They were: (i) Vakil or Prime minister, (ii) Wazir or Diwan who was the finance minister, (iii) Mir Bhaksi who was in charge of the military department and (iv) Mirsaman or the store-keeper.

REVOLTS DURING THE REIGN OF AKBAR

Various revolts took place during the reign of Akbar. The Uzbegs were the old nobility of Akbar. They were powerful and ambitious nobles and disliked the centralisation of administration by Akbar. They had another grievance that Akbar did not reward their services well. Their discontentment resulted in an open revolt in 1564 A.D., but eventually all of them were subdued. The Mirzas were part of the royal family and were among those nobles who were blood relatives of Akbar. Being members of the royal family, they desired best rewards from the emperor, failing which; they revolted during the period when Uzbegs revolted against Akbar. They were also defeated. Rebellions also took place in Bengal and Bihar and after one year of campaign, Akbar succeeded in suppressing the revolts. Thus, a number of revolts occurred during the reign of Akbar but none of them succeeded in disturbing the affairs of the state.

BATTLE OF PANIPAT (1556)

The Second Battle of Panipat was fought between the forces of Samrat Hem Chandra Vikramaditya, popularly called Hemu, and the army of Akbar, on November 5, 1556.It was a decisive victory for the Mughal Emperor Jalal ud-Din Mohammad Akbar's general Bairam Khan

Background

On January 24, 1556, Mughal ruler Humayun died and was succeeded by his son, Jalal ud-Din Mohammad Akbar who was only thirteen years old. On February 14, 1556, in a garden at Kalanaur in Punjab, Akbar was enthroned as the Emperor. At the time of his accession to the throne, the Mughal rule was confined to Kabul, Kandahar, parts of Delhi and Punjab. Akbar was then campaigning in Kabul with his guardian, Bairam Khan.

Samrat Hem Chandra Vikramaditya or Hemu was a Hindu leader who was an advisor to Sher Shah Suri's son Islam Shah earlier from 1545 to 1553 and had won 22 battles during 1553 to 1556 to quell the rebellion by Afghan rebels against Sur regime. At the time of Humayun's death in January 1556, Hemu had just quelled a rebellion in Bengal killing the Bengal ruler Mohammad Shah in the war. He made his intentions of winning Delhi for himself known to his commanders. He then started a campaign winning battles throughout northern India. When he attacked Agra, the commander of Akbar's forces in Agra ran away, leaving the state without a fight. A large area of Etawah, Kalpi and Agra states had come under Hemu's control. Hemu then moved towards Delhi and stationed his forces outside the city at Tughlaqabad. On October 6, 1556, his army encountered Mughal resistance. After a fierce fight Akbar's forces were ousted, and Tardi Beg, the commander of the Mughal forces, escaped, allowing Hemu to capture Delhi without much difficulty. Around 3000 army personnel were killed. Hemu had himself crowned at Purana Quila on October 7, 1556, established Hindu Raj in North India, and was bestowed the title of Samrat Hem Chandra Vikramaditya.

Battle

Developments in Delhi and Agra disturbed the Mughals at Kalanaur. Many Mughal Generals advised Akbar and Bairam Khan to retreat to Kabul as Mughal forces may not face Hemu's might, but Bairam Khan decided in favour of war. Akbar's army marched towards Delhi. On November 5, both armies met at the historic battlefield of Panipat, where, thirty years earlier, Akbar's grandfather Babar had defeated Ibrahim Lodi in what is now known as the First Battle of Panipat. Hemu Vikramaditya showed most heroic courage during the battle. The Mughal forces were charged repeatedly by elephants to break their lines. Hemu was himself commanding his forces from atop an elephant like a Hindu Vikramaditya King. It seemed Hemu was on a winning track and Akbar's army will run away. Then suddenly an arrow struck Hemu in the eye and knocked him senseless in his Ohda on the elephant. Not seeing Hemu in his Ohda, Hemu's army was in disarray and defeated in the ensuing confusion. Almost dead Hemu was captured by Shah Quli Khan and brought to Akbar's tent. General Bairam Khan was desirous that Akbar should slay General Hemu himself and should establish his right to the title of "Ghazi" (Champion of Faith or war veteran). But Akbar, the spirited boy that he was, refused to strike a defeated and wounded enemy. Bairam Khan irritated by Akbar's scruples beheaded Hemu himself. His head was sent to Kabul, where it was hanged outside Delhi Darwaza, while his body was placed in a gibbet outside Purana Qila in Delhi.

Aftermath

Akbar, after the Battle of Panipat, let loose a reign of terror on Hindus and Afghan supporters of Hemu Vikramaditya, who was killed in the state of unconsciousness brutally. Thousands were killed by the army of Akbar. Heads were cut and minaretts were made of such heads, at public places, to terrorise people. At least one such picture is displayed at the Panipat Wars Museum at Panipat. Akbar took Agra and Delhi without much resistance. But soon after he took possession of his capital, he had to return to Punjab when intelligence informed him of Sikandar Shah Suri's (Adil Shah Suri's brother) advancing campaign in Punjab. He was however defeated and taken captive after the siege of Fort Mankot by Mughal forces and exiled to Bengal. The victory of Akbar at the Battle of Panipat in 1556 was the real restoration of the Mughal Dynasty to Power in India. It marked the fulfillment of the destiny of the House of Timur in India as rulers.

MILITARY INNOVATIONS

Akbar was given the epithet "the Great" due to his many accomplishments, among which was his record of unbeaten military campaigns that both established and consolidated Mughal rule in the Indian subcontinent. The basis of this military prowess and authority was Akbar's skilful structural and organisational correction of the Mughal army. The Mansabdari system in particular has been acclaimed for its role in upholding Mughal power in the time of Akbar. The system persisted with few changes down to the end of the Mughal Empire, but was progressively weakened under his successors.

Organisational reforms were accompanied by innovations in cannons, fortifications, and the use of elephants. Akbar also took an interest in matchlocks and effectively employed them during various conflicts. He sought the help of Ottomans, and also increasingly of Europeans, especially Portuguese and Italians, in procuring firearms and artillery. Mughal firearms in the time of Akbar came to be far superior to anything that could be deployed by regional rulers, tributaries, or by zamindars. Such was the impact of these weapons that Akbar's Vizier, Abul Fazl, once declared that "with the exception of Turkey, there is perhaps no country in which its guns has more means of securing the Government than [India]." The term "Gunpower Empire" has thus often been used by scholars and historians in analysing the success of the Mughals in India. Mughal power has been seen as owing to their mastery of the techniques of warfare, especially the use of firearms encouraged by Akbar.

The Struggle for North India

Akbar, who had been born in 1542 while his father, Humayun, was in flight from the victorious Surs, was only thirteen when he was proclaimed emperor in 1556. His father had succeeded in regaining control of the Punjab, Delhi, and Agra with Persian support, but even in these areas Mughal rule was precarious, and when the Surs reconquered Agra and Delhi following the death of Humayun, the fate of the boy emperor seemed uncertain. Akbar's minority and the lack of any possibility of militiary assistance from the Mughal stronghold of Kabul, that was at this time in the throes of an invasion by the ruler of Badakhshan, Prince Mirza Suleiman, aggravated the situation. When his regent, Bairam Khan, called a council of war to marshall the Mughal forces, none of Akbar's chieftains approved of it. However, Bairam Khan was ultimately able to prevail over the nobles and it was decided that the Mughals would march against the strongest of the Sur rulers, Sikandar Shah Suri, in the Punjab. Delhi was left under the regency of Tardi Baig Khan. Sikandar Shah Suri, however, presented no major concern for Akbar, and avoided giving battle as the Mughal army approached. The gravest threat came from Hemu, a minister and general of one of the Sur rulers, who had proclaimed himself Hindu emperor and expelled the Mughals from the Indo-Gangetic plains.

Urged by Bairam Khan, who remarshalled the Mughal army before Hemu could consolidate his position, Akbar marched on Delhi to reclaim it. Akbar's army, led by Bairam Khan, defeated Hemu and the Sur army on 5 November 1556 at the Second Battle of Panipat, 50 miles (80 km) north of Delhi. Soon after the battle, Mughal forces occupied Delhi and then Agra. Akbar made a triumphant entry into Delhi, where he stayed for a month. Then he and Bairam Khan returned to Punjab, to deal with Sikandar Shah, who had become active again. In the next six months, the Mughals won another major battle against Sikander Shah Suri, who then fled east to Bengal. Akbar and his forces occupied Lahore and then seized Multan in the Punjab. In 1558, Akbar took possession of Ajmer, the aperture to Rajputana, after the defeat and flight of its Muslim ruler. Late in the same year, a Mughal commander defeated Ibrahim, the last Sur prince, and annexed Jaunpur, the capital of the former Sultanate of Jaunpur in the eastern Gangetic valley. The Mughals had also besieged and defeated the Sur forces in control of Gwalior Fort, the greatest stronghold north of the Narmada river.

The flurry of victories put the vital cities and strongholds located between Lahore, Delhi, Agra, and Jaunpur under Akbar's control. This was Hindustan, the old heartland of Muslim Turko-Afghan political and military power in India. The Mughals, like their predecessors, were now poised to tap the immense agricultural productivity and trade potential of the epicenter of the Indo-Gangetic plains. Royal begums, along with the families of Mughal amirs, were finally brought over from Kabul to India at the time—according to Akbar's vizier, Abul Fazl, "so that men might become settled and be restrained in some measure from departing to a country to which they were accustomed. Akbar had firmly declared his intentions that the Mughals were in India to stay. This was a far cry from the political settlements by his grandfather, Babar, and by his father, Humayun, both of whom had done little to indicate that they were anything but transient rulers.

Expansion into Central India

By 1559, the Mughals had launched a drive to the south into Rajputana and Malwa. However, Akbar's disputes with his regent, Bairam Khan, temporarily put an end to the expansion. The young emperor, at the age of eighteen, wanted to take a more active part in managing affairs. Urged on by his foster mother, Maham Anaga, and his relatives, Akbar decided to dispense with the services of Bairam Khan. After yet another dispute at court, Akbar finally dismissed Bairam Khan in the spring of 1560 and ordered him to leave on Hajj to Mecca. Bairam Khan left for Mecca, but on his way was goaded by his opponents to rebel. He was defeated by the Mughal army in the Punjab and forced to submit. Akbar, however forgave him and gave him the option of either continuing in his court or resuming his pilgrimage, of which Bairam chose the latter. Bairam Khan was later assassinated on his way to Mecca, allegedly by an Afghan with a personal vendetta. In 1560, Akbar resumed military operations. A Mughal army under the command of his foster brother, Adham Khan, and a Mughal commander, Pir Muhammad Khan, invaded Malwa. The Afghan ruler, Baz Bahadur, was defeated at the Battle of Sarangpur, and fled to Khandesh for refuge leaving behind his harem, treasure, and war elephants.

Despite initial success, the campaign proved a disaster from Akbar's point of view. His foster brother retained all the spoils and followed through with the Central Asian practice of slaughtering the surrendered garrison, their wives and children, and many Muslim theologians and Sayyids, who were the descendants of the Prophet Muhammad. Akbar personally rode to Malwa to confront Adham Khan and relieve him of command. Pir Muhammad Khan was then sent in pursuit of Baz Bahadur but was beaten back by the alliance of the rulers of Khandesh and Berar. Baz Bahadur temporarily regained control of Malwa until, in the next year, Akbar sent another Mughal army to invade and annex the kingdom. Malwa became a province of the nascent imperial administration of Akbar's regime. Baz Bahadur survived as a refugee at various courts untils until, eight years later, in 1570, he took service under Akbar.

Despite ultimate success in Malwa, the conflict however, exposed cracks in Akbar's personal relationships with his relatives and Mughal nobles. When Adham Khan confronted Akbar following another dispute in 1562, he was struck down by the emperor and thrown from a terrace into the palace courtyard at Agra. Still alive, Adham Khan was dragged up and thrown to the courtyard once again by Akbar to ensure his death. Akbar now sought to eliminate the threat of over-mighty subjects. He created specialized ministerial posts relating to imperial governance. No member of the Mughal nobility was to have unnestioned pre-eminence. When a powerful clan of Uzbek chiefs broke out in rebellion in 1564, Akbar decisively defeated and routed them in Malwa and then Bihar. He pardoned the rebellious leaders, hoping to conciliate them. But they rebelled again, so Akbar had to quell their uprising a second time. Following a third revolt with the proclamation of Mirza Muhammad Hakim, Akbar's brother and the Mughal ruler of Kabul, as emperor, his patience was finally exhausted. Several Uzbek chieftains were subsequently slain and the rebel leaders trampled to death under elephants. Simultaneously the Mirza's, a group of Akbar's distant cousins who held important fiefs near Agra, had also risen up in rebellion. They, too were slain and driven out of the empire. In 1566, Akbar moved to meet the forces of his brother, Muhammad Hakim, who had marched into the Punjab with dreams of seizing the imperial throne. Following a brief confontration, however, Muhammad Hakim accepted Akbar's supremacy and retreated back to Kabul.

In 1564, Mughal forces conquered the Gondwana kingdom. Gondwana, a thinly populated hilly area in central India was of interest to the Mughals because of its herd of wild elephants. The territory was ruled over by Raja Vir Narayan, a minor, and his mother, Durgavati, a Rajput warrior queen of the Gonds. Akbar did not personally lead the campaign because he was preoccupied with the Uzbek rebellion, but left the expedition in the hands of Asaf Khan, the Mughal governor of Kara. Durgavati committed suicide after her defeat at the Battle of Damoh while Raja Vir Narayan was slain at the Fall of Chauragarh, the mountain fortress of the Gonds. The Mughals seized immense wealth, an uncalculated amount of gold and silver, jewels and 1000 elephants. Kamala Devi, a younger sister of Durgavati, was sent to the Mughal harem. The brother of Durgavati's deceased husband was installed as the Mughal administrator of the region. Like in Malwa, however, Akbar entered into a dispute with his vassals over the conquest of Gondwana. Asaf Khan was accused of keeping most of the treasures, and sending back only 200 elephants to Akbar. When summoned to give accounts, he fled Gondwana. He went first to the Uzbeks, then returned to Gondwana where he was pursued by Mughal forces. Finally, he submitted and Akbar restored him to his previous position.

THE AGE OF SPLENDOR

AKBAR'S only surviving son, Prince Salim, succeeded to the throne on November 3, 1605, under the title of Jahangir. To prove his desire to end the bitterness that had divided the court when he had made an unsuccessful attempt to usurp power during the last years of his father's reign, he granted a general amnesty to all his former opponents. Abdur Rahman, the son of Abul Fazl (Akbar's friend who had been murdered at Jahangir's instigation), was promoted to higher rank. The nobles who had endeavored to have Jahangir's son, Khusrau, made Akbar's successor were allowed to retain their ranks and jagirs.

Despite his attempts at conciliation, Jahangir was soon faced with the task of suppressing a revolt led by Khusrau, who had fled to the Punjab. The revolt was quelled without great difficulty, with Khusrau brought back in chains, but it led, incidentally, to one important development. Khusrau had received help from Arjan Dev, the guru or leader of the Sikhs. After Khusrau's defeat, Arjan Dev was summoned to the court to answer for his conduct. Sikh historians say that the enmity of Chandu Lal, the Hindu diwan of Lahore, who had a family quarrel with the guru, was responsible for his troubles. When the guru was unable to give any satisfactory explanation for his part in the rebellion, he was put to death.

He might have ended his days in peace if he had not espoused the cause of the rebel, but this punitive action against him marked the beginning of a long and bitter conflict between the Sikhs and the Mughal government.

An event of Jahangir's private life that was to have great significance for his reign was his marriage to Nur Jahan in 1611. She was the widow of a Persian nobleman, Sher Afghan, a rebellious official of Burdwan who met his death while resisting arrest at the hands of Qutb-ud-din Khan Koka, the viceroy of Bengal.

Nur Jahan was taken to the court, and three years later, at the age of forty, she became the royal consort. A capable woman, she acquired such an ascendency over her husband that she became in effect the joint ruler of the kingdom. Coins were struck in her name, and Jahangir used to say that he had handed her the country in return for a cup of wine and a few morsels of food. Nur Jahan's relatives soon occupied the chief posts of the realm. Her brother, Asaf Khan, became the prime minister, and his daughter, Mumtaz Mahal, the Lady of the Taj, married Prince Khurram, who succeeded his father as Shah Jahan. The influence of the gifted but masterly queen and her relatives was not entirely beneficial, but they were all capable people, and until toward the end of the later part of Jahangir's reign they administered the empire efficiently. Their influence attracted a large number of brilliant soldiers, scholars, poets, and civil servants from Iran who played an important role in the administration and the cultural life of Mughal India.

One of the most fruitful achievements of Jahangir's reign was the consolidation of Mughal rule in Bengal. This province had been incorporated in the empire under Akbar, but the governors of Akbar's time had not attempted to bring the existing local chiefs—Hindu and Muslim—under the full control of the central government. The imposition of Mughal power and the crushing of local resistance was largely the work of Jahangir's foster-brother, Shaikh Alauddin, entitled Islam Khan, who was viceroy of Bengal from 1608 to 1613. He employed all possible methods—force, reward, and diplomacy—to terminate the independence of the powerful zamindars. He also enlarged the territorial limits of the empire by subjugating Cooch Behar in 1609 and Kamrup in 1612. In 1612 he shifted his capital from Rajmahal to Daccan, a singularly appropriate choice in view of the menace of Magh raids on the eastern rivers. Islam Khan died in 1613, and after an interval of four years, during which his incompetent brother was in charge of the area, his good work was continued by another capable viceroy, Ibrahim Khan Fath-i-Jung. He devoted the six years of his viceroyalty (1617–1623) to consolidating the gains already made and died fighting loyally against Prince Khurram when he revolted against his father the emperor and tried to seize the government of Bengal.

Outside Bengal, the main military events of Jahangir's reign were the victory over the Rajputs of Mewar in 1615, the reassertion of the Mughal authority in the Deccan, and the capture of Kangra in 1620. Two years later the Mughals lost the great fort of Qandahar to the Persians, and in spite of efforts made during Jahangir's and Shah Jahan's reigns, they were never able to recover it. This was also a time of internal difficulties. Hitherto, Nur Jahan, Asaf Khan, and Prince Khurram had cooperated in controlling the affairs of the country, and Khurram had been the leader of victorious expeditions in Rajputana and the Deccan. Nur Jahan, however, had now attained complete ascendency over the emperor, and tried to promote the claims of his youngest son, Prince Shahryar, to whom her daughter by Sher Afghan was married. This brought her into conflict with Prince Khurram, who revolted in 1623. He became master of Bengal and Bihar for a brief time, but was ultimately defeated and obliged to retire to the Deccan. In the end he asked his father's pardon and was reconciled in 1626.

Jahangir died in the following year on his way back from Kashmir, and was buried at Shahdara, a suburb of Lahore. Through a relay of messengers, Asaf Khan sent word to Prince Khurram, his son-in-law, who was still in the Deccan, and the succession was secured without much difficulty. Prince Shahryar, Nur Jahan's son-in-law, was captured and blinded; Nur Jahan herself retired from the world she had dominated, living quietly until her death sixteen years later.

Owing to his likable personality, the brilliance of his court, and his friendliness toward foreigners, Jahangir has been favourably treated, especially by English writers. There are, however, certain aspects of his administration which cast a shadow on his regime and darken the course of the later Mughal history. The extension of the Mughal dominion came practically to a halt in his reign, and the empire suffered a serious blow in the loss of Qandahar. In spite of vast imperial resources, no serious attempt was made to bring the great unconquered areas of the Deccan under the empire. A contemporary Dutch writer commenting on this said: The probable explanation is to be found in the sloth, cowardice, and weakness of the last emperor, Salim, and in the domestic discords of his family." There is little reason to doubt the essential truth of this harsh judgment.

A significant change took place in the composition of the nobility and the holders of high office during the years of Nur Jahan's ascendency. Akbar had made good use of the indigenous element—such men as Abul Fazl, Faizi, Todar Mal, Shaikh Farid, Man Singh, and Bhagwan Singh come to mind—and had maintained a due balance between the Irani and Turani elements. Under Jahangir this balance was upset, and the Iranis became all-powerful. This was facilitated by the early death of Shaikh Farid and by the stigma attached to Man Singh, the Rajput leader, and to Khan-i-Azam, the premier Turani noble, because of their association with Khusrau. Held in check, the Irani element was a source of strength, but this ceased to be the case in the eighteenth century, when its political role during the decline of the empire weakened the realm.

Even more objectionable was the mushroom growth of bureaucracy and the resultant increase in government expenditure. No large territory was added to the empire, but the number of mansabdars, which under Akbar numbered about eight hundred, was increased to nearly three thousand in Jahangir's reign. The author of *Maasir-ul-Umara*, himself a financial expert, in dealing with the fiscal history of the Mughal period, said: "In the time of Jahangir, who was a careless prince and paid no attention to political or financial matters, and who was constitutionally thoughtless and pompous, the fraudulent officials, in gathering lucre, and hunting for bribes, paid no attention to the abilities of men or to their performance. The devastation of the country and the diminution of income rose to such a height that the revenue of the exchequer-lands fell to five million rupees while expenditure rose to fifteen million, and large sums were expended out of the general treasury."

Jahangir must bear the ultimate responsibility for this state of affairs, but the immediate cause was the dominance and policy of Nur Jahan. She was a woman of noble impulses and good taste who spent large sums in charity, particularly for the relief of indigent women, and worked hard to relieve the drabness of Indian life. Many innovations which enhanced the grace and charm of Mughal culture can be directly traced to her, and her influence led to the maintenance of a magnificent court. But all this strained the royal resources.

The lavish style of living introduced at the royal court was initiated by the nobility, and an era of extravagance, with its concomitants of corruption and demoralization among officers of the state, was inaugurated.

This corroded the structure of the Mughal government. A contemporary Dutch account sharply criticized Nur Jahan and her "crowd of Khurasanis" for what it was costing the state to maintain "their excessive pomp," and complained that the foreign bureaucrats were particularly indifferent to the condition of the masses. To Nur Jahan herself belongs the doubtful honour of introducing the system of nazars or gifts to the court—corruption at the royal level. Asaf Khan emerges in the pages of Sir Thomas Roe's account of his negotiations at the Mughal court as exceedingly greedy for such gifts.

The era of extravagance which was ushered in during Jahangir's reign was fed from two other sources. One was the change in the prevalent philosophy of life. The old Indian emphasis on plain living and the excellence of limitation of wants was not consistent with the way of life introduced by Muslim rulers in the subcontinent, but (coupled with the Sufi philosophy) it was not without a certain influence. In Akbar's days in particular, with emphasis on the spiritual side of things, it is easy to trace a certain idealism, an other-worldliness, and the ability to rise above purely materialistic values, in spite of the elaborate grandeur of a great empire. The Irani newcomers were alien to this approach, and under their influence the gracious living became the summum bonum, the goal of human existence.

The other factor responsible for increased extravagance was the vast opportunity for spending provided by the new commercial contacts with Europe. By now the fame of the Mughal empire had spread to distant lands, and in Jahangir's day embassies came to his court from European countries. England sent Captain Hawkins in 1608, and Sir Thomas Roe, the ambassador of James I, came to conclude a commercial treaty in 1615.

By September, 1618, he was able to obtain a *farman* signed by Prince Khurram as viceroy of Gujarat which gave facilities for trade, but owing to the prince's opposition, did not allow a building to be built as a residence. The new trade, which will be noted more fully later, brought out some pathetic propensities in the Mughal nobility. Costly toys were devised to please the taste of the court. In this Jahangir led the way. He was described as "an amateur of all varieties and antiquities, and displayed an almost childish love of toys." One traveller tells how he presented the emperor with "a small whistle of gold, weighing almost an ounce, set with sparks of rubies, which he took and whistled therewith almost an hour."

THE CONQUEST OF RAJPUTANA

Having established Mughal rule over northern India, Akbar turned his attention to the conquest of Rajputana. No imperial power in India based on the Indo-Gangetic plains could be secure if a rival centre of power existed on its flank in Rajputana. The Mughals had already established domination over parts of northern Rajputana in Mewat, Ajmer, and Nagor. Now, however, Akbar was determined to drive into the heartlands of the Rajput kings that had never previously submitted to the Muslim rulers of the Delhi Sultanate. Beginning in 1561, the Mughals actively engaged the Rajputs in warfare and diplomacy. Most Rajput states accepted Akbar's supremacy; the ruler of Mewar, Udai Singh, however, remained outside the imperial fold. Raja Udai Singh was inclined from the Sisodia ruler, Rana Sanga, who had died fighting Babar at the Battle of Khanwa in 1527. As the head of the Sisodia clan, he possessed the highest ritual status of all the Rajput kings and chieftains in India. Unless Udai Singh was reduced to submission, the imperial authority of the Mughals would be lessened in Rajput eyes. Furthermore, Akbar, at this early period, was still enthusiastically devoted to the cause of Islam and sought to impress the superiority of his faith over the most prestigious warriors in Brahminical Hinduism.

In 1567, Akbar moved to reduce the Chittorgarh Fort in Mewar. The fortress-capital of Mewar was of great strategic importance as it lay on the shortest route from Agra to Gujarat and was also considered a key to holding the interior parts of Rajputana. Udai Singh retired to the hills of Mewar, leaving two Rajput warriors, Jaimal and Patta, in charge of the defense of his capital. Chittorgarh fell on February 1568 after a siege of four months. Akbar had the surviving defenders massacred and their heads displayed upon towers erected throughout the region, in order to demonstrate his authority. The total loot that fell into the hands of the Mughals was distributed throughout the empire. He remained in Chittorgarh for three days, then returned to Agra, where to commemorate the victory, he set up, at the gates of his fort, statues of Jaimal and Patta mounted on elephants. Udai Singh's power and influence was broken. He never again ventured out his mountain refuge in Mewar and Akbar was content to let him be.

The fall of Chittorgarh was followed up by a Mughal attack on the Ranthambore Fort in 1568. Ranthambore was held by the Hada Rajputs and reputed to be the most powerful fortress in India. However, it fell only after a couple of months. Akbar was now the master of almost the whole of Rajputana. Most of the Rajput kings had submitted to the Mughals. Only the clans of Mewar continued to resist. Udai Singh's son and successor, Pratap Singh, was later defeated by the Mughals at the

Battle of Haldighati in 1576. He spent the remainder of his life in exile in the Aravalli hills. Akbar would celebrate his conquest of Rajputana by laying the foundation of a new capital, 23 miles (37 km) W.S.W of Agra in 1569. It was called Fatehpur Sikri ("the city of victory").

Annexation of Western and Eastern India

Akbar's next military objectives were the conquest of Gujarat and Bengal, which connected India with the trading centres of Asia, Africa, and Europe through the Arabian Sea and the Bay of Bengal respectively. Furthermore, Gujarat had been a haven for rebellious Mughal nobles, while in Bengal, the Afghans still held substantial influence under their ruler, Sulaiman Khan Karrani. Akbar first moved against Gujarat, which lay in the crook of the Mughal provinces of Rajputana and Malwa. Gujarat, with its coastal regions, possessed areas of rich agricultural production in its central plain; an impressive output of textiles and other industrial goods, and the busiest seaports of India. Akbar intended to link the maritime state with the massive resources of the Indo-Gangetic plains. However, the ostensible casus belli was that the rebel Mirzas, who had previously been driven out of India, were now operating out of a base in southern Gujarat. Morever, Akbar had received invitations from cliques in Gujarat to oust the reigning king, which served as justification for his military mission. In 1572, he moved to occupy Ahmedabad, the capital, and other northern cities, and was proclaimed the lawful sovereign of Gujarat. By 1573, he had driven out the Mirzas who, after offering token resistance, fled for refuge in the Deccan. Surat, the commercial capital of the region and other coastal cities soon capitulated to the Mughals. The king, Muzaffar Shah III, was caught hiding in a corn field; he was pensioned off by Akbar with a small allowance.

Having established his authority over Gujarat, Akbar returned to Fatephur Sikiri, where he built the Buland Darwaza to honor his victories, but a rebellion by Afghan nobles supported by the Rajput ruler of Idar, and the renewed intrigues of the Mirzas forced his return to Gujarat. Akbar crossed the Rajputana and reached Ahmedabad in eleven days - a journey that normally took six weeks. The outnumbered Mughal army then won a decisive victory on 2 September 1573. Akbar slew the rebel leaders and erected a tower out of their severed heads. The conquest and subjugation of Gujarat proved highly profitable for the Mughals; the territory yielded a revenue of more than five million rupees annually to Akbar's treasury, after expenses.

Akbar the Great

Akbar had now defeated most of the Afghan leftovers in India. The only centre of Afghan power was now in Bengal, where Sulaiman Khan Karrani, an Afghan chieftain whose family had served under Sher Shah Suri, was reigning in power. While Sulaiman Khan meticulously avoided giving offence to Akbar, his son, Daud Khan, who had succeeded him in 1572, decided otherwise. Whereas Sulaiman Khan had the khutba read in Akbar's name and acknowledged Mughal supremacy, Daud Khan assumed the insignia of royalty and ordered the khutba to be proclaimed in his own name in defiance of Akbar. Munim Khan, the Mughal governor of Bihar, was ordered to chastise Duad Khan, but later, Akbar himself set out to Bengal. This was an opportunity to bring the trade in the east under Mughal control. In 1574, the Mughals seized Patna from Daud Khan, who fled to Bengal. Akbar returned to Fatehpur Sikri and left his generals to finish the campaign. The Mughal army was subsequently victorious at the Battle of Tukaroi in 1575, which led to the annexation of Bengal and parts of Bihar that had been under the dominion of Daud Khan. Only Orissa was left in the hands of the Karrani dynasty as a fief of the Mughal Empire. A year later, however, Daud Khan rebelled and attempted to regain Bengal. He was defeated by the Mughal general, Khan Jahan Quli, and had to flee into exile. Daud Khan was later captured and executed by Mughal forces. His severed head was sent to Akbar, while his limbs were gibetted at Tandah, the Mughal capital in Bengal.

Campaigns in Afghanistan and Central Asia

Following his conquests of Gujarat and Bengal, Akbar was preoccupied with domestic concerns. He did not leave Fatehpur Sikri on a military campaign until 1581, when the Punjab was again invaded by his brother, Mirza Muhammad Hakim. Akbar expelled his brother to Kabul and this time pressed on, determined to end the threat from Muhammad Hakim once and for all. In contrast to the problem that his predecessors once had in getting Mughal nobles to stay on in India, the problem now was to get them to leave India.

They were, according to Abul Fazl "afraid of the cold of Afghanistan." The Hindu officers, in turn, were additionally subdued by the traditional taboo against crossing the Indus. Akbar, however, spurred them on. The soldiers were provided with pay eight months in advance.

In August 1581, Akbar seized Kabul and took up residence at Babar's old citidel. He stayed there for three weeks, in the absence of his brother, who had fled into the mountains. Akbar left Kabul in the hands of his sister, Bakht-un-Nisa Begum, and returned to India. He pardoned his brother, who took up de facto charge of the Mughal administration in Kabul; Bakht-un-Nis continued to be the official governor. A few years later, in 1585, Muhammad Hakim died and Kabul passed into the hands of Akbar once again. It was officially incorporated as a province of the Mughal Empire.

The Kabul expedition was the beginning of a long period of activity over the northern frontiers of the empire. For thirteen years, beginning in 1585, Akbar remained in the north, shifting his capital to Lahore in the Punjab while dealing with challenges from beyond the Khyber Pass. The gravest threat came from the Uzbeks, the tribe that had driven his grandfather, Babar, out of Central Asia. They had been organized under Abdullah Khan Shaybanid, a capable military chieftain who had seized Badakhshan and Balkh from Akbar's distant Timurid relatives, and whose Uzbek troops now posed a serious challenge to the northwestern frontiers of the Mughal Empire. The Afghan tribes on the border were also restless, partly on account of the hostility of the Yusufzai of Bajaur and Swat, and partly owing to the activity of a new religious leader, Bayazid, the founder of the Roshaniyya sect. The Uzbeks were also known to be subsidizing Afghans.

In 1586, Akbar negotiated a pact with Abdullah Khan in which the Mughals agreed to remain neutral during the Uzbek invasion of Safavid held Khorasan. In return, Abdullah Khan agreed to refrain from supporting, subsidizing, or offering refuge to the Afghan tribes hostile to the Mughals. Thus freed, Akbar began a series of campaigns to pacify the Yusufzais and other rebels. Akbar ordered Zain Khan to lead an expedition against the Afghan tribes. Raja Birbal, a renowned minister in Akbar's court, was also given military command. The expedition turned out to be a disaster, and on its retreat from the mountains, Birbal and his entourage were ambushed and killed by the Afghans at the Malandarai Pass in Febaruary 1586. Akbar immediately fielded new armies to reinvade the Yusufzai lands under the command of Raja Todar Mal. Over the next six years, the Mughals contained the Yusufzai in the mountain valleys, and forced the submission of many chiefs in Swat and Bajaur. Dozens of forts were built and occupied to secure the region. Akbar's response demonstrated his ability to clamp firm military control over the Afghan tribes.

Despite his pact with the Uzbeks, Akbar nurtured a secret hope of reconquering Central Asia from Afghanistan. However, Badakshan and Balkh remained firmly part of the Uzbek dominions. There was only a transient occupation of the two provinces by the Mughals under his grandson, Shah Jahan, in the mid-seventeenth century. Nevertheless, Akbar's stay in the northern frontiers was highly fruitful. The last of the rebellious Afghan tribes were subdued by 1600. The Roshaniyya movement was firmly suppressed. The Afridi and Orakzai tribes, which had risen up under the Roshaniyyas, had been subjugated. The leaders of the movement were captured and driven into exile. Jalaluddin, the son of the Roshaniyya movement's founder, Bayazid, was killed in 1601 in a fight with Mughal troops near Ghazni. Mughal rule over Afghanistan was finally secure, particularly after the passing of the Uzbek threat with the death of Abdullah Khan in 1598.

Conquests in the Indus Valley

While in Lahore dealing with the Uzbeks, Akbar had sought to subjugate the Indus valley to secure the frontier provinces. He sent an army to conquer Kashmir in the upper Indus basin when, in 1585, Ali Shah, the ruling king of the Shia Chak dynasty, refused to send his son as a hostage to the Mughal court. Ali Shah surrendered immediately to the Mughals, but another of his sons, Yaqub, crowned himself as king, and led a stubborn resistance to Mughal armies. Finally, in June, 1589, Akbar himself travelled from Lahore to Srinagar to receive the surrender of Yaqub and his rebel forces. Baltistan and Ladakh, which were Tibetan provinces adjacent to Kashmir, pledged their allegiance to Akbar. The Mughals also moved to conquer Sindh in the lower Indus valley. Since 1574, the northern fortress of Bhakkar had remained under imperial control. Now, in 1586, the Mughal governor of Multan tried and failed to secure the capitulation of Mirza Jani Beg, the independent ruler of Thatta in southern Sindh. Akbar responded by sending a Mughal army to besiege Sehwan, the river capital of the region. Jani Beg mustered a large army to meet the Mughals. The outnumbered Mughal forces defeated the Sindhi forces at the Battle of Sehwan. After suffering further defeats, Jani Beg surrendered to the Mughals in 1591, and in 1593, paid homage to Akbar in Lahore.

Conquest of Baluchistan

As early as 1586, about half a dozen Baluchi chiefs had been persuaded to attend the imperial court and acknowledge the vassalage of Akbar. In preparations to take Kandahar from the Safavids, Akbar ordered the Mughal forces to conquer the rest of Baluchistan in 1595. The Mughal general, Mir

Masum, led an attack on the stronghold of Sibi, situated to the northwest of Quetta and defeated a coalition of local chieftains in a pitched battle. They were made to acknowledge Mughal supremacy and attend Akbar's court. As a result, the whole of Baluchistan, including the strategic region of Makran, the coastal strip running from India to Iran, became a part of the Mughal Empire. The Mughals now frontiered Persian ruled Kandahar from three sides.

2ND BATTLE OF PANIPAT

Lets begin with the a brief introduction of what happened before the battle. After the death of Babur the first Mughal emperor (in 1531 CE) Humayun ascended the throne of Delhi. A very learned man spent a lot of his time in royal library, but not a great ruler, as a consequence Sher Shah (the Afghan) drove him out of Delhi and sent him to exile in Persia. Sher Shah was so powerful ruler that the Mughals didn't even think of attacking India while he was alive. But after the death of Sher Shah (in 1545 CE) the Suri dynasty crumbled to its feet, Humayun seeing a chance to occupy Delhi again marched with all his troops from Persia and was successful in capturing Delhi. But his glory was short lived as he died few months after in 1556 CE, leaving Delhi again unprotected. Bairam Khan the trusted general of Humayun, enthroned Akbar as the new ruler, and remained his guardian. However even after Akbar's accession to the throne, the danger for the Mughals was not completely eliminated, that was the time of high conspiracies going all around. The battle between Afghans and Mughals to rule India gained a new height now, Sikander Shah Suri the Afghan ruler of Punjab often imposed a big threat to Akbar, hence leaving Delhi in the hands of Tardi Beg (a general in Mughal army) Akbar went to sack Sikander in Punjab.

The Second Battle of Panipat occurred in November 5,1556. Emperor Akbar, who was crowned in the same year after his father's death defeated Muhammad Adil Shah Suri of Pashtun Suri dynasty and his Prime minister Hemu (Hemchandra). This defeat of Adil Shah and Hemu initiated Akbar's reign.

Humayun, the second Mughal emperor died suddenly on 24th January, 1556 as he slipped from the steps of his library. That time his son Akbar was only thirteen years old boy. Akbar was busy in a campaign in Punjab with the Chief Minister Bairam Khan at the time of his father's death. That time Mughal reign was confined to Kabul, Kandahar, and parts of

Punjab and Delhi. Akbar was enthroned as the emperor on February 14, 1556 in a garden of Kalanaur in Punjab. Hemu or Hemchandra was the military chief of Afghan Sultan Muhammad Adil Shah. Adil Shah was the ruler of Chunar and was seeking the opportunity to expel the Mughals from India. They got the advantage of Humayun's death. Hemu occupied Agra and Delhi without much difficulty in October and became the ruler under the title `Raja Vikramaditya`. It was a short-lived victory for Adil Shah and Hemu. Bairam Khan, the Chief Minister and the guardian of Akbar proceeded towards Delhi with a large army. On November 5 both the armies met at Panipat. Hemu had a large army including fifteen hundred war elephants. He got the initial success but unfortunately a stray arrow struck his eye and he became unconscious. His troops thought that they have lost their leader and panic spread on them and they retreated. The Mughals won the battle. Shah Quli Khan captured the Hawai elephant of Hemu and presented it directly to Akbar. Hemu was brought in unconscious condition to Akbar and Bairam Khan. Akbar then severed the head of unconscious Hemu and got his cavalry sword. Some historians claimed that Akbar did not kill Hemu by himself; he just touched his head with his sword and his followers killed Hemu. Hemu's cut off head was sent to Kabul to the ladies of Humayun's harem in order to celebrate the victory.

Hemu's torso was sent to Delhi for a display on a gibbet. Iskandar Khan fromm Akbar's side chased Hemu's army and could capture about fifteen hundred elephants and a large portion of the army. Hemu's wife escaped from Delhi with the treasure she could have with her. Pir Mohammad Khan chased her caravan with a troop but his effort did not get any success. The Second Battle of Panipat changed the course of Indian History as it initiated the re-establishment of Mughal Dynasty in India.

AKBAR'S IMPERIALIST POLICY

It was Akbar who first thought of founding an all India Empire of the house of Timur. It was inspired by a longing for fame and glory. Akbar felt that for all sided development and progress of the people it was essential to end political disintegration and continuous internecine warfare. Akbar desired to found an enlightened paternal government and to initiate a policy which may inculcate a feeling of solidarity and equality among people of different creeds and classes so that a sentiment of patriotism might grow up. His policy of religious toleration bears a testimony to this.

Any accession of strength to the power of the European traders in India was considered derogatory to the interests of the country. He desired to extend his authority to the coastal regions.

He wanted to maintain friendly relations with his north-western neighbours but considered it necessary to occupy the entire Indus basin both to the east and to the west. Akbar and his successors did not aim at mere extension of territory nor did they base their authority on mere force. Up to Emperor Shah Jahan the Mughal rulers wanted to broad base their power on the consent of the governed.

They were ever intent on promoting the prosperity of the land. They tried to evoke sentiments of gratitude, loyalty and respect rather than fear and awe. Aurangzeb adopted a comparatively narrow outlook and reaped its fruit in ruin and disintegration. It was not merely the belief of Akbar that if war was not waged against one's neighbours they would themselves raise in arms against him. It was almost a universal belief that two independent rulers cannot co-exist in the same country. The rulers of the House of Timur therefore tried to establish pan India Empire.

CONQUEST OF AKBAR AND THE GROWTH OF THE MUGHAL EMPIRE

Akbar's expansion of his empire began with the conquest of northern India. First of all, he sent a strong force to Malwa. Baz Bahadur, the ruler of Malwa, was defeated and the state annexed to the Mughal Empire. Next Akbar sent his forces to Gondwana ruled by Rani Durgawati. She offered tough resistance but was overpowered. The state of Gondwana thus passed into the hands of the Mughals.

Akbar now turned his attention towards Rajputana. He was aware that the Rajputs were very brave people and it was very essential to win them over. So he first tried to have friendly relations with them. The alliance with Akbar was that of raja Bihari Mal of Amber.

He got his daughter Jodha Bai married to Akbar. The Mughal emperor honored the Raja's family by offering Bhagwan Das and Man Singh, (the son and grandson of the Raja respectively) high posts in the Mughal court. Man Singh later proved to be one of the ablest generals of medieval India. He won for Akbar most of the territories that formed a part of the Mughal empire.

But Rana Udai Singh, a scion of the Sisodias, refused to accept Akbar's offer of friendship. He instead chose to fight with Akbar. Akbar

Akbar the Great

attacked Mewar in A.D. 1567 and captured the fort of Chittor. Rana Udai Singh had to flee to the hills. After the fall of Chittor, the fort of Ranthambore too fell.

The other Rajputs of Bikaner, Jaisalmer and Jodhpur submitted in A.D. 1570. Rana Udai Singh of Mewar died in A.D. 1572 but his illustrious son Maharana Pratap Singh did not yield. He decided to carry on the struggle with the Mughals to free his motherland from them. In A.D. 1576, Akbar sent Man Singh to subdue the Maharana. A fierce battle was fought at Haldighati where the Maharana was defeated. In A.D. 1572-73, Akbar led an expedition against Gujurat. It was a port of great importance to Akbar. Akbar defeated its ruler Muzaffar Shah and to commemorate the victory, got the Buland Darwaza constructed at Sikri.

In 1576, Bengal and Bihar were annexed to the Mughal kingdom. Kabul was under the charge of Mirza Hakim. In A.D. 1580, he invade Punjab. Akbar himself marched against him and compelled Hakim to acknowledge his suzerainaty. In A.D. 1586, Hakim died and Kabul was annexed to the Mughal Empire.

Likewise Kashmir, Sind and Multan were added to the Mughal Empire. In 1595, Baluchistan and Kandhar were also annexed and thus the chain of the defense of the North-West Frontier Province was completed. Having fully secured his way over northern India, Akbar thought of conquering the Deccan. One reason was that he wanted to overthrow the Portuguese who had established their factories along the seacoast and were also building up their naval power.

From A.D. 1595-1601, Akbar sent expeditions to the Deccan to subdue the Portuguese, Chand Bibi of Ahmadnagar and to capture Asirgarh. Having completed all his conquests, Akbar thus controlled a very vast empire. It extended from Bengal in the east to Afghanistan in the west comprising Kabul and Kandhar. In the north, it extended from the mighty Himalayas to the Godavari in the Deccan. In A.D. 1605, Akbar died and was buried at Sikandra, near Agra

RAJPUT POLICY OF AKBAR

The Rajpur policy of Akbar was the result of a deliberate policy and was based on the principles of enlightened self-interest, recognition of merit, justice and fair play. The rebellions of those very people on whom depended the Mughal authority convinced Akbar, that the only way to perpetuate his power and dynasty was to seek the support of the Rajputs.

The Rajput community was the important political elements in the in India.

Moreover, the Afghan opposition to the Mughals, had not died out. The Afgans still dominated Bihar, Bengal and Orissa. Sher Khan, son of the late Sultan Muhammad Adil Shah, was preparing to overthrow the Mughal power in the eastern parts of the modern Uttar Pradesh (1561), and Sulaiman Karrani was fast becoming the leader of the Afghans in India.

Rajput policy of Akbar was based on a planned policy towards the Rajputs. Akbar was the first Mughal emperor who pursued such a policy. Akbar was an imperialist and desired to bring under his rule as much territory of India as was possible. Therefore it was necessary to bring the Rajput rulers under his suzerainty.

Akbar preferred to befriend the Rajputs instead of turning them into his enemies. He was impressed by the chivalry, faithfulness, fighting skill, etc. of the Rajputs. Akbar wanted dependable allies from among the Indian people instead of depending on foreigners. The Rajputs, therefore, became a good choice. The liberal religious policy of Akbar also directed him to be friendly with them. Akbar thus tried to befriend the Rajputs but at the same time desired to bring them under his suzerainty. Akbar captured strong forts of the Rajputs like the forts of Chittor, Ranthambhor, and Kalinjar. This weakened the power of the Rajputs to offer him resistance. Those Rajputs rulers either accepted his sovereignty or entered into matrimonial relations with him.

They were left masters of their kingdoms and were given high offices in the state and there was no interference in their administration. They were, however, asked to pay annual tribute to the emperor. Those Rajput rulers, who opposed him, were attacked and efforts were made to force them to accept his sovereignty. The case of Mewar is the best example of it. Among the rulers who voluntarily accepted the sovereignty of Akbar was Raja Bharmal of Ajmer. He met Akbar in 1562 A.D., accepted his sovereignty and married his daughter to him. This very princess gave birth to prince Salim.

Akbar gave high mansabs to Raja Bharmal, his son, Bhagwan Das and his grandson, Man Singh. After the fall of the fort of Chittor a few Rajput states like Bikaner and Jaisalmer voluntarily accepted the suzerainty of Akbar, while some of them entered into matrimonial alliances with him. After the battle of Haldi-Ghati a few more Rajput rulers like that of Banswara, Bundi and Orcha also accepted the suzerainty of Akbar.

Thus, most of the Rajput rulers submitted to Akbar without fighting, entered into his service, became his loyal allies-and a few among them became his relatives as well. The Rajput policy of Akbar was a grand success. All Rajput states, except Mewar, accepted the sovereignty of Akbar. Those very Rajputs who were fighting against the Muslim rulers for the last three hundred fifty years submitted to Akbar and participated in the expansion of the Mughal Empire. Akbar was the real founder of the Empire of the Mughals and the first successful conqueror of Rajput independence. Due to the Rajput policy of Akbar, the Rajputs forgot their ideal of maintaining their independent political existence and they gladly pulled up their strength with the Mughal emperor. It was the greatest success of Akbar. It helped in expanding and strengthening the Mughal Empire.

Akbar neither forced any Rajput ruler to enter into matrimonial alliance with him nor asked their princesses to accept Islam before marrying them. Besides, he honoured his wives, allowed them to follow their own religion, respected their Rajput relatives and gave them high offices in the state. The Rajputs became loyal supporters of the Mughal emperor because Akbar offered most liberal terms to them in exchange of their services and friendship to him. Akbar simply desired that the Rajputs should accept his sovereignty, pay him annual tribute, surrender their foreign policy to him, support him with their forces when necessary and regard themselves as one with the Mughal Empire. In return, Akbar was prepared to give them liberty in their internal matters, honour them, offer them services in the state according to their merit and provide them complete religious freedom. The liberality of Akbar was the primary reason of the success of his Rajput policy.

RELIGIOUS POLICY OF AKBAR

Religious policy of Akbar was that of complete toleration. His policy was based on the principle of universal peace. Akbar was the first among the emperors of Delhi who pursued such a policy. It was Akbar, who, from the very beginning of his reign, gradually accepted a policy of dynamic toleration and active sympathy for religious and spiritual movements. Various factors were responsible for the liberal views and policies of religious toleration of Akbar. His father was a Sunni while his mother and his protector, Bairam Khan was Shias. His tutor, Abdul Latif had so much liberal religious views that he was regarded a Sunni in Persia and a Shia in northern India. Therefore, Akbar grew up in liberal surroundings which affected his personal views. Akbar was keen to know the truth of religion. He used to remember God, came in contact with saints and went on pilgrimage to Ajmer several times at the mausoleum of Sufi saint Shaikh Muin- ud-din Chishti. He also respected very much Shaikh Salim Chishi of Fatehpur Sikri.

In 1575 A.D., he constructed Ibadat Khana, (House of worship) at Fatehpur Sikri in which regular discussion on religion took place. He wanted to ensure religious peace and security to the Empire. His abolition of pilgrimage tax and Jizya, construction of the Ibadat Khana etc. were all done with this purpose. Akbar's policy of religious toleration was based on his final belief that there is truth in every religion. To put into practice, he formed certain regulations such as people of all faiths *i.e.* Muslims, Hindus, Christians, and Jains were allowed to construct buildings for purpose of their worship, to propagate their faith peacefully and celebrate their religious fairs and festivals; state services were open to people of all faith; uniform taxation system was applied to all citizens and no social distinction was to be observed among the people on the basis of differences of their religion.

Akbar personally observed certain practices. He started the practice of Jharokha Darshan and Tula Dan and celebrated all festivals of the Hindus and the Muslims alike at the court. He stopped eating beef, reduced non-vegetarian diet, kept fire burning in his palace for twenty-four hours, stopped going on hunting and tried to stop unnecessary killing of birds. Akbar provided equal protection to all religions and the made no distinction between his subjects in any field on the basis of religion.

COINS OF AKBAR

During the reigning period of Akbar, the Mughal Empire reached to the peak of success. The Mughal emperor helped to elevate the empire by accelerating the cultural, social and the economic affairs of the era. Coins of Akbar include the gold, silver and copper coins. The Mughal emperor used to create the coins that followed the patterns of Suri coinage and gradually the weight and fabric of the coinage were also adopted. The gold coins that were created during the time of Akbar are now known as 'muhar'. According to Abul Fazl, Akbar had issued gold coins of several values. During this period, the heavy weight coins were common but with the progression of time, the light weight coins became common and the heavy weight coins became rare.

Before 988 A.H (Islamic calendar) no fractional coins in any metal came into existence. Later some fractional coins were used in all metals though they were rare. Besides, these coins meant for the entire empire, some coins were also issued on the local pattern in gold and silver. Gold coins were similar to those issued in the time of Humayun and silver coins were issued from Gujarat, Malwa and Kashmir. These coins followed the patterns that were popular then in the respective territories. The shape of the coins of Akbar was round and later was changed to square for gold and silver coins. The round and square coins were issued simultaneously during 993 A.H. to 998 A.H. Later the square shaped coins were abandoned and almost all the coins of the later period were issued in round shape. Akbar had also issued some commemorative gold coins in Mihrabi shape *i.e.* hexagonal with oblong upper and lower sides and left and right sides of the shapes of domes.

The coins of Akbar were distinguished for the styles he incorporated along with the shape and weight of the coins. The coins gained the distinct characteristics due to the content of their inscriptions. Till 1585 A.D. the gold and silver coins were issued in the `Kalima` type. They followed the earlier `Shahrukhi` coins of the early Mughal emperors like Babar and Humayun. The coins were issued with the `Kalima` on the obverse with the names of the four Khalifas. On the reverse side of the coin was the emperor with or without the titles, the pious wish, the name of the mint with or without an epithet and the date in the Hijri era. The dates in the Hijri era were inscribed in a regular manner till 98 A.H. then the word `Alif` was put on them to represent 1000. The coins of Akbar also reflect the change in the religious thinking of the emperor. During this period the `Kalima` was removed from the coins and its place was given to the Ilahi creed Allah Akbar Jalla jalalah. Including these, the name and titles of the emperor were also withdrawn. The Ilahi coins issued after 1585 A.D. may be distinguished into four types. The earliest coins bear the Ilahi creed exclusively. The coins bore the inscription of Allah Akbar on one side and Jalla jalalah on the flip side of the coin. These coins were issued in the thirteenth year of the reign of Akbar. The second type has a similarity with the first type but had the year with the word Ilahi on the Jalla jalalah side. Later the third type was introduced and the full Ilahi creed was placed on one side of the coin and the dates in two lines were engraved on the other side of the coin. In these coins, Akbar introduced an innovative way which is remarkable in the Indian numismatic history. From this time onwards, the coins issued bore the names of the month of issue. Though the suspension of the mint name continued, with the issue of the third type, the mint name was reintroduced. Akbar introduced the use of metrical legends on some of his gold and silver coins and after Akbar this was practised by most of his successors as well. The earliest coins with a couplet were issued but were suspended shortly after.

They were reissued and were continued till the end of his reign. Another metrical legend on gold was used on the coins of Agra mint and the metrical legend is observed on silver coins on the Allahabad issues. Silver coins with the metrical legend were issued on the conquest of Bandhogarh. Akbar also reintroduced the pictorial motifs on some of his coins.

The gold coins that were issued to commemorate the conquest of the fortress of Asirgarh, the stronghold of Khandesh, bear a hawk on one side and the mint name and the date on the other side of the coin. Some silver coins of another type manifesting Akbar riding a horse with a hawk were perhaps issued on this occasion. In later years, the mint less gold and silver coins were issued. The effigy of Ram and Sita with the words `Rama Siya` in Nagari was observed on the top of one side of the coin.

Another pictorial coin was also issued in the same year, which bore the picture of duck on the coin. The copper coins which were also known as `dam`, was the fortieth part of a silver rupee. The fractional coins of it were `nisfi` or `adhelah` (half), `paula` or `rabi` or `damra` (quarter) and `damri` (one eighth). Akbar issued this type of coins till the forty fourth year of his reign. After these coins a new coin termed as `tankah` was introduced and it was just twice the weight of the `dam` (664 grains). The `dam` was given a fractional status with the introduction of these new denominations and it was termed as `nim tankha` (half tankah).

After a short span of time, another series of copper coins were issued from Ahmedabad, Agra, Delhi and from some places outside India and they came to be known as `tanki`. With some exceptions, the copper coins of Akbar followed the copper coinage of Babar and Humayun in respect of the legends. They only had the name of the mint with the words `fulus` or `Sikka fulus` on the obverse and the date in Persian words on the reverse. Later with the introduction of Ilahi era, the Ilahi month and year were placed on this side. When the `tankah` and `tanki` coins were introduced, the obverse had the value suffixed with the word `Akbar Shahi`. The mint name was now placed on the reverse along with the date. In time of Akbar, the mint names got importance and since then they became an integral part of the Mughal coins. The steady territorial expansion of Akbar's empire was accompanied by the expansion of the mints. Over twenty names are seen on the gold coins and about forty five on the silver coins. In the beginning, regular mints for gold were situated at the provincial capitals and afterwards Delhi was added to the list. But the mint at Delhi was soon closed and Ahmedabad took the position when Gujarat was conquered. Similarly, coins were issued from Patna after Bihar was attached to the empire.

These mints, which struck gold coins, also issued silver and copper coins. In addition to that, there were three or four mints which issued only silver and copper coins. Apart from that, copper coins were issued from many other places. The time of Akbar was remarkable as the designs of the coins during the time of Akbar had got the originality with technical designs and minting process. Mughal coinage during Akbar truly reflects originality and innovative technique. Innovations like ornamentation of the background of the coin with floral scrollwork were introduced during this time.

SCULPTURES DURING AKBAR ERA

Art and architecture received handsome patronage under the reign of Mughal emperor, Akbar. Though he was not a prolific builder but he did commission some of the most impressive Mughal monuments in India. The main contribution of Akbar in the field of architecture and sculpture can be witnessed in the form of the Fatehpur Sikri.

One of the main features of architecture and sculpture during Akbar era is the wide use of sandstone as the building material. As far as the architectural elements are concerned, these have been inspired from the Mughal architecture. Arches, domes, pillars, chhatris, chhajjas and jharokhas have been utilized to build the Fatehpur Sikri and the Agra fort. The latter, though commissioned by Akbar, was finally completed during the rule of Shah Jahan.

Another important monument built by Akbar is the tomb of Humayun. The sculpture of Humayun's Tomb is quite simple yet the splendor of the building is evident. The sculptures during Akbar era comprise intricate inlay works. The sculpture of Fatehpur Sikri is a living example of the Mughal sculpture and architecture that evolved during this period. The same idiom was followed by the later Mughal emperors including Jahangir and Shah Jahan.

PAINTING IN THE COURT OF AKBAR

As per the historical record, it is said that the first painting of a portrait of Akbar was done by Abd al-Samad in 1551. In the Berlin album of Akbar, there is a painting of him with Hindal Mirza. A later period painting of Akbar's court depicts Humayun in a tent. The painters recruited by Humayun had to change their individual style as per Akbar's taste. During Akbar's time, the Persian style of painting disappeared gradually. Akbar is regarded as the actual patron of Mughal painting even though he was reported to be illiterate and even dyslexic. The paintings of Akbar's court included the album leaves and a bizarrely dressed, blue-eyed, wandering dervish somewhat figure. Akbar's first and greatest project was said to be the copying and illustration of a romance already popular in India, the Hamza-name, the heroic developments of the Emir Hamza, a kinsman of the Prophet. This painting was done on cloth, with a stout paper backing, and its giant format is exceptional in Islamic painting. It was not possible at the Akbar's period to display the paintings for public exhibition even though Akbar had desired so. The small staff of Persian members recruited by Humayun could not do that. The creators of the beautiful paintings of Akbar's court were not known exactly. But, it is assumed that the Muslim painters from Malwa and the Muslim courts of the Deccan (Ahmadnagar, Bijapur and Golconda), would have been done those paintings in markedly differing styles. They were also trained in wall painting (a probable source for many of the illustrations) but not in book illustration at all probably. Most of the paintings surviving today are not variable in quality and many must have been experiments without a practical sequel.

The great painters of Akbar's time, Abd al-Samad and Mir Sayyid All were mainly responsible for executing the paintings. They used to work cut out in the administration of the studio, obtaining the paper and pigments, issuing them as necessary to the painters and accounting for them to the Treasury, and then seeing that the work was satisfactory and completed on time. The characteristic painting of Akbar was full with scenes flourished with adventure and drama, giants, monsters and demons, in a smoky palette of colours and this style continued till the end of his reign. The effect of these paintings was often brilliant, but bold rather than refined, combining Persian compositions and figures with the dark, jingly landscapes of the painting of pre-Islamic India. One of the finest paintings of Akbar's court is the one, which depicts the 15 miraculous rescue of Hamza's son, Nur al-Dahr, from drowning. In this particular painting, the work of at least four separate hands can be detected. It includes the water, painted in bravura linear style with white highlights, the figures, the forest landscape and some or all of the birds. Some paintings of Akbar's court have found place in the palace libraries, astronomical and astrological treatises, particularly star books and other works relevant to medicine, works of cosmography and geography. But now only few of these have survived. The earliest copy of the 'Anvdri Suhayll' was made for him, which shows marked reminiscences of contemporary painting at Tabriz or Meshed. It contains twenty-seven full-page miniatures, but the margins of some of the other pages have pounced sketches in charcoal. During Akbar's time, even the non-Muslim painters used to practice various works in his royal scriptorium. The painters were of Hindu, Jain, and even of Christian origin. The painters of Akbar's court like Manohar and Mansur illustrated double-page spreads and depicted the episodes from Babar's campaigns, his visits to his relatives, his feasts and his hunts. Sometimes these paintings spread up to three or four pages, which depicted the gardens ordered by Babar, particularly near Kabul, the flora and fauna of India as the cameos. The subjects for illustration in most of the paintings also included Babar's visit to the rock-carved idols below the fortress of Urwa, which showed his wide sympathies, which Akbar himself shared.

The Persian origins of the painters supervising the palace studio of Akbar and their ready access to Persian and Central Asian manuscripts figured largely in their paintings. In these paintings, primary colours were rare and there was a vast spectrum of smoky tones and figures were highly modeled. As most of these painters were trained in Europe, the European effect was very much evident in their paintings. These paintings had elegant gloss binding, margins illuminated in gold inks of contrasting tones with an almost infinite variety of detail, magnificently illuminated medallions and headpieces. Most of the painters of Akbar's court used to treat standard subjects exceptionally. In one of such painting by Mukund, Bahram Gur is shown hunting gazelles with a background of a Flemish seascape with ships and mountains distantly sunlit.

The painting at Akbar's court was so rich and diverse that it is difficult to single out one aspect but portraiture should be mentioned specially. These paintings also depict the historical narratives since the early fifteenth century under the successors of Tamerlane. But in spite of his heroic status in their eyes, there are no known portraits either of him, or of his son Shah Rukh or of his grandson Ulugh Beg. A concept of the dynastic portrait developed gradually during the Akbar's time and it was at least done for the public audience halls of his palaces. Most of his portraits were in profile or half-profile style. Akbar was very much attached to paintings and once in a private discussion of painting he remarked to Abul Fazl, "There are many that hate painting, but such men I dislike. It appears to me as if a painter had a quite peculiar means of recognising God; for a painter in sketching anything that has life, and in devising its limbs, one after the other, must come to feel that he cannot bestow individuality upon his work, and is thus forced to think of God, the giver of life, and will then be increased in knowledge."

AKBARNÂMA, THE BOOK OF AKBAR

The Akbarnâma, which literally means Book of Akbar, is an official biographical account of Akbar, the third Mughal Emperor (r. 1542–1605), written in Persian. It includes vivid and detailed descriptions of his life and times. The work was commissioned by Akbar, and written by Abul Fazl, one of the Nine Jewels (Hindi: Navaratnas) of Akbar's royal court. It is stated that the book took seven years to be completed and the original manuscripts contained a number of paintings supporting the texts, and all the paintings represented the Mughal school of painting, and work of masters of the imperial workshop, including Basawan, whose use of portraiture in its illustrations was an innovation in Indian art.

FINAL YEARS

The closing years of Akbar's reign were troubled by the misconduct of his sons. Two of them died in their youth, the victims of intemperance; and the third, Salim, who succeeded him as Emperor Jahangir (ruled 1605 until 1627), was frequently in rebellion against his father. Asirgarh, a fort in the Deccan proved to be the last conquest of Akbar, taken in 1599 as he proceeded north to face his son's rebellion. Reportedly, Akbar keenly felt these calamities, and they may even have affected his health and hastened his death, which occurred in Agra on October 27, 1605. His body was deposited in a magnificent mausoleum at Sikandra, near Agra.

5

Jahangir

Born as Prince Mohammad Salim, he was the third and eldest surviving son of Mughal Emperor Akbar. Akbar's twin sons, Hasan and Hussain, died in infancy. His mother was the Rajput Princess of Amber, Jodhabai (born Rajkumari Hira Kunwari, eldest daughter of Raja Bihar Mal or Bharmal, Raja of Amber, India).

Jahangir was a child of many prayers. It is said to be by the blessing of Shaikh Salim Chishti (one of the revered sages of his times) that Akbar's first surviving child, the future Jahangir, was born. He was born at the dargah of the Shaikh Salim Chishti, within the fortress at Fatehpur Sikri near Agra. The child was named Salim after the darvesh and was affectionately addressed by Akbar as Sheikhu Baba.

Akbar developed an emotional attachment with the village Sikri (abode of Chishti). Therefore, he developed the town of Sikri and shifted his imperial court and residence from Agra to Sikri, later renamed as Fatehpur Sikri. Shaikh Salim Chishti's daughter was appointed Jahangir's foster mother as a mark of respect to the Shaikh. Jahangir's foster brother Nawab Kutb-ud-din Khan was private secretary to the emperor Jahangir and afterwards governor of Bengal. Nawab Kutb-ud-din Khan's son Nawab Mohtashim. Khan was granted by Jahangir 4,000 bigas of land in Badaun District (United Provinces) where he built a small fort named Sheikhupur, Badaun after Jahangir, who was caned Sheikhu-baba in his childhood.

Revolt

In 1600, when Akbar was away from the capital on an expedition,

Salim broke into an open rebellion, and declared himself Emperor. Akbar had to hastily return to Agra and restore order. There was a time when Akbar thought of putting Khusraw on the throne instead of Salim. Prince Salim forcefully succeeded to the throne on November 3, 1605, eight days after his father's death. Salim ascended to the throne with the title of Nur-ud-din Mohammad Jahangir Badshah Ghazi, and thus began his 22-year reign at the age of 36. Jahangir soon after had to fend off his son, Prince Khusraw, when he attempted to claim the throne based on Akbar's will to become his next heir. Khusraw was defeated in 1606 and confined in the fort of Agra. As punishment Khusraw was blinded, and the Sikh Guru Arjun (the religious spiritual head of the sect at the time) was put to death, for giving the then fugitive Khusraw money when he visited Guru Arjun. Jahangir's rule was characterized by the same religious tolerance as his father Akbar, with the exception of his hostility with the Sikhs, which was forged so early on in his rule.

In 1622, Khurram (Shah Jahan), younger brother of Khusraw, had Khusraw murdered in a conspiracy to eliminate all possible contenders to the throne. Taking advantage of this internal conflict, the Persians seized the city of Qandahar and as a result of this loss, the Mughals lost control over the trade routes to Afghanistan, Persian and Central Asia and also exposed India to invasions from the north-west.

Reign

An aesthete, Jahangir decided to start his reign with a grand display of "Justice", as he saw it. To this end, he enacted Twelve Decrees that are remarkable for their liberalism and foresight. During his reign, there was a significant increase in the size of the Mughal Empire, half a dozen rebellions were crushed, prisoners of war were released, and the work of his father, Akbar, continued to flourish. Much like his father, Jahangir was dedicated to the expansion of Mughal held territory through conquest. During this regime he would target the peoples of Assam near the eastern frontier and bring a series of territories controlled by independent rajas in the Himalayan foothills from Kashmir to Bengal. Jahangir would challenge the hegemonic claim over Persia by the Safavid rulers with an eye on Kabul, Peshawar and Qandahar which were important centers of the central Asian trade system that northern India operated within. In 1622 Jahangir would send his son Prince Khurram against the combined forces of Ahmednagar, Bijapur and Golconda. After his victory Khurram would turn against his father and make a bid for power. As with the insurrection of his eldest son Khusraw, Jahangir was able to defeat the challenge from within his family and retain power.

Jahangir promised to protect Islam and granted general amnesty to his opponents. He was also notable for his patronage of the arts, especially of painting. During his reign the distinctive style of Mughal painting expanded and blossomed. Jahangir supported a flourishing culture of court painters. Jahangir is most famous for his golden "chain of justice." The chain was setup as a link between his people and Jahangir himself. Standing outside the castle of Agra with sixty bells, anyone was capable of pulling the chain and having a personal hearing from Jahangir himself.

Furthermore, Jahangir preserved the Mughal tradition of having a highly centralized form of government. The son of a Hindu Rajput mother who converted to Islam, Jahangir made the precepts of Sunni Islam the cornerstone of his state policies. A faithful Muslim, as evidenced by his memoirs, he expressed his gratitude to Allah for his many victories. Jahangir, as a devout Muslim, did not let his personal beliefs dictate his state policies. Sovereignty, according to Jahangir, was a "gift of God" not necessarily given to enforce God's law but rather to "ensure the contentment of the world." In civil cases, Islamic law applied to Muslims, Hindu law applied to Hindus, while criminal law was the same for both Muslims and Hindus. In matters like marriage and inheritance, both communities had their own laws that Jahangir respected. Thus Jahangir was able to deliver justice to people in accordance of their beliefs, and also keep his hold on empire by unified criminal law. In the Mughal state, therefore, defiance of imperial authority, whether coming from a prince or anyone else aspiring to political power, or a Muslim or a Hindu, was crushed in the name of law and order.

Jahangir's relationship with other rulers of the time is one that was well documented by Sir Thomas Roe, especially his relationship with the Persian King, Shah Abbas. Though conquest was one of Jahangir's many goals, he was a naturalist and lover of the arts and did not have quite the same warrior ambition of the Persian king. This led to a mutual enmity that, while diplomatically hidden, was very clear to observers within Jahangir's court. Furthermore, Abbas had, for many years, been trying to recover the city of Kandahar, which Jahangir was not keen to part with, especially to this king whom he did not particularly care for, despite seeing him as an equal.

In this state, Jahangir was also open to the influence of his wives, a weakness exploited by many. Because of this constant inebriated state, Nur Jahan, the favourite wife of Jahangir, became the actual power behind the throne.

Marriage

Salim was made a Mansabdar of ten thousand (Das-Hazari), the highest military rank of the empire, after the emperor. He independently commanded a regiment in the Kabul campaign of 1581, when he was barely twelve. His Mansab was raised to Twelve Thousand, in 1585, at the time of his betrothal to his cousin Manbhawati Bai, daughter of Bhagwan Das of Amber. Raja Bhagwant Das, was the son of Raja Bharmal and the brother of Akbar's wife Rajkumari Hira Kunwari, also known as Mariam Zamani.

The marriage with Manbhawati Bai took place on February 13, 1585. Manbhawati gave birth to Khusrau Mirza. Thereafter, Salim was allowed to marry, in quick succession, a number of accomplished girls from the aristocratic Mughal and Rajput families. One of his favourite wives was a Rajput Princess, known as Jagat Gosain and Princess Manmati, who gave birth to Prince Khurram, the future Shah Jahan, Jahangir's successor to the throne. The total number of wives in his harem was more than eight hundred.

Jahangir married the extremely beautiful and intelligent Mehr-ul-Nisa (better known by her subsequent title of Nur Jahan), in May 1611. She was the widow of Sher Afghan. She was witty, intelligent and beautiful, which was what attracted Jahangir to her. Before being awarded the title of Nur Jahan ('Light of the World'), she was called Nur Mahal ('Light of the Palace'). Her abilities are said to range from fashion designing to hunting. There is also a myth that she had once killed four tigers with six bullets.

JAHANGIR AND ART

Jahangir was fascinated with art and architecture. Jahangir himself is far from modest in his autobiography when he states his prowess at being able to determine the artist of any portrait by simply looking at a painting. As he said: "...my liking for painting and my practice in judging it have arrived at such point when any work is brought before me, either of deceased artists or of those of the present day, without the names being told me, I say on the spur of the moment that is the work of such and such a man. And if there be a picture containing many portraits, and each face is the work of a different master, I can discover which face is the work of each of them. If any other person has put in the eye and eyebrow of a face, I can perceive whose work the original face is, and who has painted the eye and eyebrow."

Jahangir took his connoisseurship of art very seriously. Paintings created under his reign were closely catalogued, dated and even signed, providing scholars with fairly accurate ideas as to when and in what context many of the pieces were created, in addition to their aesthetic qualities.

He was not only an admirer of Christian artwork but also a purveyor of it. This was largely due to earlier Jesuit missions during his father's reign. Jesuits had brought with them various books, engravings, and paintings and, when they saw the delight Akbar held for them, sent for more and more of the same to be given to the Mughals, as they felt they were on the "verge of conversion," a notion which proved to be very false. Instead, both Akbar and Jahangir studied this artwork very closely and replicated and adapted it, adopting much of the early iconographic features and later the pictorial realism for which Renaissance art was known. Jahangir was notable for his pride in the ability of his court painters. A classic example of this is described in Sir Thomas Roe's diaries, in which the Emperor had his painters copy a European miniature several times creating a total of five miniatures. Jahangir then challenged Roe to pick out the original from the copies, a feat Sir Thomas Roe could not do, to the delight of Jahangir.

Jahangir was also revolutionary in his adaptation of European styles. A collection at the British Museum in London contains seventy-four drawings of Indian portraits dating from the time of Jahangir, including a portrait of the emperor himself. These portraits are a unique example of art during Jahangir's reign because before, and for sometime after, faces were not drawn full, head-on and including the shoulders as well as the head as these drawings are. During his time, Jahangir also pioneered several ornate genealogies illustrated with portraits of each family member in the style of Italian Renaissance painters. Jahangir's love for hunting met his love for art as he commissioned artists on multiple occasions to paint him while hunting and would even paint scenes himself, from time to time. Jahangir was also known for his vast collection of illuminated Persian albums that contained writings as well as paintings.

RAJPUT POLICY OF JAHANGIR

Jahangir continued the Rajput policy of his father Akbar exactly in the same manner. He was extremely liberal towards the Rajputs but he also attempted to force Mewar to submission which had refused it so far. He sent several Mughal forces, one after another, to invade Mewar right from the beginning of his reign. Rana Amar Singh fought against the Mughals with the zeal like his father. He refused to submit though entire Mewar was practically destroyed and the Mughals established military posts everywhere. But, ultimately, he agreed for peace on the advice of his son prince Karan and few of his nobles and the treaty was signed with the Mughals in 1615 A.D. According to the treaty the Rana accepted the sovereignty of the Mughal emperor Jahangir and, instead of himself, deputed his son and successor, prince Karan to attend the Mughal court. Jahangir returned to the Rana all territory of Mewar including the fort of Chittor on condition that it would not be repaired. Thus, the long conflict between Mewar and the Mughals finally came to an end.

The Ranas of Mewar observed this treaty till Aurangzeb attempted to conquer Mewar during his reign. It would be wrong to conclude that Rana Amar Singh had no tried to safeguard the honour of Mewar and had disgraced the name of his father, Rana Pratap by accepting the peace treaty with the Mughals. Amar Singh also fought as valiantly as Rana Pratap against the Mughals and submitted only when he was advised by his son and successor, prince Karan and a few of his nobles. Besides, the subjects of the Rana needed peace, and fight between the Mughals and Mewar had been so long and hard that Mewar was practically ravaged. Peace was necessary for its reconstruction. Jahangir, on his part, offered very liberal terms to Rana. Jahangir in no way, tried to dishonour the Rana. On the contrary, he returned all territory of Mewar and the fort of Chittor to him.

JAHANGIR AND RELIGION

While Sunni Islam was the state religion, there was no widespread pressure to convert; indeed, Jahangir specifically warned his nobles that they "should not force Islam on anyone." In the first century of Islamic expansion this attitude was taken partially because of concerns that an absence of non-Muslims would deprive the state of a valuable source of revenue. However, as the jizya was not imposed by Jahangir, there might have been more behind this policy of toleration than mere economic reasoning. Jahangir was certainly willing to engage with other religions, and Edward Terry, an English chaplain in India at the time, saw a ruler under which "all Religions are tolerated and their Priests [held] in good esteeme." Brahmins on the banks of the Ganges received gifts from the emperor, while following a meeting with Jadrup, a Hindu ascetic, Jahangir felt compelled to comment that "association with him is a great privilege." He enjoyed debating theological subtleties with Brahmins, especially about the possible existence of avatars. Both Sunnis and Shias were welcome at court, and members of both sects gained high office. When drunk, Jahangir swore to Sir Thomas Roe, England's first ambassador to the Mughal court, that he would protect all the peoples of the book. Many contemporary chroniclers were not even sure quite how to describe his personal belief structure.

Roe labelled him an atheist, and although most others shied away from that term, they did not feel as though they could call him an orthodox Sunni. He relied greatly on astrologers, though that was not seen as unusual for a ruler at the time, even to the extent that he required that they work out the most auspicious time for the imperial camp to enter a city. Roe believed Jahangir's religion to be of his own making, "for he envyes Mahomett, and wisely sees no reason why he should not bee as great a prophet as he, and therefore proffeseth him selfe soe ... he hath found many disciples that flatter or follow him." At this time, one of those disciples happened to be the current English ambassador, though his initiation into Jahangir's inner circle of disciples was devoid of religious significance for Roe, as he did not understand the full extent of what he was doing: Jahangir hung "a picture of him selfe sett in gold hanging at a wire gold chaine, with one pendent soule pearle" round Roe's neck. Roe thought it "an specially favour, for that all the great men that were the Kings image (which none may doe but to whom it is given) receive no other then a meddall of gold as bigg as six pence."

Had Roe intentionally converted, it would have caused quite a scandal in London. But since there was no intent, there was no resultant problem. Such disciples were an elite group of imperial servants, with one of them being promoted to Chief Justice. However, it is not clear that any of those who became disciples renounced their previous religion, so it is probable to see this as a way in which the emperor strengthened the bond between himself and his nobles. Despite Roe's somewhat casual use of the term 'atheist', he could not quite put his finger on Jahangir's real beliefs. Roe lamented that the emperor was either "the most impossible man in the world to be converted, or the most easy; for he loves to heare, and hath so little religion yet, that he can well abide to have any derided." Broad toleration for other religions made little sense to Europeans forged in the heat of religious conflict, while the lifestyle and pretensions Jahangir afforded himself meant that it was difficult to see him as a devout Muslim. Sri Ram Sharma argues though that contemporaries and some historians have been too disparaging about Jahangir's beliefs, simply because he did not persecute non-believers and enforce his views on others. This should not imply that the multi-confessional state appealed to all, or that all Muslims were happy with the situation in India.

In a book written on statecraft for Jahangir, the author advised him to direct "all his energies to understanding the counsel of the sages and to comprehending the intimations of the 'ulama." At the start of his regime many staunch Sunnis were hopeful, because he seemed less tolerant to other faiths than his father had been. At the time of his accession and the elimination of Abul Fazl, his father's chief minister and architect of his eclectic religious stance, a strong orthodox nucleus of noblemen had gained power in administration." Jahangir did not always benevolently regard some Hindu customs and rituals. On visiting a Hindu temple, he found a statue of a man with a pig's head, which was supposed to represent God, so he "ordered them to break that hideous form and throw it in the tank." If the Tuzuk is reliable on this subject (and there is no reason to suspect that it is not), then this was an isolated case.

J. F. Richards argues that "Jahangir seems to have been persistently hostile to popularly venerated religious figures." This is perhaps misleading. Hindu ascetics like Jadrup were treated with respect, and it was only those who upset the order of the state that were seen as a threat to the state, with their popularity making them even more dangerous. A Muslim, who had gained some followers by claiming that he had surpassed the understanding of the companions of Mohammad, was imprisoned in Gwalior Fort. If he had been allowed to spread his message there was potential for serious disturbance, so he had to be stopped.

Most notorious was the execution of the Sikh Guru Arjun. It is unclear that Jahangir even understood what a Sikh was, referring to Guru Arjun as a Hindu, who had "captured many of the simple-hearted of the Hindus, and even of the ignorant and foolish followers of Islam, by his ways and manners ... for three or four generations (of spiritual successors) they had kept this shop warm." The trigger for Guru Arjun's execution was his support for Jahangir's rebel son Khusrau, yet it is clear from Jahangir's own memoirs that he disliked Guru Arjun before then: "many times it occurred to me to put a stop to this vain affair or bring him into the assembly of the people of Islam."

Guru Arjun was handed over to the Mughal governor of Lahore, and was tortured to death for refusing to convert to Islam. Jahangir ordered his execution, but it is unlikely that he also ordered Guru Arjun to be tortured and converted, for two reasons; one, because we have no other examples from Jahangir's generally tolerant reign to support the idea that he forced people to convert to Islam, and two, because Jahangir makes no note of Guru Arjun's torture, yet cheerfully describes the torture of two other rebels, as well as Guru Arjun's execution. Jahangir maintained his hostility towards the Sikhs, imprisoning Guru Hargobind, the successor of Guru Arjun, for several years.

A rana was described as an infidel, but only because he was fighting against the Mughals, and infidel was used as an everyday phrase to describe all non-Muslims anyway. Admittedly Muslims were discouraged from performing most Hindu rites, with Jahangir lamenting that many Muslims prayed at a temple dedicated to Durga, and worshipped at a black stone. With Jahangir himself occasionally taking part in Hindu ceremonies, the aforementioned example was probably one way of showing support for the idea that Muslim and Hindus should not mix their rituals. His attitude to religion in his domain was relaxed yet diligent. He saw himself as doing Allah's bidding, yet he was inquisitive enough to explore new ideas about religion, intelligent enough to understand that Hindus were in the majority and grand enough in his pretensions not to need to obey every line of the Qur'an.

Such a religious situation allowed the more recently arrived form of Christianity to have opportunity to grow. Jahangir did not seem to have anything against Christianity. He wrote fondly of Akbar's reign, when "Sunnis and Shias met in one mosque, and Franks and Jews in one church, and observed their own forms of worship." Roe noted that "of Christ he never utters any word un-reverently."

His prayer room in Agra contained pictures of "our Lady and Christ." In the imperial palace in Lahore, over one of the doors, according to William Finch, a merchant, was "the Picture of our Sauiour," with an image of the Virgin Mary facing it. Elsewhere, the emperor had pictures of angels and demons, with the demons having a "most ugly shape, with long hornes, staring eyes ... with such horrible difformity and deformity, that I wonder the poore women are not frightened therewith."

It is possible that Jahangir might have seen these images in their Islamic persona, as the Qur'an features such creatures, yet depiction of living things was harem (forbidden), so the images could well have been created by a Christian artist. However, as Mughal art was still heavily Persian-influenced, images of living beings were allowed, and widespread, so perhaps the other worldly images had nothing to do with Christianity at all; they nonetheless caught Finch's eye. Muqarrab Khan sent to Jahangir "a European curtain (tapestry) the like of which in beauty no other work of the Frank painters has ever been seen." One of his audience halls was "adorned with European screens." Christian themes attracted Jahangir, and even merited a mention in the Tuzuk. One of his slaves gave him a piece of ivory into which had been carved four scenes. In the last scene "there is a tree, below which the figure of the revered (hazrat) Jesus is shown. One person has placed his head at Jesus' feet, and an old man is conversing with Jesus and four others are standing by." Though Jahangir believed it to be the work of the slave who presented it to him, Sayyid Ahmad and Henry Beveridge suggest that it was of European origin, and possibly showed the Transfiguration. Wherever it came from, and whatever it represented, it was clear that a European style had come to influence Mughal art, otherwise the slave would not have claimed it as his own design, nor would he have been believed by Jahangir.

There was even some baseless suggestion that Jahangir had converted to Christianity. Thrown by the religious tolerance of Akbar and Jahangir's rule, the Jesuits had long thought that they were always on the verge of conversion. Finch recounted how there "was much stirre with the King about Chrytianitie, he affirming before his Nobles, that it was the soundest faith, and that of Mahomet lies and fables." This is an extremely implausible story, yet the fact that Finch told it at all shows the extent to which Christianity was evident in the Mughal court. Jahangir apparently allowed a Jesuit to teach some Indian boys Portuguese and elements of Christian doctrine, and the Jesuits were also allowed to open churches in Ahmadabad and Hooghly. Christians were allowed to openly celebrate Christmas, Easter and other such festivals, and the Jesuits were even given an allowance and gifts in order to carry on with their work, with a few Indians converting to Christianity. Given the toleration of Hinduism, such imperial leeway was not shocking. Christianity occupied a special place in Islamic canon, as did Isa (Jesus), who was considered to be amongst the greatest prophets. What did surprise some observers was the forcible conversion of three sons of Jahangir's brother, Prince Daniyal, to Christianity, followed by a parade to celebrate their conversions. This was seen by the Jesuits as a gigantic step forward, but the English and the locals knew better. Hawkins dryly commented that Jahangir made his nephews Christian "not for any zeale he had to Christianitie, as the [Jesuit] Fathers, and all Christians thought; but upon the prophecie of certain learned Gentiles [Hindus], who told him that the sonnes of his should be disinherited, and the children of his brother should raigne. And therefore he did it, to make these children hatefull to all Moores." This highlighted the likely limits of Christianity in India. Its inhabitants already had mono-and polytheistic religions from which to choose, and the European Christians had done little to demonstrate the attractiveness of conversion. A few did convert, though Terry believed that this was only for Jesuit money, as they did not appear to know anything about their new religion, and Roe agreed on this matter. Even Jahangir's nephews were allowed to return to the Islamic fold, because "the King of Portugall sent them no presents nor wives." Christianity was tolerated because it posed no real threat. It certainly had an effect on the arts, but it is difficult to discern any other lasting impact on Mughal India.

DECCAN POLICY OF JAHANGIR

Jahangir's Deccan policy was a continuation of that of Akbar's which, following ancient Hindu traditions, treated the north and south as indivisible parts of one country. It was the emperor's desire to annex Ahmadnagar and, if possible, the two remaining independent states of Bijapur and Golkunda. Jahangir placed his son, Prince Khurram, in command of his army in 1613 and ordered him to lead a number of campaigns against Rajput forces in Mewar and Kanga, and the Deccani sultanates of Ahmadnagar, Bijapur, and Golkonda.

The long siege of Kanga was brought to a successful end in 1629. This was the most notable military achievement of Jahangir's reign, prompting him to visit the place of conquest and build mosques there. The complete success of the Mughal army over the forces of Ahmadnagar was not possible, however, owing in part to the strength of the Deccan kingdom and in part to the inferiority of Mughal weapons. Not only did Ahmadnagar defy the Mughal advance, but successful opposition came from an able Abyssinian named Malik Ambar, a former slave, who prepared for a war by training the mountaineers of Maharasthra in guerrilla tactics (later perfected by the great Hindu ruler Shivaji to the despair of Emperor

Aurangzeb). When the Mughals had partial success in 1616, Prince Khurram was rewarded by Jahangir with the title of Shah Jahan ("King of the World"). But the Deccan was far from conquered.

RELIGIOUS POLICY OF JAHANGIR

Religious policy of Jahangir has been placed between his father, Akbar and his son, Shah Jahan. He had faith in God and observed principles of Islam in a normal way. He was not a religious man. He did not practice principles of Islam strictly. He came in contact with people of all faiths which liberalised his views.

He believed in the unity of God. He mostly pursued the religious policy of Akbar and gave equal facilities to all his subjects without discriminating between them on grounds of religion. The Hindus were not burdened by additional taxation and received services in the state according to merit. However, there are certain instances which prove that, at times, Jahangir favoured Islam. Jahangir punished the Hindus in the state of Kashmir because they used to marry Muslim girls and convert them to Hinduism.

In the same way, threw away the idol of Varaha at Ajmer into a pond and destroyed Christian churches when he was at war with the Portuguese. One reason of punishing the Guru Arjan Dev, the Sikh religious leader, was certainly the religious views of the Guru which he disliked.

He also ordered expulsion of all Jains from Gujarat when he felt dissatisfied with them. But, these instances are examples of his occasional frenzy.

Jahangir did not pursue a policy of religious persecution against any sect. He punished Guru Arjun because of the financial help which he gave to the rebel prince Khusrav. He even punished Muslim preachers like Shaikh Rahim, Qazi Nurulla, Shaikh Ahmad Sarhindi etc. when he felt unhappy with them. So there remains no reason to charge him for fanaticism against the Sikhs, the Hindus, the Jains or the Christians. Mostly, Jahangir maintained the spirit of religious toleration with all his subjects and no change was brought about by him in the policy of Akbar.

COINS OF JAHANGIR

The Mughal Empire, primarily, witnessed the zenith of success in the time of Akbar. However coins were given due heed during the reign of

Jahangir as well. In fact he took a personal interest to develop his coinage. Jahangir included his innovative qualities in issuing coins and later those became the characteristic of his coinage.

In 1605 A.D., after the demise of Akbar, Jahangir came to the throne. Though he was announced the ruler of the empire, Jahangir ordered not to issue any coin before his formal coronation. During this time, some gold coins were issued from Agra with a couplet and these coins are considered as the posthumous issues in the name of Akbar. Even some gold coins were issued during this time bearing the first regnal year of Jahangir and the Hijri year.

During the interim period of 1605 to 1606 A.D., silver coins were issued with his name as Prince Salim. After the formal coronation of Jahangir, he ordered to increase the weight of gold and silver coins. Later when it was realized that the heavy weight coins were inconvenient in transactions, the old weight of the coins was restored. And till the end of his reigning period, gold and silver coins of these weights were issued. Though in the time of Akbar, coins were issued from numerous places, in the time of Jahangir, a few places issued coins.

Agra, Ahmedabad, Ajmer, Burhanpur and Delhi issued coins in silver, gold and copper. Ahmadnagar, Fathpur, Jahangirnagar, Kashmir, Patna and some other places issued gold coins and the silver coins were also issued from places like Surat, Ujjain etc. To establish his reigning period and make a mark of his own, he ordered to include a couplet in the gold and silver coins. But this order was not faithfully carried out and only during the first three years this legend was placed on the coins issued from Agra, Delhi and some other places. The coins issued during this period carried 'Kalima' on one side and 'Nuruddin Muhammad Jahangir Badshah Ghazi' on the flip side of the coin.

Jahangir, in his ruling period, introduced his regnal year in the place of the Ilahi era and his coins bore the regnal year and the Hijri year. The coins that were issued in the time of Jahangir bore the name 'Nuruddin Jahangir Shah Akbar Shah' on one side and the other side followed the Ilahi coins of Akbar. These coins bore the mint's name, the Ilahi (Persian) month, the regnal and the Hijri years. Apart from these coins, couplets inscribed on the coins were also issued from different places of India and some other places outside India. These issues from each of these mints had couplets of their own with some individual characteristics. Later in his ruling period, Jahangir issued some gold coins that had portraits of his own, for being presented to his favourites. These coins were in the same tradition in which he had earlier issued the coin with the portrait of his father. Some coins were issued at the time of Jahangir that bore the bust of the emperor in profile.

On some of the coins his posture with a flower or a cup in his right hand was seen. On the reverse side of the coin was a lion either to the right or to the left. Some coins displayed the emperor seated cross legged on the throne with a cup on the right hand and a legend on the reverse side of the coin. Later the coins issued displayed the seated emperor on one side and the lion on the other side of the coin.

Each side of the coin occupied a hemistich of the metrical legend in the exergue. These coins did not carry the names of the place from where they were issued. The coins issued in the ruling period of Jahangir also manifested the portrait of the emperor holding a cup and each hemistich of the metrical legend is placed to the right and the left in the blank space. On the reverse side of the coin was a small sun in the centre, the name of the mint, the regnal year, the Hijri year and an invocation `Ya Muin` on its left and right of the coin. As per the historical evidences, Jahangir had mentioned in his diary about the replacement of the name of the month by the figure of configuration, which belonged to the month. After the announcement of this order of the emperor, the gold and silver coins issued from his camp mints contained the zodiacal signs on one side of the coin.

During the later days of his reign, Jahangir lost his mental and physical stability and then the administration was entrusted to his queen Nurjahan. The coins that were issued from places like Agra, Ahmedabad, Akbarnagar, Allahbad, Kashmir, Patna, Surat etc bore a couplet that signified that `by order of Shah Jahngir gold attained a hundred beauties when the name of Nurjahan Badshah Begum was placed on it`. These coins continued till the termination of Jahangir's reigning period and later during the time of Shah Jahan, these coins were returned to the mint and melted for carrying the zodiac signs.

As a matter of fact, these coins are very rare. The coins of Jahangir had simple legends and the copper coins that were issued in the beginning of the reign follow the pattern of Akbar with the only change that the words `Shah Salimi` took the place of `Akbar Shahi`. These coins were issued from Ahmadabad. Some of the coins of Jahangir bore the words like `Sikka Jahangir` on the obverse and `Sikka Rawani` on the reverse.

The coins of the later years from the same mint had `Sikka Jahangiri` on the obverse and the mint name and the date on the reverse. On some coins, the word `raji` (current), or `raij-ul-wakt` (current in the period) or `rawan shud` (in currency) are seen on one side.

DEATH

He was trying to restore it by visiting Kashmir and Kabul. He went from Kabul to Kashmir but returned to Lahore on account of a severe cold. Jahangir died on the way back from Kashmir near Sarai Saadabad in 1627. To preserve his body, the entrails were removed and buried in the Chingus Fort, Kashmir. The body was then transferred to Lahore to be buried in Shahdara Bagh, a suburb of Lahore, Punjab. He was succeeded by his third son, Prince Khurram who took the title of Shah Jahan. Jahangir's elegant mausoleum is located in the Shahdara locale of Lahore and is a popular tourist attraction in Lahore.

6

Shah Jahan

The period of his reign was the golden age of Mughal architecture. Shah Jahan erected many splendid monuments, the most famous of which is the Taj Mahal at Agra built as a tomb for his wife Mumtaz Mahal (birth name Arjumand Banu Begum). The Pearl Mosque at Agra, the palace and great mosque at Delhi also commemorate him. The celebrated Peacock Throne, said to be worth millions of dollars by modern estimates, also dates from his reign. He was the founder of Shahjahanabad, now known as 'Old Delhi'. The important buildings of Shah Jahan were the Diwan-i-Am and Diwan-i-Khas in the fort of Delhi, the Jama Masjid, the Moti Masjid and the Taj. It is pointed out that the Palace of Delhi is the most magnificent in the East.

The Mughals attempted to conquer south India as part of their policy right from the reign of Akbar. Shah Jahan pursued the same policy. Besides, the states of south India provided shelter to the rebels against the Mughals. Shah Jahan desired to conquer these states. Ahmednagar became a part of the Mughal Empire in 1633 A.D. The ruling-family of Golconda was Shia and its rule had refused to acknowledge the suzerainty of the Mughals. Shah Jahan desired to conquer Golconda. He was able to manage this when Abdullah Qutub Shah ascended the throne, and he agreed to the terms and conditions of the Mughals Emperor. In 1636 A.D., Shah Jahan attacked Daulatabad.

Bijapur was weak at that time due to rebellious attempts of its nobles. Therefore, Muhammad Adil Shah readily agreed for peace and a treaty was signed between the two parties. The Deccan policy of the Mughals proved fairly successful during the reign of Shah Jahan. The existence of Ahmednagar was wiped away while both Bijapur and Golconda accepted the suzerainty of the emperor. Besides, they were forced to pay the annual tribute from time to time and part of their territories and a few of their forts were occupied by the Mughals. Some minor conquests were also made during the reign of Shah Jahan. The Bhils of Malwa and Gonda, Raja Pratap of Palam and the Raja of Little Tibet accepted the suzerainty of the Mughal Emperor while Assam was forced to establish trade relations with the Mughal Empire after constant fighting between the years 1628-39 A.D.

Biography

Birth And Early Years: Shah Jahan was born as Prince Khurram Shihab-ud-din Mohammad, in 1592 in Lahore as the third and favourite son of the emperor Jahangir, his mother being a Rathore Rajput Princess, known as Princess Jagat Gosain who was Jahangir's second wife. The name Khurram-Persian for 'joyful'- was given by his grandfather Akbar. His early years saw him receive a cultured, broad education and he distinguished himself in the martial arts and as a military commander while leading his father's armies in numerous campaigns-Mewar (1615 CE, 1024 AH), the Deccan (1617 and 1621 CE, 1026 and 1030 AH), Kangra (1618 CE, 1027AH). He was responsible for most of the territorial gains during his father's reign. He also demonstrated a precocious talent for building, impressing his father at the age of 16 when he built his quarters within Babar's Kabul fort and redesigned buildings within Agra fort.

Marriage: In 1607 CE (1025 AH), at the age of fifteen, Khurram was to marry Arjumand Banu Begum, the grand daughter of a Persian noble, who was 14 years old at the time. She would become the unquestioned love of his life. They would, however, have to wait five years before they were married in 1612 CE (1021 AH). After their wedding celebrations, Khurram "finding her in appearance and character elect among all the women of the time," gave her the title Mumtaz Mahal (Jewel of the Palace).

She had 18 children. Despite her frequent pregnancies, Mumtaz Mahal travelled with Shah Jahan's entourage throughout his earlier military campaigns and the subsequent rebellion against his father. Mumtaz Mahal was utterly devoted — she was his constant companion and trusted confidante and their relationship was intense. She is portrayed by Shah Jahan's chroniclers as the perfect wife with no aspirations to political power. This is in direct opposition to how Nur Jahan had been perceived.

EARLY LIFE

Born on 5 January 1592, Shah ab-ud-din Muhammad Khurram which was Shah Jahan's birth name, was the third son born to Emperor Jehangir, his mother was a Rajput princess from Marwar called Princess Manmati – her official name in Mughal chronicles being Bilquis Makani. The name "Khurram" was chosen for the young prince by his grandfather, Emperor Akbar, with whom the young prince shared a close relationship. When Khurram was only six days old, Akbar, ordered that the prince be taken away from his Rajput mother and handed him over to his first wife and chief consort, Empress Ruqaiya Sultan Begum, who was childless. Ruqaiya assumed the primary responsibility for Khurram's upbringing and he grew up under her care. Her step-son, Jahangir, noted that Ruqaiya loved Khurram "a thousand times more than if he had been her own son."

As a child, Prince Khurram received a broad education befitting his status as a Mughal prince, which included martial training and exposure to a wide variety of cultural arts, such as poetry and music, most of which was inculcated, according to court chroniclers, under the watchful gaze of his grandfather and his grandmother, Empress Ruqaiya. In 1605, as the Emperor Akbar lay on his deathbed, Prince Khurram, who at this point was 13, remained by his bedside and refused to move even after his mother tried to retrieve him. Given the politically uncertain times immediately preceding Akbar's death, Prince Khurram was in a fair amount of physical danger of harm by political opponents of his father and his conduct at this time can be understood to be a precursor of the bravery that he would later be known for.

In 1605, his father succeeded to the throne, after crushing a rebellion by Prince Khausrau – Prince Khurram remained distant from the court politics and intrigues in the immediate aftermath of that event, which was apparently a conscious decision on Jahangir's part. As the third son, Prince Khurram did not challenge the two major power blocs of the time, his father's and his step-brother's; thus he enjoyed the benefits of Imperial protection and luxury, while being allowed to continue with his education and training. This relatively quiet and stable period of his life allowed Prince Khurram to build his own support base in the Mughal court, which would be useful later on in his life.

Due to the long period of tensions between his father and step-brother, Prince Khurram began to drift closer to his father and over time

Shah Jahan

started to be considered the de-facto heir apparent by court chroniclers. This status was given official sanction when Jahangir granted the jagir of Hissar-Feroza, which had traditionally been the fief of the heir apparent, to Prince Khurram in 1607.

MARRIAGE

In 1607, Prince Khurram was engaged to Arjumand Banu Begum - when they were 15 and 14 years old, respectively. The young girl belonged to an illustrious Persian noble family which had been serving Mughal Emperors since the reign of Akbar, the family's patriarch was Itimad-ud-Daulah, who had been Emperor Jahangir's finance minister and his son; Asaf Khan - Arjumand Banu's father - played an important role in the Mughal court, eventually serving as Chief Minister. Her aunt was the Empress Nur Jahan and is thought to have played the matchmaker in arranging the marriage.

But for some reason, the Prince was not married to Arjumand Banu Begum for five years, which was an unusually long engagement for the time. However, Shah Jahan married a Hindu princess during this time, whose name has not been recorded by contemporary chroniclers, with whom he had his first child - a daughter – who died in infancy.

Politically speaking, the betrothal allowed Prince Khurram to be considered as having officially entered manhood, and he was granted several jagirs, including Hissar-Feroze and ennobled to a military rank of 8,000, which allowed him to take on official functions of state, an important step in establishing his own claim to the throne.

In 1612, aged 20, Prince Khurram married Arjumand Banu Begum on an auspicious date chosen by court astrologers. The marriage was a happy one and Prince Khurram, while married to her, remained devoted to her and she bore him fourteen children, out of whom the seven survived into adulthood. In addition, Khurram had two children from his first two wives.

The Mughal Emperor Shah Jahan is accompanied by his three sons: Dara Shikoh, Shah Shuja and Aurangzeb, including their maternal grandfather Asaf Khan IV. Mumtaz Mahal died, aged 40, while giving birth to Gauhara Begum in Burhanpur, the cause of death being post-partum haemorrhaging, which caused considerable blood-loss and after a painful labour of thirty hours. Contemporary historians note that Princess Jahanara, aged 17, was so distressed by her mother's pain that she started distributing gems to the poor, hoping for divine intervention and Shah Jahan, himself, was noted as being "paralysed by grief" and weeping fits. Her body was temporarily buried in a walled pleasure garden known as Zainabad, originally constructed by Shah Jahan's uncle Prince Daniyal along the Tapti River. Her death had a profound impact on Shah Jahan's personality and inspired the construction of the Taj Mahal, where she was later reburied.

The intervening years had seen Khurrum take two other wives known as Akbarabadi Mahal (d.1677), and Kandahari Mahal (b. c1594), (m.1609). But according to court chroniclers, his relationship with his other wives was more out of political consideration and they enjoyed only the status of being royal wives. After his death came Aurangzeb and other weak rulers.

Though there was genuine love between the two, Arjumand Banu Begum was a politically astute woman and served as a crucial advisor and confidante to her husband, she even is said to have implored Prince Khurram not to have children with his other wives, a call he listened. Later on, as Empress, Mumtaz Mahal (Persian: the chosen one of the Palace) wielded immense power, such as being consulted by her husband in state matters and being responsible for the imperial seal, which allowed her to review official documents in their final draft.

REIGN OF SHAH JAHAN

The reign of Shah Jahan was marked as the golden age of the Mughal dynasty. Shah Jahan was well-educated and cultured, and his is known to have provided protection to scholars. Persian and Sanskrit literature flourished during his reign. He also patronised fine arts like music, painting and architecture. He had several wives, yet he was devoted to them. His love for Mumtaz Mahal has become almost legendary. He loved his children and gave them all necessary training and comforts. He was a hard fighter and a capable commander. He participated in all important campaigns during the life-time of his father and planned all military campaigns himself when he became the emperor. He extended the boundary of the Mughal Empire. While Ahmednagar was completely annexed to the Mughal Empire, Bijapur and Golconda were forced to accept the suzerainty of the emperor. He even attempted to conquer Central Asia and recover Qandahar. Shah Jahan was a just ruler and earnestly desired the welfare of his subjects. Trade, industry and agriculture flourished and the state as well as the subjects enjoyed prosperity during his reign. He worked hard and personally supervised the administration of the empire. He brought about improvement in the Mansabdari System. He helped his subjects generously in times of famines and natural calamities. With regard to religious affairs, he was certainly orthodox when compared with Jahangir and Akbar, yet he did not interfere in the daily lives of the Hindus and the Christians. He participated in fairs and festivals of the Hindus and continued the practices of Jharokha Darshan and Tula Dan as before.

He continued the policy of his father and grand father in his relations with the Rajputs and commanded their loyalty. The regime of Shah Jahan was marked by the birth of trade and commerce in Delhi, Agra, Lahore, and Ahmedabad through an improved network of roads and waterways. The greatest accomplishment of this great connoisseur of art was the architectural structures and monuments created in that period. A major change that was noticed is in the substitution of sandstone as a building material in Akbar's Red Fort with costly marble as in the Diwan-i-am (hall of public audience) or the black marble pavilion of the Shalimar Gardens in Srinagar. The Jami Masjid, the Moti Masjid, the tomb of Jahangir in Lahore definitely deserves mention. Finally, the architectural masterpiece, embodying Shah Jahan's eternal romance with his beloved wife Mumtaz Mahal is the exquisite Taj Mahal, situated in Agra.

REVOLT OF SIKHS UNDER SHAH JAHAN

Revolt of the Sikhs during the reign of Shah Jahan took place due to several reasons and is an important part of the medieval history of India. The relations of the Sikhs were spoiled with the Mughals just in the beginning of the reign of Shah Jahan.

The discord began with a minor incident. Shah Jahan was camped near Amritsar for the purpose of hunting. One of his hunting hawks flew into the camp of Guru Har Govind and was captured by his disciples. When the Mughals asked the Guru to return it, he refused and foiled several attempts of the Mughals to recover it by force. However, a few friends of the Guru who were in Mughal service pleaded in favour of him to Shah Jahan who left the matter as it was. Another quarrel between the Sikhs and the Mughuls arose when Guru Har Govind started constructing the city of Sri Govindpur near the bank of the Beas River.

The Mughals attacked but were defeated. The Mughals came in conflict with the Sikhs for the third time when Vidhi Singh, one of the disciples of the Guru and a famous dacoit, stole two fine Imperial horses and presented them to the Guru. The Mughals demanded them back but the Guru refused. A strong Mughal force attacked the Guru in 1613 A.D. but was defeated. Another force of the Mughals was defeated by the Guru near Kartarpur. But the Guru realised the futility of constant fighting against the Mughals. He feared that it might result in the extinction of the nascent Sikh religion. Therefore, he left and settled down at Kiratpur in the hills of Kashmir where he died in 1645 A.D. Thus, the relations between the Mughals and the Sikhs became strained during the reign of Shah Jahan.

DECCAN POLICY OF SHAH JAHAN

During his early age, Prince Khurram was able to muster his strength in Deccan. It was Deccan that Aurangzeb, fourth son of prince Khurram and Mumtaj Mahal rose like a serpent and devoured the throne of Delhi. We have seen that the later wars of Jahangir were fought by prince Khurram, similarly, the later wars of Shah Jahan were fought by Aurangzeb.

Deccan policy of the Mughals during the reign of Shah Jahan remained quite successful. Shah Jahan attempted either to annex the kingdoms of the Deccan or force them to accept the suzerainty of the emperor.

He was a capable commander and understood the politics of the Deccan well. The death of Malik Ambar, the wazir of Ahmednagar, provided him good opportunity to put pressure on Ahmednagar. Hussain Shah sat on the throne of Ahmednagar. He opened negotiations with the Mughals and at the same time tried to befriend Bijapur. His unscrupulous diplomacy resulted in the loss of many loyal nobles like Shahji Bhonsle. Hussain Shah was imprisoned in the fort of Gwalior and Ahmednagar was annexed to the Mughal Empire. It meant the end of the state of Ahmednagar though Shahji Bhonsle continued to fight against the Mughals on behalf of another child of the ruling dynasty of Ahmednagar, named Murtaza III. However, he surrendered the child to the Mughals in 1636 A.D. and accepted the service of Bijapur. Qutub Shah, ruler of Golconda died in 1626 A.D. He was succeeded by a child of eleven years of age named Abdullah Qutub Shah. In 1636 A.D., Golconda was forced to accept the suzerainty of the Mughals. Aurangzeb, when appointed as governor of the Deccan for the second time in 1652 A.D., again pressurised Golconda because it had failed to pay the annual tribute to the Mughals.

Aurangzeb waited for an opportunity and he got it when Mir Jumla, one of the most prominent nobles of the Sultan, quarreled with him and sought protection from Aurangzeb. Aurangzeb captured Hyderabad and besieged the fort of Golconda. But before he could capture it he received orders of Shah Jahan to raise the siege. Therefore, a treaty was signed between the two parties. Golconda accepted the suzerainty of the Shah Jahan, married one of his daughters to prince Muhammad, son of Aurangzeb, gave rupees ten lakhs as dowry and yet another rupees seventeen lakhs as war-indemnity to the Mughals. Thus, though Golconda was weakened but its existence remained. Sultan Ibrahim Shah was succeeded by Muhammad Adil Shah I in Bijapur.

Adil Shah had no fixed plan against the onslaughts of the Mughals while his nobles were divided among themselves. The attempt of the Mughals to capture Bijapur in 1631 A.D., however, failed. The Mughals again attacked it in 1636 A.D. and forced Bijapur to accept their suzerainty. In 1656 A.D, Adil Shah died. It was believed that he had no son but his wife, Bari Sahiba declared one child as his son and succeeded in placing him on the throne, with the name of Adil Shah II.

Shah Jahan tried to take advantage of it. He charged Bijapur for different things and ordered Aurangzeb to attack it. Aurangzeb besieged the fort of Bijapur but before he could capture it, he received orders of Shah Jahan to raise the siege. A treaty was, therefore, signed between the two by which Bijapur accepted the suzerainty of the Mughal emperor and agreed to pay rupees one and a half crores to the Mughals.

The forts of Bidar and Kalyani also remained with the Mughals. The state of Ahmednagar was completely annexed to the Mughal Empire and Bijapur and Golconda were forced to accept the suzerainty of the emperor, surrender part of their territories and a few important forts and pay annual tribute and war-indemnity. Probably, even Bijapur and Golconda could be annexed if Shah Jahan himself would not have stopped Aurangzeb from attempting so. Shah Jahan understood well the politics of the Deccan. Probably, he felt that the annexation of these two states would complicate matters for the Mughals. Thus, the Deccan policy of the Mughals during the reign of Shah Jahan remained quite successful.

WAR OF SUCCESSION

Shah Jahan's last days were made highly tragic by the outbreak of a terrible war of succession among his s-ons. It broke out as soon as he fell ill in September, 1657, and subjected the old Emperor to extreme humiliation and agony till his exit from this world. Shah Jahan had four sons, all of mature age at that time-Dara Shukoh aged 43, Abuja aged 41, Aurangzeb aged 39, and Murad aged 3 and two daughters, Jahanara, who aided with Dara Shikoh, and Raushnara, who joined the party of Aurangzeb. AU the brothers had by that time gained considerable experience in civil and military affairs as governors of provinces and commanders of armies, but there were differences among them in personal qualities and capacities. The eldest of them, Dara, Shikoh, was in the confidence of his father, who d him to be his successor.

A man of eclectic views, liberal disposition, and of scholarly instincts, Dara, Shukoh mixed with the followers of other faiths and studied the doctrines of the Scholary, the Talmud, the New Testament and the works of Sufi writers. He caused a Persian version of the Atharva Veda and the Upanishads to be made with the assistance of some Brahmana scholars' and aimed at finding, a modus vivendi among the apparently hostile creeds. For this he naturally incurred the displeasure of the orthodox members among his co-religionists, who went against him. But he was not a heretic. He never "discarded the essential dogmas of Islam; he only displayed the eclecticism of the Sufis, a recognised school of Islamic believers. If he showed contempt for the external rites of religion, he only shared the, standpoint of many noble thinkers of all Churches, such as John Milton".

His latest biographer has aptly remarked: "It is hardly an exaggeration to say that any one who intends to take up the solution of the problem of religious peace in India must begin the work where Dara had left it, and proceed on the path chalked out by that prince.

" But the excessive fondness of his father for him, and his constant presence at the court, prevented the growth in him of the qual-.ties of an astute politician or the abilities of a brave general and also bred in him a sense of pride, which made him contemptuous of advice. His anger was, however, "seldom more than momentary. The second brother, Shuja, then governor of Bengal,intelligence and was a brave soldier. But his excesser love of ease and pleasure made him "weak, indolent, and negligent, incapable of sustained effort, vigilant caution, and profound combination".The youngest, Murad, then governor of Gujarat, was no doubt, liberal and brave, but was addicted to hard g and could not therefore develop the qualities needed for leadership.

Aurangzeb, the third brother, was the ablest of au. He possessed uncommon industry and profound diplomatic and military skill, and an unquestionable capacity for administration. Further, as a, zealous Sunni

Mussalman, he naturally obtained the support of the orthodox Sunnis. As we shall see, the differences in the character of the rival princes did much to influence the course of the struggle. Dara Shukoh, a liberal man but an ill-qualified general and statesman, was a poor match for the clever and intelligent Aurangzeb; Shuja and Murad had also to suffer for their incompetence before the superior generalship of Aurangzeb.

Dara Shukoh alone of the four brothers was present at Agra when Shah Jahan fell ill in September, 1657. The illness was indeed serious and it was suspected by the three absentee brothers that their father had really expired and the news had been suppressed by Dara, Shikoh. So precarious is the position of an autocracy that even the illness of the Emperor gave rise to confusion and disorder in the kingdom, which became more intense as soon as the fratricidal contest commenced. Shuja, proclaimed himself Emperor at Rarajmahal, the then capital of Bengal, and marched towards the metropolis of the Empire. But on arriving near Benares be was defeated by an army sent against him under Dara Shijkoh's son, Sulaiman Shukoh, and was forced to retire to Bengal. Murad also crowned himself at Ahmedabad (5th December, 1657). He joined Aurangzeb at Malwa and formed an alliance with him. They entered into an agreement to partition the Empire, which was solemnized in the name of God and the Prophet.

THE PORTUGUESE AND CAPTURE OF HUGLI

The Portuguese had established themselves above Satgaon in Bengal in or about A.D. 1579 on the strength of an imperial firman, and had gradually strengthened their position by the erection of large buildings round about Hugli, which became consequently more important than Satgaon from the commercial point of view. But far from remaining satisfied with peaceful commercial pursuits, they gave offence to Shah Jahan by some objectionable practices. They not only exacted heavy duties from the Indian traders, especially on tobacco (which had become by that time an important article of trade), at the cost of the revenues of the State, but also became arrogant enough to begin the abominable and cruel practice of slave trading, for which they kidnapped many orphan Hindu or Muslim children, whom they converted to Christianity. Their audacity rose so high that they captured two slave girls of Mumtaz Mahal's. This must have been sufficient to incense the Mughul'. Emperor. The conversion of Indians to Christianity by some of the Jesuit missionaries added to his resentment against the Portuguese.

After his accession to the throne, Shah Jahan appointed Qasim 'Ali Khan governor of Bengal and charged him 'with the duty of punishing the Portuguese. Hugli was accordingly besieged by a large army, under the command of Qasim 'Ali Khan's son, on the 24th June, 1632, and was captured after three months. Many of the Portuguese, as we know from the court-chronicler, 'Abdul Hamid Lahori, were killed and a large number of them were taken as prisoners to Agra, where they suffered terribly.

THE DECCAN AND GUJARAT, 1630-1632

In the Deccan Famine of 1630 to 1632 some 2 million Indians had died by 1633. The famine was the result of three consecutive staple crop failures, leading to intense hunger, disease, and displacement in the region.In the fourth and fifth years of the reign of Shah Jahan an appalling famine of the most severe type desolated the Deccan and Gujarat. The horrors of this terrible calamity have been thus described by 'Abdul Hamid Lahori: "The inhabitants of these two countries were reduced to the direst extremity. Life was offered for a loaf, but none would buy; rank was to be sold for a cake, but none cared for it; the ever-bounteous hand was stretched out to beg for food; and the feet which had always trodden the way of contentment walked about only in search of sustenance. For a long time dog's flesh was sold for goat's flesh, and the pounded bones of the dead were mixed with flour and sold. When this was discovered, the sellers were brought to justice.

Destitution at length reached such a pitch that men began to devour each other, and the flesh of a son was preferred to his love. The numbers of the dying caused obstructions in the roads, and every man whose dire sufferings did not terminate in death and who retained the power to move wandered off to the towns and villages of other countries." An English merchant-traveller, Peter Mundy, who went on business from Surat to Agra and Patna and came back while the famine was raging, has also left a detailed account of its horrors.

REVOLT IN BUNDELKHAND UNDER SHAH JAHAN

The revolt in Bundelkhand (1628-1635 A.D.) under the reign of Shah Jahan is an important part of the medieval history of India. During the reign Jahangir, Bir Singh Bundela was the ruler of Bundelkhand. He had killed Abul Fazl at the instigation of Jahangir when Akbar was the Mughal emperor. When Jahangir became the ruler, Bir Singh was given high honour and rank. After his death his son, Jujhar Singh was accepted as a successor by Jahangir. Jujhar Singh was in the service of the the court while his son, Bikramajit looked after the administration of Bundelkhand. Bikramajit oppressed his subjects during the collection of revenues. When the news reached Shah Jahan, he ordered an enquiry into the past collections. That alarmed Jujhar Singh and he fled away from the court to Bundelkhand.

Shah Jahan ordered the Mughal army to attack Bundelkhand from different directions in 1628 A.D. and himself reached Gwalior to supervise the operations. Jujhar Singh realised the futility of fighting against the emperor and surrendered himself in 1629 A.D. and offered one thousand gold mohurs, fifteen lakh rupees, forty elephants and a part of his Jagirs to the emperor. Shah Jahan pardoned him and sent him in the campaign of the Deccan. Jujhar Singh served the emperor loyally for five years and played an important part in the wars of the Deccan. In 1634 A.D. he returned to his capital, Orcha. In 1635 A.D., he conquered Gondwana and killed the ruler Prem Narayan. This was a crime in eyes of the emperor as no Mughal emperor allowed fighting among his vassal rulers. The son of Prem Narayan also appealed to emperor for justice. Shah Jahan ordered Jujhar Singh either to pay rupees ten lakhs or give up Gondwana to him or hand over his Jagir which may be equal to Gondwana. Jujhar Sir refused to accept any of these conditions. Shah Jahan then sent Aurangzeb to attack Bundelkhand. Jujhar Singh and his Bikramajit abandoned the capital Orcha, and proceeded towards the Deccan. Orcha was occupied by Aurangzeb, Hindu-temples were destroyed and mosques were raised in their places. Jujhar Singh and Bikramajit were killed in the jungle by the Gonds and their heads were produced before Shah Jahan. Two of the sons of Jujhar Singh and one of his grandsons were converted to Islam. The Bundela ladies who were captured during the war were either taken over to the Mughal harem or were distributed among the Mughal nobles. Bundelkhand was handed over to Devi Singh, one of the relatives of Bir Singh, who had sided with the Mughals during the war. Thus the revolt of Bundelkhand under Shah Jahan's reign was brutally suppressed in 1635 A.D.

COURT OF SHAH JAHAN

Court of Shah Jahan followed a daily routine of a series of complicated and monotonous rituals laid down by the Emperor. Sometimes, however, Shahzadi Jahanara Begum Sahib provided a break from the regular pattern, when she organized some entertainment or function for the Emperor or the royal household. Also, she often showed her generosity by distributing presents. The Emperor believed in his duty to his subjects, both courtiers and commoners. Every morning, first he would offer his prayers alone in a minuscule mosque adjoining his private chambers, then emerge reading a rosary of pearls and collecting his thoughts for the day's work. From then on till nightfall he no longer belonged to himself, but would attend to the duties a king owes to his subjects. First he would present himself for public view to the people of Agra by appearing on the Jharoka-i-Darshan, an open balcony on the sandstone wall of the fort. The folk gathered underneath would be reassured by his presence and at seeing him in good health; he would reciprocate by returning their greetings and assuring them of the continuity of the Empire.

After that he would take a round of the palace, meeting the grand officers of his army and the stable-master and inspecting newly-acquired horses and war elephants. Following this morning ritual, he would grant audiences in the grand Diwan-i-Am (the hall of common audience). This was a huge pavilion with enormous pillars of red sandstone supporting the ornate arches which sheltered the imperial terrace a dais skirted the grilles of wrought silver. When the emperor entered, there would be a fanfare of trumpets and a great beating of drums which would penetrate to the furthest corners of the Zenana. Then he would sit on his gold and silver throne, encrusted with precious stones, magnificent in its own right but a pale precursor to the future Peacock Throne. He would sit with his legs crossed in a posture called 'Pharaoh's mode' which was the privilege only of people of high status. At his feet, the Omrahs, or nobles and grand officers of the Empire, would stand around according to rank. Ushers with gold maces would announce ambassadors and visiting dignitaries. Shah Jahan had simplified the sycophantic practices, particularly the Sajda (bowing low). It was abolished as it involved prostration, which according to the tenets of Islam is due to God alone. A second form of prostration which did not involve bowing in Sajda, but which was somewhat complex, was introduced.

This involved bowing (from the waist) and touching one's forehead, eyes, and arms four times. Even this was considered against Muslim tradition. There seems to have been created a controversy between the Imperial grandeur and orthodoxy. It remained the court ceremony of salutation but an exception was made in regard to theologians of various degrees. They used only the common Muslim formula of wishing peace.

Apart from granting audiences, Shah Jahan would receive emissaries from the provinces and dictate letters to his scribes, send reprimands, grant compensations, and attend to other administrative functions of his office. Each Wednesday, he presided over the Chamber of Justice, judging cases that were beyond the capability of ordinary tribunals. These were usually disputes regarding finance, religious questions, and general affairs. This duty was close to his heart, as he liked to consider himself as having a special ability to administer true justice. Some historians hold that he proved to be a strong and fair judge.

After attending to the Diwan-i-Am, the Emperor would go to the Diwan-i-Khas, which consisted of three sections decorated with dentated arches. The throne here was simpler than the one in the Diwan-i-Am, sculpted from a single block of grey marble and lined with brocade cushions. When the Emperor had seated himself and was ready to hold audience, the ambassadors and grand officials waiting to meet him would rush to his feet and make their petitions. He also received his architects, with whom he would discuss the progress of the construction of his monuments, and painters and upholsterers would present their work to him, hoping for a commission. For secret meetings he would retire with his vizier, Dara Shikoh, and other officials who enjoyed his confidence, to the Shah Burj in the north-east corner of the fort. This was an octagonal tower surrounded by a gallery, from where there was a view of the Taj Mahal. Since this was still under construction, the sounds of the labourers, masons, and carvers of marble working could probably be heard. At the court of Agra, there were seats of gold, of silver and of precious woods inlaid with ivory pieces.

After lunch, the Emperor and the ladies would rest for the afternoon. Following this, Shah Jahan would hold court in the Zenana to hear the grievances and petitions of female supplicants, and also to deal with any matter relating to the harem which needed his attention. Charity was one of the state duties of the princesses. In fact, it was a matter of prestige among them to contribute funds or construct buildings like mosques, wells, bazaars, etc., for public benefit, and often the royal ladies would request an increase in their allowances from Shah Jahan in order to distribute more alms. The female staff of the Mughal Zenanas was managed by a Mahaldar, a formidable matron who ruled her domain with an iron hand. Usually she would have only one rival, the chief eunuch or Nazir. These retainers would give orders to the ladies-in-waiting and servants, granting them leave according their rank: one month a year for the 1st grade, seven months for the 3rd, etc. The Mahaldar also disbursed salaries, each woman receiving, according to her rank, a salary that varied from 1,160 rupees per month down to 10. Her role was also political, for she was supposed to maintain a network of spies and keep watch over the activities of the royal family, reporting anything significant directly to the Emperor himself. It was important for these managers to be vigilant in everything and supervise each matter. If any of the lower-rank servants were found guilty of serious misdemeanours, they would be punished. The Mahaldar or Nazir would report the crime and the culprit would be tried by a domestic tribunal presided over by the Emperor himself. The Zenana would witness the more severe punishments. Disobedience was severely penalized by Shah Jahan. He would not tolerate a nobleman sitting in his presence even inadvertently, nor if the subject was fatigued. He was a very strict disciplinarian.

On the other hand, he appreciated brave retorts and courtiers defending themselves in a clever and judicious manner. In the evening, after attending to the Zenana, the Emperor would retire to the Moti Masjid to offer his prayers with his chosen courtiers. As he left the harem, the female members of his household would be murmuring respectful blessings and patting him, and often some lady petitioner whose request had been granted would be loudly calling down benefactions upon him. After prayers he would return to his duties with his viziers and ministers in the Diwan-i-Khas. With evening setting in, the tapers of the heavy, silver candelabra would be lit and the silk and gold tapestries would glitter brilliantly. When his day's work was done, he would come back to the Zenana for supper.

Finally, at ten at night, he would recline on his couch and listen to the scribes reading his favourite poems or other literary works to him, or to Qaris reciting verses from the Holy Quran. The princesses, ladies, and courtiers would be free for the evening. All the visitors, noblemen, and officials would leave the palace. The Rajput guards would be sent away to the outer walls and be replaced by Tartar, Uzbek, and Kashmiri guards. Female members of these mountain tribes would guard the harem. They would patrol the Zenana and gardens by the light of the stars or the moon. Thus ended a typical day in court of the Mughal Emperor.

MILITARY COMMANDER

The first occasion for Prince Khurram to test out his military prowess was during the Mughal campaign against the Rajput state of Mewar, which had been a hostile force to the Mughals since Akbar's reign. In

1614, commanding an army numbering around 200,000, Prince Khurram began the offensive against the Rajput kingdom. After a year of the harsh war of attrition, Maharana Amar Singh II surrendered to the Mughal forces and became a vassal state of the Mughal Empire.

In 1617, Prince Khurram was directed to deal with the Lodi in the Deccan, to secure the Empire's southern borders and to restore imperial control over the region. His successes in these conflicts led to Jahangir granting him the title of Shah Jahan (Persian: Glory of the World) and raised his military rank and allowed him a special throne in his Durbar, an unprecedented honour for a prince, thus further solidifying his status as crown prince.

REBEL PRINCE

Jahangir receives prince Khurram of his returns from deccan. Inheritance of power and wealth in the Mughal empire was not determined through primogeniture, but by princely sons competing to achieve military successes and consolidating their power at court. This often led to rebellions and wars of succession. As a result, a complex political climate surrounded the Mughal court in Prince Khurram's formative years.

In 1611 his father married Nur Jahan, the widowed daughter of an Afghan Noble. She rapidly became an important member of Emperor Jahangir's court and, together with her brother Asaf Khan, wielded considerable influence. Arjumand was Asaf Khan's daughter and her marriage to Prince Khurram consolidated Nur Jahan and Asaf Khan's positions at court.

Court intrigues, however, including Nur Jahan's decision to have her daughter from her first marriage wed Shah Jahan's youngest brother Shahzada Shahryar and her support for his claim to the throne led Khurram, supported by Mahabat Khan, into open revolt against his father in 1622.

The rebellion was quelled by Jahangir's forces in 1626 and Khurram was forced to submit unconditionally. Upon the death of Jahangir in 1627, Prince Khurram succeeded to the Mughal throne as Shah Jahan, King of the World, the latter title alluding to his pride in his Timurid roots and his ambitions. Shahanshah Shah Jahan's first act as ruler was to execute his chief rivals and imprison his step mother Nur Jahan. This allowed Shan Jahan to rule without contention.

CONTRIBUTIONS TO ARCHITECTURE

The Shalimar Gardens, Lahore comprising over four-hundred fountains, were built by the Mughal emperor. The Taj Mahal is the most notable example of Islamic architecture in South Asia; it was constructed according to the commands of the famous Mughal Emperor Shah Jahan.

Shah Jahan left behind a grand legacy of structures constructed during his reign. He was one of the greatest patrons of Islamic architecture. His most famous building was the Taj Mahal, now a wonder of the world, which he built out of love for his wife the empress Mumtaz Mahal.

Its structure was drawn with great care and architects from all over the world were called for this purpose. The building took twenty years to complete and was constructed from white marble underlaid with brick. Upon his death, his son Aurangazeb had him interred in it next to Mumtaz Mahal. Among his other constructions are the Red Fort also called the Delhi Fort or Lal Qila in Urdu, large sections of Agra Fort, the Jama Masjid, the Wazir Khan Mosque, the Moti Masjid, the Shalimar Gardens, sections of the Lahore Fort, the Jahangir mausoleum—his father's tomb, the construction of which was overseen by his stepmother Nur Jahan and the Shahjahan Mosque. He also had the Peacock Throne, Takht e Taus, made to celebrate his rule. Shah Jahan also placed profound verses of the Quran on his masterpieces of architecture.

A famous seamless celestial globe was produced in 1659–1660, by the Sindhi astronomer Muhammad Salih Tahtawi of Thatta with Arabic and Persian inscriptions.

Contribution to the Arts

The imperial Pearl Mosque of the Mughal Emperor Shah Jahan. All the inscriptions on the Taj Mahal tombs of Shah Jahan and his wife are in Persian Calligraphy on the tombs and on the Agra Fort in quranic calligraphy and a Persian poem in Nasta¿lîq. Shah Jahan's cenotaph is bigger than that of his wife, but reflects the same elements: a larger casket on a slightly taller base, again decorated with astonishing precision with lapidary and calligraphy that identifies him.

The pen box and writing tablet were traditional Persian funerary icons decorating the caskets of men and women respectively. The Ninety Nine Names of God are found as calligraphic inscriptions in Persian nast Nastalîq inscription style of calligraphy on the sides of the actual tomb of Mumtaz Mahal, in the crypt including "O Noble, O Magnificent, O Majestic, O Unique, O Eternal, O Glorious... ". The tomb of Shah Jahan bears a calligraphic inscription that reads: "He traveled from this world to the banquet-hall of Eternity on the night of the twenty-sixth of the month of Rajab, in the year 1076 Hijri."

Jama Masjid, Delhi one of the largest mosques in the Mughal Empire was completed during the reign of Shah Jahan.

Written in Persian: the bright tomb of arjmand banou beegom famous as Mumtaz Mahal (the best of the region) died year...

the purified shrine of his majesty resident of paradise the highness Shahjahan the Magnificent rest his soul in peace. year 1076 H.G. Shah Jahan was very interested in Persian inscription and a Persian poet who requested a famous Persian calligrapher to decorate his palace and castles.

DEATH OF EMPEROR SHAH JAHAN COMMEMORATED AT TAJ MAHAL

Shah Jahan built the Taj Mahal as a memorial to his wife following her death. This week saw thousands of people gather at the Taj Mahal in India to mark the anniversary of the death of the emperor who oversaw the construction of the spectacular monument.

Each year the death anniversary - or Urs - of Mughal emperor Shah Jahan is commemorated in a three-day event, with thousands coming from all around to pay homage to the emperor who lived from 1592 to 1666.

The event culminated in the offering of tributes to Shah Jahan and his wife Mumtaz Mahal at the Taj Mahal. Entrance to the monument was made free today to enable people to visit the graves of the royal couple, which are normally kept closed throughout the year in an underground chamber. Another highlight of the ceremony was the presentation of the 'chadar' - a vast multi-coloured cloth - which was carried in a procession to the tomb by hundreds of people. This year's chadar was a record 450-metres long, reports the ANI news agency.

"Every year, we offer this cloth, and this year too, it has happened," said Tahiruddin Tahir, president of the Khuddam-E-Roja Committee, which oversaw the ceremony. "People from all communities and religions, including Hindus, Muslims, Sikhs and Christians have all made this and presented the special cloth. So, I pray that the message of peace and brotherhood is spread during this festival." Meanwhile, the event highlights the extraordinary story behind the construction of the Taj Mahal - a spectacular monument that never fails to wow those on tours through India. Shah Jahan is understood to have built the Taj Mahal as a monument to his third wife Mumtaz Mahal.

The emperor reportedly fell in love with Mumtaz after spotting her for the first time at the marketplace in his royal complex. He was so grief stricken when she died that he decided to build her an everlasting memorial and resting place, drawing inspiration from the Koran's detailed description of heaven.

To ensure that no other structure would ever rival the beauty of the Taj Mahal, Shah Jahan made an agreement with the building's artists that they would not create anymore art or design in their lifetime. The Taj Mahal took over twenty years to build and covers an area of some 1003 acres.

7

Rise of Aurangzeb

Shah Jahan was a bigoted Muslim and a confirmed nepotist. He provided for the imperial princes before anyone else in the matter of administrative and judicial postings regardless of age, capability and talent. He also started the practice of conferring the cream of the offices on each prince; like Dara Shikoh was made the governor of Punjab and Multan, Aurangzeb was appointed governor of all the four provinces of the Deccan and so on. This might have been just a clever way to keep them occupied, but that was not how the nobility viewed it. The nobles saw this, and rightfully so, as an obstacle in the path of their promotions. However, the end of Shah Jahan's reign did not live up to the beginning; it saw one of the messiest battles of succession that Indian history ever witnessed.

In September 1657, Shah Jahan fell ill. The prognosis was so unoptimistic that the rumors had it that the emperor was dead. This was enough to spark off intense intrigue in the court. All the four claimants to Shah Jahan's throne were the children of the same mother although one would never have guessed that from their temperaments and their determination to make it to the throne. In 1657, Dara Shikoh was 43, Shah Shuja 41, Aurangzeb 39 and Murad 33. All of them were governors of various provinces: Dara was the governor of Punjab, Murad of Gujrat, Aurangzeb of the Deccan and Shah Shuja of Bengal. Two of them emerged clear frontrunners in the battle for the throne quite early: Dara Shikoh and Aurangzeb. Aurangzeb was with doubt the ablest of Shah Jahan's sons and a clear favourite for the throne.

His credentials both in battle and administration were legendary. He was also an orthodox Muslim of the oldest school possible, which made him a hot favourite with the clergy. As stated earlier, the actual events, which unfolded around Shah Jahan's illness, were confused. Aiding and abetting the confusion with every word and gesture, for his own aims and purposes, was the favourite son Dara Shikoh. Aurangzeb did not waste much time. Acting on Dara Shikoh's behalf, Aurangzeb along with Murad met the Mughal armies twice in battle, and beat them each time while moving on relentlessly towards Agra, where Shah Jahan was convalescing. When Shah Jahan heard of Aurangzeb's advance, he expressed a wish to meet Aurangzeb and talk to him. It was the emperor's belief that upon seeing him alive, his son would turn on his heels and go back. Clearly the old king had been ailing only in body and not in mind, for certainly the appearance of Shah Jahan himself would have laid to rest the whole issue of succession. Even the most ardent of Aurangzeb's supporters would have had second thoughts about defying the great Mughal's authority openly. However, Dara Shikoh lacked the potentate's easy confidence in his son. He was not so convinced that Aurangzeb would meekly go back to where he had come from once the king had reassured him.

In panic he also gave out that he was the heir-apparent. So with suspicion and rumors ruling the day and power having the last laugh, Aurangzeb was the most amused of them all. Within a year he had all his brothers out of the way, father permanently in custody in the Agra Fort (where he hung on for eight years before dying in 1666) and was firmly entrenched on the Mughal throne. If Shah Jahan has been over-romanticized by scholars, his son and successor Aurangzeb has been unduly denigrated. Aurangzeb, it seems, could do nothing right. Later writers were to contrast his bigotry with Akbar's tolerance, his failure against the Marathas rebels with Akbar's successes against the Rajputs; in fact he has been set up as the polar opposite of everything that earned one the Akbarian medal of genius.

One writer has said about him, rather tongue-in-cheek, "His life would have been a blameless one, if he had no father to depose, no brothers to murder and no Hindu subjects to oppress." This picture of him has left such an impact on popular imagination that even today he is regarded as the bad guy of the Mughal regime, the evil king who slayed all Hindus and Sikhs. Hardly anyone remembers that he governed India for nearly as long as Akbar did (over 48 years) and that he left the empire larger than he found it. In fact, Aurangzeb ruled the single largest state ever in Mughal history. Aurangzeb's rise to the throne has been criticized as being ruthless.

However, he was no crueler than others of his family. He succeeded not because he was crueler but because he was more efficient and more skilled in the game of statecraft with its background of dissimulation; and if it's any consolation, he never shed unnecessary blood. Once established, he showed himself a firm and capable administrator who retained his grip of power until his death at the age of 88. True, he lacked the magnetism of his father and great-grandfather, but commanded an awe of his own. In private life he was simple and even austere, in sharp contrast to the rest of the great Mughals. He was an orthodox Sunni Muslim who thought himself a model Muslim ruler.

AURANGZEB: A POLITICAL HISTORY

The four sons of the Mughal Emperor, Shah Jahan, all laid claim to the throne when their father fell seriously ill in 1658. Each had considerable administrative experience and military skills, each commanded a considerable military force, and each had a loyal following. Dara Shikoh (1615-58), the eldest son, was resident at Shah Jahan's court as the designated heir; Shuja was Governor of Bengal, Bihar, and Orissa; Aurangzeb governed the Deccan; and Murad was Governor of Gujarat and Malwa. Dara's forces were defeated by Aurangzeb, who occupied the imperial capital of Agra; and Aurangzeb took his own father prisoner. Shuja's army was routed in battle; and Murad was lured into a false agreement and taken prisoner. Dara eventually collected together another force, suffered defeat as before, and once again he fled; but soon he was betrayed by one of his allies, and handed over to his brother. Accused of idolatry and apostasy from Islam, Dara was condemned to death, and the sentence was carried out on the night of 30 August 1659, one year after Aurangzeb took over the Fort at Agra and assumed the throne. Aurangzeb delivered the head of his brother to their father.

Aurangzeb Alamgir ("World Conqueror"), whose reign lasted for forty-nine years until his death in 1707, conducted vigorous military campaigns to extend the frontiers of the vast Mughal empire which he had inherited. Both in the northwest and northeast, the imperial armies gained ground, but the losses, which were very considerable, drained the treasury. Already under his father, the revenue of the crops had been raised from a third to a half, and the extensive and interminably long military campaigns he waged required him to keep the peasantry heavily taxed. Some notable victories were likewise achieved in the Deccan. Aurangzeb retained Shahjahanabad as his capital, but after some two decades the capital, in a manner of speaking, shifted to wherever Aurangzeb would set camp during his long military campaigns, which in the Deccan alone lasted some 26 years and perhaps cost him his life. Aurangzeb's mobile army consisted of some 500,000 camp followers, 50,000 camels, and 30,000 war elephants; and when this gargantuan force moved, bands of Maratha guerrillas would strike the rear, attacking the stragglers and fleeing with booty.

A considerable part of Aurangzeb's energies were consumed in keeping his numerous opponents at bay, and he had to deal with the Rajputs, the disloyalty of his son Akbar, and the Sikhs, whose leader, Guru Tegh Bahadur, was killed at Aurangzeb's command when he refused to convert to Islam. Neither could Aurangzeb forgive the Sikhs for having supported his brother and principal rival, Dara. (There is another, though related, view of the question of Dara's relationship to the Sikhs: it is not so much that the Sikhs supported Dara, but rather they sheltered him, given that they were bound to the principle that they were obligated to give asylum to whoever came seeking their assistance). The most effective opposition to Aurangzeb's rule, however, came from the Marathas, whose chief, Shivaji, could not be contained. Only Shivaji's premature death at the age of 53, in 1680, appeared to offer the Mughal Emperor some relief, but that very year the Rajputs of Jodhpur and Mewar forged an alliance against Aurangzeb and declared themselves free from his sovereignty. The army that Aurangzeb sent under his son Akbar to subdue them was formidable, but the emperor had perhaps not reckoned with his son's traitorous conduct. However, Akbar, who had rather vainly declared himself the emperor, was compelled to flee to the Deccan, where he enlisted the help of Shivaji's son, Sambhaji. Aurangzeb decided to take to the field himself, and eventually drove his own son into exile in Persia, from where Akbar never returned. The Sultanates of Bijapur and Golconda were also reduced to utter submission, and Sambhaji was captured in 1689 and tortured before being murdered.

Towards the end of his reign, Aurangzeb's empire began to disintegrate, a process which would be considerably accelerated in the years after his death, when "successor states" came into existence. Aurangzeb's harsh treatment of Hindus, and the reversal of the liberal religious policies of his predecessors, particularly Akbar, have been cited as principal reasons for the disintegration of his empire. [For a more detailed consideration, see the accompanying article on "Aurangzeb and the Encounter with Religion."] More likely, the peasantry was bled to death, and the system of political alliances established by Akbar was allowed to go to seed. The empire had become far too large and unwieldy, and Aurangzeb did not have enough trustworthy men at his command to be able to manage the more far-flung parts of the empire. Many of the his political appointees broke loose and declared themselves independent, and Aurangzeb's preoccupation with affairs in the Deccan prevented him from meeting political challenges emanating from other parts of the empire. Shortly after the death of Aurangzeb, the Mughal Empire ceased to be an effective force in the political life of India, but it was not until 1857-58, when the Indian Rebellion was crushed and the Emperor Bahadur Shah was put on trial for sedition and treason, that the Mughal Empire was formally rendered extinct.

AURANGZEB'S VIEWS ON THE JIZYA

From Aurangzeb's Fatwa: [Jizyah] refers to what is taken from the Dhimmis, according to [what is stated in] al-Nihayah. It is obligatory upon the free, adult members of [those] who are generally fought, who are fully in possession of their mental faculties, and gainfully employed, even if [their] profession is not noble, as is [stated in] al-Sarajiyyah. There are two types of [Jizyah]. [The first is] the Jizyah that is imposed by treaty or consent, such that it is established in accordance with mutual agreement, according to [what is stated in] al-Kafi. [The amount] does not go above or below [the stipulated] amount, as is stated in al-Nahr al-Faiq. [The second type] is the Jizyah that the leader imposes when he conquers the unbelievers (kuffar), and [whose amount] he imposes upon the populace in accordance with the amount of property [they own], as in al-Kafi. This is an amount that is pre-established, regardless of whether they agree or disagree, consent to it or not.

The wealthy [are obligated to pay] each year forty-eight dirhams [of a specified weight], payable per month at the rate of 4 dirhams. The next, middle group (wast al-hal) [must pay] Twenty-four dirhams, payable per month at the rate of 2 dirhams. The employed poor are obligated to pay twelve dirhams, in each month paying only one dirham, as stipulated in Fath al-Qadir, al-Hidayah, and al-Kafi. [The scholars] address the meaning of "gainfully employed", and the correct meaning is that it refers to one who has the capacity to work, even if his profession is not noble.

The scholars also address the meaning of wealthy, poor, and the middle group. Al-Shaykh al-Imam Abu Jafar, may Allah the most high have mercy on him, considered the custom of each region decisive as to whom the people considered in their land to be poor, of the middle group, or rich. This is as such, and it is the most correct view, as stated in al-Muhit. Al-Karakhi says that the poor person is one who owns two hundred dirhams or less, while the middle group owns more than two hundred and up to ten thousand dirhams, and the wealthy [are those] who own more than ten thousand dirhams...The support for this, according to al-Karakhi is provided by the fatawa of Qadi Khan (d. 592/1196). It is necessary that in the case of the employed person, he must have good health for most of the year, as is stated in al-Hidayah. It is mentioned in al-Idah that if a dhimmi is ill for the entire year such that he cannot work and he is well off, he is not obligated to pay the Jizyah, and likewise if he is sick for half of the year or more. If he quits his work while having the capacity [to work] he [is still liable] as one gainfully employed, as is [stated in] al-Nihayah. No Jizyah is imposed upon their women, children, ill persons or the blind, or likewise on the paraplegic, the very old, or on the unemployed poor, as is stated in al-Hidayah.

Expansion of the Empire

Emperor Aurangzeb seated on a golden throne holding a hawk in the Durbar. Such scenes would be rare in the latter part of his reign as he was permanently camped in the Deccan, fighting wars. From the start of his reign up until his death, Aurangzeb engaged in almost constant warfare. He built up a massive army, and began a program of military expansion along all the boundaries of his empire. Aurangzeb pushed north-west into the Punjab and what is now Afghanistan; he also drove south, conquering Bijapur and Golconda, his old enemies. He attempted to recover those portions of the Deccan territories where the Maratha king Shivaji was sparking rebellions. This combination of military expansion and religious intolerance had deeper consequences. Though he succeeded in expanding Mughal control, it was at an enormous cost in lives and treasure. And, as the empire expanded in size, Aurangzeb's chain of command grew weaker. The Sikhs of the Punjab grew both in strength and numbers, and launched rebellions. The Marathas waged a war with Aurangzeb which lasted for 27 years. Even Aurangzeb's own armies grew restive — particularly the fierce Rajputs, who were his main source of strength. Aurangzeb gave a wide berth to the Rajputs, who were mostly Hindu. While they fought for Aurangzeb during his life, on his death they immediately revolted against his successors.

With much of his attention on military matters, Aurangzeb's political power waned, and his provincial governors and generals grew in authority.

AURANGZEB: A POLITICAL HISTORY

The four sons of the Mughal Emperor, Shah Jahan, all laid claim to the throne when their father fell seriously ill in 1658. Each had considerable administrative experience and military skills, each commanded a considerable military force, and each had a loyal following. Dara Shikoh (1615-58), the eldest son, was resident at Shah Jahan's court as the designated heir; Shuja was Governor of Bengal, Bihar, and Orissa; Aurangzeb governed the Deccan; and Murad was Governor of Gujarat and Malwa. Dara's forces were defeated by Aurangzeb, who occupied the imperial capital of Agra; and Aurangzeb took his own father prisoner. Shuja's army was routed in battle; and Murad was lured into a false agreement and taken prisoner. Dara eventually collected together another force, suffered defeat as before, and once again he fled; but soon he was betrayed by one of his allies, and handed over to his brother. Accused of idolatry and apostasy from Islam, Dara was condemned to death, and the sentence was carried out on the night of 30 August 1659, one year after Aurangzeb took over the Fort at Agra and assumed the throne. Aurangzeb delivered the head of his brother to their father. Aurangzeb Alamgir ("World Conqueror"), whose reign lasted for forty-nine years until his death in 1707, conducted vigorous military campaigns to extend the frontiers of the vast Mughal empire which he had inherited.

Both in the northwest and northeast, the imperial armies gained ground, but the losses, which were very considerable, drained the treasury. Already under his father, the revenue of the crops had been raised from a third to a half, and the extensive and interminably long military campaigns he waged required him to keep the peasantry heavily taxed. Some notable victories were likewise achieved in the Deccan. Aurangzeb retained Shahjahanabad as his capital, but after some two decades the capital, in a manner of speaking, shifted to wherever Aurangzeb would set camp during his long military campaigns, which in the Deccan alone lasted some 26 years and perhaps cost him his life. Aurangzeb's mobile army consisted of some 500,000 camp followers, 50,000 camels, and 30,000 war elephants; and when this gargantuan force moved, bands of Maratha guerrillas would strike the rear, attacking the stragglers and fleeing with booty. A considerable part of Aurangzeb's energies were consumed in keeping his numerous opponents at bay, and he had to deal with the

Rajputs, the disloyalty of his son Akbar, and the Sikhs, whose leader, Guru Tegh Bahadur, was killed at Aurangzeb's command when he refused to convert to Islam.

Neither could Aurangzeb forgive the Sikhs for having supported his brother and principal rival, Dara. (There is another, though related, view of the question of Dara's relationship to the Sikhs: it is not so much that the Sikhs supported Dara, but rather they sheltered him, given that they were bound to the principle that they were obligated to give asylum to whoever came seeking their assistance). The most effective opposition to Aurangzeb's rule, however, came from the Marathas, whose chief, Shivaji, could not be contained.

Only Shivaji's premature death at the age of 53, in 1680, appeared to offer the Mughal Emperor some relief, but that very year the Rajputs of Jodhpur and Mewar forged an alliance against Aurangzeb and declared themselves free from his sovereignty. The army that Aurangzeb sent under his son Akbar to subdue them was formidable, but the emperor had perhaps not reckoned with his son's traitorous conduct. However, Akbar, who had rather vainly declared himself the emperor, was compelled to flee to the Deccan, where he enlisted the help of Shivaji's son, Sambhaji. Aurangzeb decided to take to the field himself, and eventually drove his own son into exile in Persia, from where Akbar never returned. The Sultanates of Bijapur and Golconda were also reduced to utter submission, and Sambhaji was captured in 1689 and tortured before being murdered. Towards the end of his reign, Aurangzeb's empire began to disintegrate, a process which would be considerably accelerated in the years after his death, when "successor states" came into existence.

Aurangzeb's harsh treatment of Hindus, and the reversal of the liberal religious policies of his predecessors, particularly Akbar, have been cited as principal reasons for the disintegration of his empire. [For a more detailed consideration, see the accompanying article on "Aurangzeb and the Encounter with Religion."] More likely, the peasantry was bled to death, and the system of political alliances established by Akbar was allowed to go to seed. The empire had become far too large and unwieldy, and Aurangzeb did not have enough trustworthy men at his command to be able to manage the more far-flung parts of the empire. Many of the his political appointees broke loose and declared themselves independent, and Aurangzeb's preoccupation with affairs in the Deccan prevented him from meeting political challenges emanating from other parts of the empire. Shortly after the death of Aurangzeb, the Mughal Empire ceased to be an effective force in the political life of India, but it was not until 1857-58, when the Indian Rebellion was crushed and the Emperor Bahadur Shah was put on trial for sedition and treason, that the Mughal Empire was formally rendered extinct.

AURANGZEB'S RELATIONS WITH BRITISHERS

The behaviour of the English East India Company was another element that has to be added to the complex situation created by internal rebellion, the activities of the Sikhs, and the long-drawn-out war with the Marathas. The East India Company opened its first factory, or trading post, at Surat on the west coast in 1612, and in the next half century established a chain along the coast. Trouble first arose in Bengal, where Shayista Khan was trying to introduce some order and regard for the Mughal government in place of the lax administration of his predecessor, Shah Shuja. The foreign settlements of the Portuguese, the Dutch, and the British, emboldened by their superiority on the sea, had become truculent, and in distant regions considered themselves subject to no checks from the Mughal government. Shah Shuja, partly out of his general indifference to financial considerations and partly to gain support in the coming struggle for the throne, was particularly generous to the foreign traders.

To the English factory which was opened at Hugli in 1651, he gave an order in 1652 permitting open trade in Bengal on a payment of three thousand rupees annually in lieu of customs dues. In the succeeding years the Company's trade multiplied many times, but, insisting on the authority of Shuja's order, it refused to increase its contribution or pay any of the normal taxes. When Shayista Khan objected, difficulties arose between him and the English. The attitude of the Company's officers may be judged from a letter addressed to London in 1665:

- Your Worship must consider that these people are grown more powerful than formerly, and will not be so subject to us as they have been, unless they be a little beaten by us, that they may understand, if they impede us by land, it lieth in our power to requite them by sea. ... In fine ... your affairs will be quite ruined if this Nabob [Shayista Khan] lives and reigneth long."

The first attempt by the English to wage war against the Mughals was made in 1686 when Sir Josiah Child, the powerful governor of the East India Company, persuaded the government to send a small fleet to

India to seize and fortify Chittagong. The expedition was an utter failure; and far from gaining any territory, English traders were expelled from all their factories in Bengal. Meanwhile on the west coast, the English had also angered Aurangzeb. English pirates operating out of Bombay were seizing ships taking pilgrims to Mecca; among them was the Ganj-i-Sawai owned by the emperor himself. They were also minting coins in Bombay with a superscription containing their own king's name. Aurangzeb ordered the seizure of the Surat factory and the expulsion of all Englishmen from his dominions. He relented because of the English control of the pilgrim trade in the Arabian Sea, and also, it appears, because they had a powerful advocate at court in the wazir, Asad Khan. After levying a fine of one and a half lakhs of rupees Aurangzeb allowed them to return to their factories; and for the next fifty years, the English merchants refrained from any further attempts to establish themselves as a territorial power.

RELIGIOUS POLICY OF AURANGZEB

Aurangzeb was the third son of the Mughal emperor Shah Jahan; his mother was Mumtaz Mahal, who is buried in the Taj Mahal. Aurangzeb showed his ability in administrative and military matters in various appointments, which gradually caused him to envy his eldest brother Dara Shikoh, the designated successor to the throne. In 1657 Shah Jahan became seriously ill, and the rivalry between Dara Shikoh and Aurangzeb turned into open confrontation. Shah Jahan recovered unexpectedly, but the struggle for succession continued. Aurangzeb placed his father under house arrest, drove one brother into death, had two other brothers executed and in 1658 declared himself emperor of the Mughal empire, assuming the name 'Alangir ("the World Seizer"). Aurangzeb did not share the interest of his ancestors and relatives in the arts, drink and the good life generally but was serious-minded and religious. He inherited an empire that had flourished for nearly a century under the wise administrative and economic procedures introduced by his great-grandfather Akbar the Great. The economic boom had led to the development of artisanal activity in all villages, and the municipalities had become economically much less dependent on the central power. Aurangzeb tried to stem the growing independence of the different parts of his empire by returning to autocratic rule. He abandoned the policy of separation of religion and state and turned away from the policy of religious tolerance that during the previous three generations had kept Muslims, Hindus, Sikhs, Christians and others together in peace and common destiny. In 1675 he executed the Sikh guru

Tegh Bahadur because of his refusal to convert to Islam. The Sikh rebellion that followed continued throughout Aurangzeb's reign; relations between Sikhs and Muslims have been strained ever since. In 1679 Aurangzeb reintroduced the jizya, a poll tax for non-Muslims that had been abolished by Akbar the Great a century earlier. The result was a revolt of the Hindu Rajputs, supported by Aurangzeb's third son Akbar, in 1680 - 1681.

In the south of the empire the Maratha kingdom was conquered and broken up and its ruler Sambhaji executed in 1689, which started a long and exhausting guerilla campaign by the Maratha Hindu population. The ongoing struggles placed severe strain on the empire's finances, and increased taxation led to several peasant revolts, often but not always under the guise of religious movements. At Aurangzeb's death the empire was larger than before but severely weakened. It survived for another 150 years but was in constant religious strife. What Akbar the Great had so splendidly begun collapsed 300 years later under the colonial onslaught, because the empire's economic progress did not lead to the political reform that would have allowed further development.

Aurangzeb: Religious Policies

The disintegration of the Mughal Empire followed rapidly after the death of Aurangzeb in 1707. During his long reign of 49 years, Aurangzeb had done much to extend the frontiers of the empire he had inherited from his father, Shah Jahan, but the extensive military campaigns he conducted, particularly in the Deccan, created a severe financial drain on his resources. The burden of oppressive taxation fell on the peasantry, and political feudatories who owed their positions to Aurangzeb were constantly breaking loose from the emperor's control. But more often than not, it is the religious policies pursued by Aurangzeb that have been cited as one of the principal reasons for Aurangzeb's undoing, and among many Hindus the name of Aurangzeb evokes the same passionate hatred as do the names of Mahmud of Ghazni and Muhammad of Ghori. With the ascent of the Hindu right to political power in India, a great many people have been emboldened to further attack Aurangzeb. A brief consideration of Aurangzeb's policies, consequently, is in order, but not only to understand the nature of his reign, or the state of Hindu-Muslim relations in India over a period of time, important as are these questions; it is also imperative to ask questions about how our histories are written and how notions of 'minority' and 'majority' get constructed and become part of the political vocabulary.

A year after he assumed power in 1658, Aurangzeb appointed muhtasaibs, or censors of public morals, from the ranks of the ulema or clergy in every large city. He was keen that the sharia or Islamic law be followed everywhere, and that practices abhorrent to Islam, such as the consumption of alcohol and gambling, be disallowed in public. But he was at the outset faced with one problem, namely that the treatment he had meted out to his own father, subjecting him to imprisonment, was scarcely consistent with the image he sought to present of himself as a true believer of the faith. Accordingly, Aurangzeb sought recognition of his ascent to the Mughal Emperor's throne from the ruler of the holy places in the Hijaz, and he became a great patron of the Holy Places. He is reported as well to have spent seven years memorizing the Koran, and unlike his predecessors, his reign was marked by austerity. The monumental architecture that characterized the reigns of Akbar and Shah Jahan -- the Agra Fort, Fatehpur Sikri, the Taj Mahal, Shahjahanabad, among others -- held little interest for Aurangzeb, and similarly the musicians who had adorned the courts of his predecessors were dismissed.

From the standpoint of Aurangzeb's Hindu subjects, the real impact of his policies may have started to have been felt in 1668-69. Hindu religious fairs were outlawed in 1668, and an edict of the following year prohibited construction of Hindu temples as well as the repair of old ones. Also in 1669, Aurangzeb discontinued the practice, which had been originated by Akbar, of appearing before his subjects and conferring darshan on them, or letting them receive his blessings as one might, in Hinduism, take the darshan of a deity and so receive its blessings. Though the duty (internal customs fees) paid on goods was 2.5%, double the amount was levied on Hindu merchants from 1665 onwards. In 1679, Aurangzeb went so far as to reimpose, contrary to the advice of many of his court nobles and theologians, the jiziya or graduated property tax on non-Hindus, and according to one historical source, elephants were deployed to crush the resistance in the area surrounding the Red Fort of Hindus who refused to submit to jiziya collectors. The historian John F. Richards opines, quite candidly, that "Aurangzeb's ultimate aim was conversion of non-Muslims to Islam. Whenever possible the emperor gave out robes of honor, cash gifts, and promotions to converts. It quickly became known that conversion was a sure way to the emperor's favor" (p. 177).

It can scarcely be doubted, once the historical evidence is weighed, that the religious policies of Aurangzeb were discriminatory towards Hindus, Sikhs, and other non-Muslims. Nonetheless, numerous inferences have been drawn from the literature which are not warranted by the historical record. Though many historians have written of conversions of Hindus, surprisingly little, if any, evidence has been offered to suggest how far the conversion of Hindus took place, and whether there was any official policy beyond one of mere encouragement that led to the conversion of Hindus. Then, as now, conversion would have been more attractive to the vast number of Hindus living under the tyranny of caste oppression, and it isn't clear at all how the kind of inducements that Aurangzeb offered -- if indeed he did so for the purposes of conversion, as Richards maintains -- are substantially different from the inducements that modern, purportedly secular, politicians offer to people in their electoral constituencies. And what of the popular representation of Aurangzeb as a ferocious destroyer of Hindu temples and idols?

Hindu temples in the Deccan were seldom destroyed, notwithstanding Aurangzeb's extensive military campaigns in that area. True, in north India, some Hindu temples were undoubtedly torn down, but much work needs to be done to establish the precise circumstances under which these acts of destruction took place. The famed Keshava Rai temple in Mathura was one such temple, but here Aurangzeb seems to have been motivated by a policy of reprisal, since the Jats in the region had risen in revolt.

Like his predecessors, Aurangzeb continued to confer land grants (jagirs) upon Hindu temples, such as the Someshwar Nath Mahadev temple in Allahabad, Jangum Badi Shiva temple in Banaras, and Umanand temple in Gauhati, and if one put this down merely to expediency, then why cannot one view the destruction of temples as a matter of expediency as well, rather than as a matter of deliberate state policy? Moreover, recent historical work has shown that the number of Hindus employed as mansabdars, or as senior court officials and provincial administrators, under Aurangzeb's reign rose from 24.5% in the time of his father Shah Jahan to 33% in the fourth decade of his own rule. One has the inescapable feeling that then, as now, the word 'fanaticism' comes rather too easily to one's lips to characterize the actions of people acting, or claiming to act, under the name of Islam. It is also notable that as a firm Sunni, Aurangzeb dealt as firmly with the Shia kingdoms of Bijapur and Golconda as he did with the Hindus or Muslims. One can safely assert that Aurangzeb acted to preserve and enhance the interests of his own Muslim community, and restored the privileges of the Sunni ulema, but his actions with respect to the Hindus, Shias, and others are more open to interpretation.

Jizyah according to Satish Chandra

Aurangzeb introduced the jaziya, but, cautions Satish Chandra, "it was not meant to be an economic pressure for forcing Hindus to convert to Islam, for its incidence was to be light." For this assertion Satish Chandra gives two bits of proof, so to say.

First, "women, children, the disabled, the indigent, that is, those whose income was less than the means of subsistence, were exempted as were those in government service." How could even Aurangzeb have exacted a tax from those "whose income was less than the means of subsistence?"

And why would he exact a discriminatory and humiliating tax from those who were in government service, that is, from those who were already serving his interests and those of the Islamic State? The second proof that Satish Chandra gives is that "in fact, only an insignificant section of Hindus changed their religion due to this tax" -- but could that not have been because of the firm attachment of Hindus to their faith, because of their tenacity rather than because of the liberality of Aurangzeb? The jaziya was not meant either to meet "a difficult financial situation". Its reimposition was in fact, says Satish Chandra, "both political and ideological in nature."

Political in the sense that "it was meant to rally the Muslims for the defence of the State against the Marathas and the Rajputs who were up in arms, and possibly against the Muslim States of Deccan, especially Golconda, which was in alliance with the infidels." A parity twice-over -- one, that Aurangzeb was only trying to rally the Muslims just as those opposing him had rallied the Marathas and Rajputs. And, in any case, the ones who were opposing him were "infidels" "Jaziya was to be collected by honest; God-fearing Muslims who were specially appointed for the purpose and its proceeds were reserved for the Ulema." As the proceeds went to Ulama, there was a secular reason for exacting the tax -- it was to be "a type of bribe for the theologians among whom there was a lot of unemployment,"

Aurangzeb's Administration

Aurangzeb ruled for almost 50 years. During his long reign, the Mughal Empire reached territorial climax. Aurangzeb proved to be a hardworking ruler and never spared himself or his subordinates in the task of government. He was a stirct disciplinarism who did not spare his own sons, during his reign he introduced few administrative changes.

Rise of Aurangzeb

According to histories, Aurangzeb brought changes in administration. Those were that the senior Hindu officers in the finance ministry were retained and even promoted, although in Banaras and some other places and Brahmans were harassed, and Hindu temples were also demolished by orthodox mobs. Aurangzeb stopped this desecration, but, in accordance with Islamic Sharia rules no new temples would be elected. A high proved mansabdar was appointed as censor of morals (muhtasib) to prevent drinking and to make Muslim changes to Quranic Laws. There were many changes regarding festival's celebration also. Like celebration of Iranian Naw festival, which falls on the day the sun enters Aries was banned The "Kalima", or the confession of faith, was no longer stamped on coins, to prevent the holy words from being defiled by unbelievers or heretics. These reforms in no way undermined Hindu political and economic interests. Aurangzeb also used to send gift to holy men of Mecca-Madina & those were suppose to be distributed among poor or needy but to Aurangzeb's disappointment the funds were misused. In other words some historiams used different way of describing Aurangzeb's reign. They divided his reign into two phases.

First phase was from 1658-1679 and second was from 1679 to his death 1707. And these were divided again into severed sub-phases. Other Historians defines economy measures, tax, Hindu temples etc in the reign of Aurangzeb. There were many ceremonies, which were used to perform, were also stopped like the practices of the Emperor putting a Tika or saffrom paste on the forehead of a new raja was stopped. Practices, which were considered against Islamic spirit, were banned. Public displays of Holi and Muharram procession were also stopped. The courtiers were also asked not to wear silk gowns or gowns of mixed silk and cottons.

Taxs

There were taxes. Basically there were many taxes and we are told that Khalisa areas alone, rahdari had yielded 25 lakhs of rupees a year. Another tax was pandari or ground rent for stalls in the bazar in the capital and others towns. Another vexation tax, which was abolished in 1666, was the octroi duty on Tobacco.

Economy Measures

According to the history of Aurangzeb, in thirteenth years, it was reported that expenses had exceeded income during the preceding twelve years. Some of the measures of economy adopted by Aurangzeb were the retrenchment of many items in the expenditure of the Emperor, the princes and Begums. It seems that Aurangzeb was keen to promote trade among Muslim who depended almost exclusively on the state support. In 1665, he reduced the duty on import of goods by Muslim traders from 5 per cent to 2 ½ per cent and two years later abolished it altogether. But he had to reimpose it when he found Muslim traders were abusing it by presenting goods of Hindu traders as theirs. So ultimately it was kept 2½ per cent for the Muslims. Many temples were being destructed by him also. So this was Aurangzeb's way of administrating the Mughal.

Aurangzeb's Religious Policy

According to historians Aurangzeb reversed Akbar's Policy of religious toleration. He basically used those policies which were already introduced by his predecessor but those were not that strong so again Aurangzeb during his reign again used those policies and one of them in Religious policy. Aurangzeb's religious policy was largely based on his analysis of the first half of Aurangzeb's reign, which in his opinion was climaxed by the reinposition of Jizyah (poll tax). The other orthodox measures of Aurangzeb were insidious attempts on his part to establish an Islamic state in India which in effect implied conversion of the entire population to Islam and the extinction of every form a dissent. The religion policy of Mughal was largely the reflection of the personal religious views etc. It was a very narrow and orthodoxy kind of policy taken by Aurangzeb.

He put ban on the practice, which were considered as against Islamic spirit. And many ceremonies and festivals were banned that time. Many temples were also destroyed that time. It was earlier found that long standing temple should not be demolished but no new temples allowed to be built. But later on it was found that many temples were demolished. And this was so because Aurangzeb started fearing for his political existence because there were some temple where both Hindu & Muslim used to go and learn teachings and Aurangzeb thinking that these kind of practice may hamper therefore, there should be stopped so demolishment took place. There was also tax, which was imposed on non-Muslims like Jizyah.

Jizyah

It was that tax which was reimposed by Aurangzeb on the non-muslims. Aurangzeb considered reimpostion of Jizyah, but postponed the matter due to "certain political exigencies". That it was reimpossed twenty-

Rise of Aurangzeb

two years after Aurangzeb's accession to the throne is clear indication that its institution was on account of political considerations. Jizyah was used to be collected by honest God-fearing Muslims, who were especially appointed for this purpose. Because of this tax many got converted and enjoyed benefits but many did not left their religion and were being harassed. There were exception in this tax was that the women, children and the person who can not earn even for his own livelihood will be taken into consideration. So basically Jizyah was not an Income Tax but was a kind of property tax, which is imposed only in non-Muslim. These many let Islam grow.

Policy's Impact

There been several bad impacts of Aurangzeb's policies. Some historians had said that Aurangzeb's policies made Mughal very weak. Earlier there was no respect left for Islam and its adherents; mosques were without splendor, while idol-temples flourished; the requisites of canonical practice remained closed under bolts, while the gates of irreligious practices were flung open. That time Aurangzeb was the defender of the truth faith, converts to Islam were made much of. Many temples were given order of destruction and instead mosques built. But now because of this religious policy Mughal State had failed to yield the expected dividends. Now Aurangzeb faced difficult task of bringing under Imperial control the extensive country extending up to Jinji, populated by Hindu population and simultaneoudy he had to deal with Marathas. And situation became so worst that there seem like Aurangzeb need to make some modification in his policy. His attitude towards Hindu temples also varied from time to time according to circumstance that is political exigencies. And his attitude towards Marathas also varied. But policy was not changed. During that time many festivals & ceremonies banned and all practice, which is found against Islamic spirit, were also banned. Jizyah's impact was also very bad. Altogether, Jizyah came into picture because of religious policy. This tax was for non-Muslims. And basic impact of this Jizyah was that people got converted into Islamic religion so as to escape from Jizyah and enjoy profits of being Islamic. But many people who were not Islamic were treated badly. Many people used to close their shops and observe hartals against the measure. But even though Jizyah had not led to any large conversion. And in this Jizyah there started lot of corruption. Aurangzeb's religious policy led to series of contractions, which he found hard to resolve.

RELIGIOUS POLICIES UNDER AURANGZEB IN THE MUGHAL EMPIRE

As an orthodox Sunni Muslim, Aurangzeb felt that his empire should be a land of pure Islam, administered according to the restrictive rules and regulations laid down by the early Khalifas. He was astute and shrewd enough not to be unaware of the administrative and political fallouts of his zealous and in a sense bigoted following of the precepts of Islam.

Some historians are of the view that Aurangzeb's conscience goaded him into taking a stance of uncompromising hostility towards unbelievers and that he was willing to incur any political danger or loss of revenue in order to follow his ideals.

They are of the opinion that it is not correct to accuse Aurangzeb of sanctimonious hypocrisy and of feigning religious sentiments which he did not feel in his heart. Explaining this point, V.A. Smith writes: "Although his religion did not hinder him from committing actions in the field of statecraft which are repugnant to the moral sense of mankind, his creed, as a creed, was held in all sincerity, and he did his best to live upto it. He resembled most other autocrats in assuming that rules of morality do not apply to matters of state.

There is no reason to suppose that he felt any remorse for his treatment of his father, and it is certain that his conscience was perfectly easy concerning the penalties which he inflicted on his brothers, sons and other relatives. The safety of the state, as identified with the maintenance of his personal authority, was sufficient justification in his eyes for acts which we are disposed to call unfeeling crimes. Those acts in no way conflicted with his religions sentiments" (The Oxford History of India).

Two events apparently set Aurangzeb on his path of bitter opposition and violence against the Hindu religion. The first is the death of Raja Jai Singh in Deccan in 1667, presumably due to poisoning by his son, Kirat Singh, who did so at the behest of Aurangzeb. As the leading Hindu officer of the realm, Raja Jai Singh had some restraining influence on the anti-Hindu policies of Aurangzeb.

On 18 April 1669, the emperor was informed that in the provinces of Thatta, Multan and Benaras, but more noticeably, in the last, brahmans were bold enough to give public lectures on their holy books and scriptures to which even Muslim students from distant places were attracted. The emperor regarded such open propaganda of Hindu idolatry as nothing but scandalous.

Then and there commands were issued "to all the governors of provinces to destroy with a willing hand the schools and the temples of the infidels; and they were strictly enjoined to put an entire stop to the teaching and practice of idolatrous forms of worship."

After Raja Jai Singh's death in the Deccan, Raja Jaswant Singh of Marwar (Jodhpur) was deputed to his place. As, however, there was no improvement in the situation, he was sent in disgrace to the west of the Indus, a region where the Hindus preferred not to go. He was appointed commandant of a small post at Jamrud, at the mouth of the Khyber, where he died towards the end of 1678.

Aurangzeb thought that the death of the Raja had provided him with a further opportunity to advance in his policy of humiliating the Rajas and the Hindus in general. He reimposed the jiziya, the hated poll-tax on non-Muslims, which the wise and compassionate Akbar had abolished early in his region. The historian, Khafi Khan defined the objectives of Aurangzeb as the curbing of the infidels and the demonstration of the difference between a land of Islam (Darul-Islam) and a land of the unbelievers (Dar-ul-harb).

It was the orthodox reform movement in Indian Islam started by Mujaddid Alf-i-Sani Shaikh Ahmad Sirhindi (1563-1624) which, probably, had a great influence on the life and activities of Aurangzeb.

The aims of this reform movement were regeneration and rejuvenation of Islam in strict accord with the shariyat and the "establishment of a true Islamic State conforming to Islamic ideas and practices in all its activities..." Aurangzeb came into contact with Khwaja Muhammad Masum, son of Mujaddid Ahmad Sirhindi, while he was a prince.

Aurangzeb was very respectful to Masum and asked for his advice on important matters of Muslim theology. On ascending the throne, Aurangzeb continued to be in touch with the Khwaja as also his son Muhammad Saifuddin.

Aurangzeb claimed the throne against his liberal-minded, elder brother Dara because he considered Dara to be a heretic. As a diehard sunni Muslim he believed in the Islamic theory of kingship and wanted to follow its precepts. The essential feature of this theory is that the ruler should strictly enforce the Quranic law in the administration of his empire.

In 1659, he took the first step in this direction by issuing a number of ordinances to restore the Muslim law of conduct as per the teaching of the Quran. The practice of inscribing the Kalima (the Muslim confession of faith) on the coins were discontinued to prevent defilement in the hands of the infidels.

The celebration of Nauroz, the Zoroastrian New Year's day, was stopped, thus discontinuing a custom followed by his predecessors in imitation of the Persian kings. Bhang or cannabis Indica was no more to be cultivated because of its addictive harmful properties. Muhtasibs or the moral police were placed in all big cities to check on and curb the practice of un-Islamic habits such as drinking, gambling and illicit traffic of women.

They also had the power to punish the Muslims for heresy, blasphemy, failure to say the prayers (namaz) and to observe the fast of the Ramzan. The Sufis and Shias were not spared. The Ismailia or Bohra community of Gujarat suffered serious persecutions for heresy among the Muslim communities.

Music was banned in the court in 1668 and the musicians were told to go away. They were, however, given pensions. An exception was made for the royal band and it continued. Tuladan or the ceremony of weighing the emperor on his two birthdays (according to the solar and lunar calendars) was discontinued as it was un-Islamic.

Likewise, Jharokadarshan, a custom according to which the Mughal emperors used to appear at the outer balcony of their palaces in the morning to receive felicitations from their subjects, was also stopped. The rejoicings and merry-making on the anniversary of coronation as also on birthdays were prohibited by the emperor.

Drinking and gambling were so widespread that it was almost impossible for the moral police to stamp them out. Likewise, the dictate ordering courtesans and dancing girls to abandon their vocation and to get married was observed more in breach than in compliance. The eminently sensible order prohibiting sati was also not obeyed because of the strong opposition of the Hindus.

Aurangzeb declared in a farman granted to a priest of Benaras in 1659, that his religion forbade him to allow construction of new temples, but there was no bar on the destruction of old ones. The repair works of old temples were prohibited in 1664 and on 9 April 1669 came the order (mentioned earlier) to destroy all schools where brahmans were lecturing on the Hindu scriptures in public. The widespread destructions of temples all over the country followed this order.

The reimposition of jizya on the Hindus came on 2 April 1679 with the avowed objective of spreading Islam and overthrowing idolatrous practices. By reimposing this hateful tax, Aurangzeb went against the courageous and compassionate decision of his illustrious great grandfather, Akbar abolishing it. Commenting on the nature of the tax, Dr J.N. Chaudhuri states: "It was a commutation tax, i.e., the price of indulgence, and had to be paid by an assessee with marks of humility. For its assessment and collection, the non-Muslim population was roughly divided into three grades: the first grade having an income above 10,000 dirhams had to pay 48 dirhams; the second, whose income was 200 to 1000 dirhams paid 24 dirhams, and the third with incomes below 200 dirhams, 12 dirhams, a dirham being equivalent to a quarter of a rupee.

It appears that the jizya hit the poor-non-Muslim population most, as the rate of taxation in their case was heavy in proportion to their income. Women, children below fourteen, beggars and paupers were exempted from their tax. Of the monks, the heads of wealthy monasteries only had to pay; government officials were, however, exempted from paying this tax" [The Mughal Empire).

By an order in 1671 all Hindu head-clerks and accountants were removed from their posts so as to fill those vacancies with Muslims. As, however, not many experienced and qualified Muslims were available to fill in, the order was modified allowing 50 per cent of such posts to be retained by the Hindus. Then, in 1668 there was a blanket ban on all Hindu fairs, and in March 1695 an order prohibited all Hindus (excepting the Rajputs) to ride in palanquins, elephants and pedigree horses. They were also forbidden to carry arms.

The consequence of all these discriminatory, demeaning and humiliating measures of Aurangzeb was far-reaching and ultimately disastrous for the stability of the empire.

Narrating all the anti-Hindu acts of Aurangzeb (as reviewed earlier), Dr Mira Singh strikes a different note by stating: "It would be...irrational to term Aurangzeb as a fanatic purely on the basis of (above) statements just as it would be ridiculous to interpret all his acts as religion-oriented solely. (Moreover) all discussions, on the spread of Islam in India must be preceded by the contention that while the establishment of a theocratic state continued to remain the ideal of the Islamic state, in reality its interpretation varied from state to state according to the existing political exigencies. Hence, in a predominant Hindu India, no ruler but an imbecile could hope to debar Hindus from the state service, civil and military, leave alone attempt their total annihilation.

In fact, in India, since Mahmud Ghaznavi's time, the Muslim rulers had realized the essential difference between the ideal Din Panahi and the functional Din Dari and had perforce preferred to enforce the latter in the country. The diligent utilization of the Hindu potential to the maximum advantage of the Muslim ruler may have differed from ruler to ruler, but the impossibility of bringing about a total extermination of Hinduism was universally recognized by all. Against such background, as also keeping in view Aurangzeb's brilliant political record under Shah Jahan, it seems inconceivable and entirely irrational that Aurangzeb, when a sultan, threw all political caution to wind and attempted to establish a fanatic rule" [Medieval History of India].

Dr Singh, therefore, argues that it is necessary to make a logical interpretation of Aurangzeb's motives and policies which she believes were based upon:

(a) the personal religious views of the emperor;
(b) his policy towards the ulemas and theologians who consistently endeavoured towards the creation of an Islamic state; and
(c) his policy towards the non-Muslim subjects and the handling of those issues which were primarily political in nature but involved certain religious elements too.

Dr Singh observes that in the sixteenth and seventeenth centuries, the Muslim ruling class in the country could be categorized as belonging to three main religious streams. The progressives among them were, like Akbar and Dara Shikoh, believers in the universality of religion, regarded religions as different paths for the attainment of the same goal and recommended (and practised) mutual tolerance among all faiths. Next were the liberals who more or less followed the Islamic path, but ruled according to the political exigencies of the state.

Usually, they kept the state separate from religion as Jahangir did during his rule. Shah Jahan adhered to the essentials of a liberal rule, but compared to Jahangir he was more inclined to orthodoxy. And finally there were the orthodox bigots like Ahmad Sirhindi, Aurangzeb's mentor, who were against associating Hindus in any manner with the Islamic state and demanded their persecution. Thus Aurangzeb, by nature and association, was inclined towards orthodoxy from his youth and the debate to chose between orthodoxy and liberalism as state policy was apparently always in his mind. Inheriting a more or less liberal administration from his father Shah Jahan, he continued to keep it going. During this time, he tried to solve various problems according to their political weightage and made efforts to keep the state above religion.

However, as political and economic problems drew the country more and more to a deepening political crisis, his frustrations became more and more acute and apparently he turned towards religion believing it to be the cause as also the resolution of all problems. Once he had crossed the thin line between orthodoxy and fanaticism, Aurangzeb lost the innate sense of keeping the state separate from politics.

A spate of anti-Hindu measures were enacted, but Dr Singh argues that they were spread over a long period of time and that it would be a grave mistake to regard these as examples of Aurangzeb's fanaticism. She says that there were an equal number of instances to prove Aurangzeb's initial tolerance. Khafi Khan refers to the abolition of some eighty cesses and taxes. It seems Aurangzeb was quite aware of the political importance of the Rajputs and his attempts to win over Raja Raj Singh of Mewar show clearly his intent. With regard to the blanket order dismissing all Hindus in the revenue department and replacing them by Muslims, the Akham-i-Alamgiri refers to the emperor's reprimand of Amir Khan in 1669 for suggesting the sack of one of the two Hindu bakhshis and replacing him by a Muslim instead.

Moreover, there are farmans, dated after the infamous order for the destruction of schools and temples, sanctioning grants for the maintenance of such Hindu religious institutions. Writing during the closing years of Aurangzebi reign, Bhimsen provides an interesting account of numerous temples which were constructed in the Deccan during those years. Likewise, Ishwardas in his Futuhat-i-Alamgiri has given an account of the various temples which existed during Aurangzeb's reign as well as the Sikh Gurudwara in Dehradun for which the emperor provided a gate.

Also, Athar Ali has shown by his research that contrary to popular belief the numbers of Hindu/ Rajput nobles did not go down during the reign of Aurangzeb. It would appear the percentages of such nobles went down marginally from 22.9 per cent (in 1628-58) to 20.6 per cent (1658-78) and then rose to 27.8 per cent (1679-1701).

AURANGZEB; RELIGIOUS POLICY AND THE IDEAS

Muhi-ud-din Muhammad Auranzeb was born on 3rd November, 1618(N.S) at Dohad near Ujjain. At early age he became a good scholar of Arabic and Persian, and learned Turki and Hindi as well. While he did not care for painting, music and other fine arts. At the end of 1634 A.D, he was appointed mansabdar of 10,000 Zat and 4,000 Sawar. Then he was given charge of Bundela expedition against Jujhar Singh of Orchha, which was his first experience of war and diplomacy. So, from the very early age he acquired reputation as a good soldier, administrator and diplomat.

Aurangzeb was staunch Muslim who could not go against the law of Islam. This orthodoxy misinterpreted by historians, i.e he was intolerant to other religions. While in his own book (Waqi-i-Alamgiri) he stated, "No person shall in unlawful way interfere with or disturb the Brahmins and the other Hindus resident in their places."

The "Ideas" of Aurangzeb can be judged from his personality. His personality can be studied from two dimensions; as a religious man and as a statesman.

As a religious man he was staunch Muslim and careful and conciliatory to non-Muslims. As a statesman Aurangzeb attended in person every detail of state's administration. Due to his long term, campaigns and reduction of taxes, financially he became weak. Toward rebels and his opponents he was conciliatory in a limit while he was more conciliatory and merciful toward his allies.

THE SUCCESSORS OF AURANGZEB

The successors of Aurangzeb: Bahadur shah and others, Mohammed shah; invasion of Nadir Shah ; growth of Maratha power ; Ahmad shah Durrani; the third battle of panipat.

War of succession. Aurangzeb left behind him four sons, the princes Muazzam, Azam, Akbar, and Kambakhsh. Akbar, a rebel and exile, no longer counted ; the three others were all equally eligible candidates for the vacant throne. A document in the nature of a will found under the pillow of the dead emperor suggested a division of the empire between these three sons, but none of them had the slightest intention of being content with anything less than the whole.

The eldest, prince Muazzam, had himself proclaimed at kabul, while his brother, prince Azam, assumed the imperial dignity in the Deccan camp. Both of these claimants assembled large armies, which met at Jajau, to the south of Agra, in June 1707. The battle ended in the total defeat of prince Azam, who was killed, along with two adult sons. Shah Alam or Muazzam thus secured possession of Agra, the treasure city of the empire, and the command of abundant cash, which he distributed freely among his followers . In February 1708 Prince Kambakhsh was defeated in the Deccan, and died from his wounds. Thus prince Muazzam became undisputed Padshsh. He is known to history as either Bahadur shah I or shah Alam I.

Reign of Bahadur Shah I. He conciliated the Marathas by the release of their Raja, Shahu (ante,p.219), and patched up a peace with the Rajputs. The most important event of his short reign was a severe conflict with the Sikh sectaries of the Panjab, and it will be convenient to notice briefly in this place the origin and early stages in the development of the Sikh power.

Origin and rise of the Sikhs. The Sikhs, or 'disciples', are one of the many reformed sects of Hinduism which have arisen from time to time.

The teaching of Nanak, the first guru oif the sect, late in the fifteen century, which was based on that of Kabir(ante,p.143), did not attract much official attention until the beginning of the seventeenth century in Jahangir's reign, when the guru of of the day was put to death. That act of severity roused the zeal of the martyr's adherents, who took up arms under the leadership of his son Har Gobind and became the declared enemies of the government.

Sikh organisation. Guru Gobind Singh (1675-1708), grandson of Har Gobind, converted the sect into a political power by means of an organization (known as the Khalsa) and rule of life which sharply separated the sikhs from the rest of the population and united them closely among themselves. The disciples, who were fobidden to use tobacco in anyform, were required to wear their hair long, and to practise sundry other special onservances. The fact that most of the Sikhs were jats by caste supplied another bond of union, and the reult was that during the eighteenth century the sect gradually became a ruling power. But, although the jats have furnished the majority of sikh converts, it must be clearly understood that people of all castes may be initiated as Sikhs, and that within the sect no distinction of caste is recongnized.

War of Banda, the sikh leader. When Bahadur Shah died at Lahore, in February 1712, he was engaged in endeavours to check the barbarous ravages commited by the Sikhs at Sahrind and other places in the Panjab, under the leadership of Banda, the nominee of Guru Gobind Singh. Bahadur shah was a good-natured, generous man, but lacking in the strength needed by a ruler in troublous times. He was nicknamed the 'Heedless king' (Shah-i-bekhabar).

War of succession ; Jahandar shah ; Farrukhsiyar. The death of the emperor was followed by the usual war between his four sons. The most competent claimant, Azim-ush-shan, governor of Bengal, had the ill luck to be the first killed in battle. Two others perished in further fighting. The survivor, Jahandar shah, a worthless debauchee of low tastes, was proclaimed emperor by Zulfikar khan, apowerful noble, who became Vazir (1712).

After a few months Jahandar Shah was put out of the way, and Farrukhsiyar, son of Azim-ush-shan-, was placed on the throne (January 1713) by the influence of two Saiyids of Barha. For some years this clan of Saiyids enjoyed the position of king-makers, and appointed whom they chose to occupy the seat of Aurangzeb. The imperial dignity was quickly becoming an empty although dangerous honour.

Defeat of the sikhs. The principal event in Farrukhsiya's reign was the crushing defeat of the Sikhs, whose leader Banda was captured and executed with the most inhuman tortures. About a thousand of his followers also were slain. This severity kept the Sikhs quiet for a generation. Allusion has been made above (ante, p.162) to the important trading privileges gained for the English merchants by the surgeon Hamilton, who attended Farrukhsiyar. The emperor, a timid, helpless creature, not personally of any importance, was murdered early in 1719.

Accession of Mohammed shah ; break-up of the empire. Several nonentities, who lasted only a few moths, having been set up, the Saiyids selected another insignificant prince, who ascended the throne as Mohammed shah, in October 1719. During his reign, which was long, and continued until 1748, the empire began to break to pieces. The emperor of Delhi was gradually reduced to a position like that of the later members of the Tughlak dynasty(ante,p.119), while the outlying powers, Hindu, Mohammedan, and foreign, came to the front, with the ultimate result that the sceptre passed into English hands.

Independence of the Deccan ; the Nizam. A Turki noble, named Chin Kilich khan, generally known by his title of Asaf jah, the son of a favourite officer of Auragzeb, had become viceroy of the Deccan. For a time he held the office of vazir at Delhi, but in 1723 he retired from court, and after that date may be regarded as an independent sovereign. He was the ancestor of the present Nizam of Hyderabad. Before the withdrawal of Asaf Jah to the south, the king-making clan of saiyids had lost their power through the murder of Husain Ali and the imprisonment of his brother Abdullah, who had been their leaders.

Practical independence of oudh ; Saadat khan. About this tiem, Saadat khan, governor of Oudth, likewise made himself practically independent and founded the line of Nawab-Vazirs, who were recognized later as kings of oudh.

Bengal ; Allahvardi Khan. The Suba of Bengal, including Bihar and Orissa, although nominally under the control of the emperor, was really as little subject to his authority as the Afghan kings of Bengal had been before the time of Akbar. Allahvardi (Alivardi) khan, the Subadar from 1740 to 1756, an able despot, ceased to pay tribute to the imperial court.

The Rohillas ; general revolt of provinces. To the north of the Ganges, the Rohillas, a clan of Afghan immigrants, made themselves masters of the rich tract now called Rohikhand. In short, everywhere a general revolt of the provinces began in the reign of Mohammed shah, was completed in the time of his successors.

Shahu and Balaji Visvanath Peshwa. Tara Bai was the last natable member of sivaji's line. Shahu, who became Raja early in 1708 (ante,p.219), had been brought up at the Mogul court, and was more Mohammedan than Hindu un his habits. He preferred pleasure to business, and was glad to leave affairs of state in the hands of ministers, especially in those of a clever Brahmin named Balaji Visvanath, who was appointed his Peshwa in 1714, and tried to introduce some order into the confused Maratha Government.

Baji Rao I, Peshwa. When Balaji Visvanath died, in 1720, he was succeeded by his elder son, Baji Rao I, after an interval of some months. The dignity of Peshwa thus became hereditary. Owing to shahu's easy-going disposition, the minister overshadowed his nominal master, and from 1727, when the peshwa was granted full powers, the Raja ceased to count. Shahu surveyed until 1748, but Baji Rao was the real head of the government, and was able to pass on his authority to his son. Baji Rao was an able soldier as a leader of plundering bands; but woth no taste for civil administration. He largely extended Maratha influence in the dominions still under the nominal authority of the emperor of Delhi.

Balaji ; the peshwa dynasty. On the death of Baji Rao I, in 1740, his place as peshwa was taken, after a struggle, by his son Balaji, who became practically the sovereign of the Marathas. Nobody asks who succeeded shahu as Raja of satara. All readers of history rightly think of the government of the Marathas in the eighteenth century as that of the Peshwas. Their position was the same as that of the ministers in modern Nepal, who have thrust their nominal sovereigns into the background.

The name of the Maharajadhiraj in that country has no interest for anybody. Thus the line of the Peshwas became substantially a ruling dynasty, which may be taken to date from 1727, when Shahu bestowed full powers on Baji Rao I. The dynasty lasted until the general settlement of India effected by the Marquess of Hastings in 1818, but retained little power after the treaty of Bassein, in 1802.

Change in Maratha government. During the rule of the first three peshwas the character of the Maratha government changed. The hereditary dominions in the ghats and Konkan left by Sivaji became of comparitively small importance. The main efforts of the Maratha rulers were directed to securing their power over the dominions of the Mogul emperor and the Nizam, by compelling the sovereigns of those countries to pay tribute to the Marathas. countries which consented to pay chauth, or one-fourth of the land revenue, plus the sardesmukhi, or one-tenth, were supposed to be protected from plunder. The emperor Mohammed shah, in 1720, during the lifetime to Balaji Visvanath peshwa, had been forced not only to acknoledge the maratha title to the hereditary dominions of shivaji (swaraj), but to recognize formally the Maratha right to levy Chauth and sardesmukhi from the six Subas of the Deccan.

Origin of existing maratha states. About this time the chiefs who founded the still-existing maratha dynasties of the Gaikwar of Baroda, of Holkar at Indore, and of sindia at Gwalior, come into notice. The ancestor of the Gaikwar was an adherent of a defeated opponent whom Baji Rao I though it prudent to conciliate.

The chiefs of Indore and Gwalior are descended from men of humble origin who became officers of Baji Rao and gradually rose to distinction in his service. At the great settlement of 1818 those three dynasties were lucky enough to be confirmed in their possessions. But the Bhonsla Raj of Nagpur or Berar lost its independence at the same date, and was finally extinguished by Lord Dalhousie in 1853. The Raj had been founded in 1743 by a Maratha leader named Raghuji, who acquired Cuttack (Katak) in 1751, and claimed from Bengal twelve lakhs of rupees as chauth. Raghuji is not to be confounded with Raghoba or Raghunath Rao, the younger son of Baji Rao I, who became prominent in the first Maratha war.

Foreign invasion ; Nadir shah. Unhappy India, already bleeding to death from internal disorders, had yet a calamity still greater to suffer. For more than two centuries she had been spared the misery caused by serious invasions from beyond the passes of the north-western frontier, but was now to undergo experiences which recalled the days of Mahmud and Timur. Early in 1736, the throne of persia was seized by Nadir shah, an adventure who had earned a right to the highest place by the display of extraordinary abilities as a general. Being dissatisfied at the delay of the Delhi government in redressing certain grievances of which he complained, he occupied Ghazni and Kabul, and, advancing without meeting serious resistance, was within a hundred miles of Dehi before Mohammed shah could do anything to stop him.

Battle of karnal; massacre at Delhi. Early in 1739, at karnal, not far from the historic field of Panipat, the imperial forces ventured to bar the invaders path, and were easily routed. Mohammed shah submitted , and, being courteously received, entered Delhi with the Victor. Nadir shah at first held his troops in check and protected the city, but when the populace attacked him and his men, he let loose twenty thousand soldiers to burn, plunder, and kill. Not less than thirty thousand people perished in the massacre, which lasted for half a day. Return home of Nadir shah, 1739. Nadir shah wanted something more than blood.

The seizure of the crown jewels and the peacock throne (ante,p.200) alone was sufficient to enrich the robber beyond the dreams of avarice, but he was not content until he had extorted from the surviving citizens, great and small, the larger part of their possessions, every form of cruelty being used to compel payment. He then made a treaty with Mohammed shah, providing for the throne, and after a stay of fifty-eight days returned to his own country, laden with coin, plate,jewels, and prcious things of every kind to the value of many millions sterling. Like the early invaders, he also took away with him hundreds of skilled artisans.

The court of Delhi. The imponent court of Delhi continued to be the scne of endless intrigues and assassinations. The most prominent personages there were the Vazir Kamar-ud-din khan and Ghazi-ud-din, son of Asaf jah, viceroy of the Deccan.

Ahmad shah Durrani. In 1747 Nadir shah, king of persia, who had become an insane tyrant, was murdered, and succeeded in his eastern territories by a chieftain named Ahmad KHan, head of the Abdali or Durrani clan of Afghans, who took the title of Ahmad shah. Next year the Durrani invaded the panjab, and was driven back, after a hard fight at Sahrind, by the imperial forces under the command of the heir-apparent, prince ahmad, and the Vazir, who was killed in action.

Ahmad shah of Delhi, 1748. In April of the same year, Mohammed shah died and was succeeded by his son, Ahmad shah, who must not be confounded with his Durrani namesake and contemporary.

Annexation of the Panjab by the Durrani. During the reign of Ahmad shah, Ghazi-ud-din and other nobles were engaged in constant fighting with one another, and ahmad shah Durrani annexed the panjab. In 1754 Ghazi-ud-din blinded his nominal sovereign, and selected as his successor a son of Jahandar shah.

Sack of Delhi by Ahmad shah Durrani. This prince was enthroned under the title of Alamgir II, but had nothing beyond the title in common with Aurangzeb. In 1756 Ahmad shah Durrani sacked Delhi and repeated the horrors of Nadir shah's massacres seventeen years before. He also disgraced himself by a cruel slaughter of unarmed Hindus at Mathura. Next year the heat caused sickness among his troops and obliged him to retire to hsi own country.

Maratha conquest of the panjab. The son of Ghazi-ud-din, who bore the ame name as his father, called in the marathas to help him against his rivals, and the imperial city and the panjab were occupied by a Maratha chief named Raghoba, the younger son of Baji Rao I(1758). Maratha empire at its greatest extent, 1760. This bold advance of the upstart Hindu power alarmed the Mohammedan princes, and induced them to combine for the empulsion of the intruders, by whom almost the whole of India, from the Himalayas and the Indus to Tanjore, was dominated for the moment. The maratha army now included a large park of artillery and ten thousand disciplined infantry, modelled on European principles.

The Bhao Sahib at Delhi. In 1760, the Peshwa, hearing that Ahmad shah Durrani had defeated the marathas in the panjab, or gained a great expeditionary force under his cousin,Sadashei Rao, commonly known as the Bhao Sahib, to march on Delhi. As the Peshwa's army slowly advanced, it was joined by sindia and Holkar and other chieftains, and by the jats under Suraj Mal. They begged the Bhao Sahib to adopt the traditional guerilla tactics of the Marathas, but the Brahmin general haughtily refused. This caused great offene, and after this, the jats took no further part. The Bhao Sahib captured Delhi on 2 August, and completed the ruin of the palace and city, stripping the silver plating from the ceiling of the Hall of Audience. It was generally realized that if the marathas were victorious, they would establish a Hindu Raj on the ruins of the Mogul empire. Meanwhile, the Afghan commander was encamped at some distance away, on the banks of the jumna, unable to cross owing to the swollen state of the river.

Rise of Aurangzeb

Third battle of Panipat, January 1761. Ultimately on 6 january 1761, the Maratha host, with little or no support from the jats and Rajputs, confronted the army of Ahmad shah Durrani, who was supported by the troops of oudh and other mohammedan principalities, on the plain of panipat, where the fate of India has been so often decided. Delay in bringing on a battle had reduced the Maratha army to a state of famine, and at last the Bhao sahib was compelled either to fight or to starve. He was utterly routed with enormous slaughter, in which most of the MAratha chiefs fell. The peshwa died soon after. The third battle of panipat was the death-blow to the power of the peshwa as the sovereign of the Marathas, the temporary revival of maratha influence a few years later being chiefly the work of Sindia, Holkar, and other independent princes.

Withdrawal of the Durrani. The Durrani made no use of his victory, and was constrained by mutiny to go home with his plunder. In april 1767, after inflicting several defeats on the sikhs, he reappeared once more for a moment near panipat with fifty thousand Afghan cavalry, and then retired, troubling himself no more with the affairs of Hindustan.

Causes of the decline of the Mogul empire. Akbar, Jahangir, shahjahan, and Aurangzeb were all strong, hardy men of dauntless personal courage, able and willing to meet man or beast in deadly combat, as many anecotes prove. But the sons of Aurangzeb seemed to be of a different breed. All the spirit was crushed out of them by their father. Their sons and grandsons grew up as nerveless weaklings in the society of women, eunuchs, and the riff-raff of the palace. The nobles became as debased as the members of the royal family, and were better fitted to buy over a commandant than to storm his fort. They went to war riding in palankeens, attended by a swarm of worthless followers of both sexes, and were served in camp with all the pomp and luxury of the Delhi court. Such people could not be successful. The rule of a despotic monarch cannot not be successful. The rule of a despotic monarch cannot be maintained except by a man who knows how to rule. The succesors of Aurangzeb had no such knowledge.

IT is not surprising that in the course of a century and a half the Mogul dynasty should have lsot its vigour; the wonder rather is that the padshahs for four successive generations possessed character and ability sufficient to hold together a vast empire and to govern it is such a fashion that it made at least a show of strength. The Deccan wars exposed the internal rottenness of the imperial organization. In the whole of India there wasnot a capable of effecting the necessary reforms. The weakness of the empire was palinly seen by European observers. Manucci, the Italian physician, writes, late in Aurangzeb's reign:

'Having set forth all the grandeur and power of the moguls, I will, with the reader's permission, assert from what I have seen and tested, that to sweep it entirely away and occupy the whole empire, nothing is required beyond a corps of thirty thousand trusty European soldiers, led by competent commanders who would thereby easily acquire the glory of great conquerors.'

That opinion probably was quite sound. It was held a little lter by Clive, although he did not care to act upon it. Condition of India under Aurangzeb's Successors. The condition of India during the half-century following the death of Auragzeb may be summed up in one word-misery. Even before his death, the french physician Bernier, not an unfriendly critic, declared that 'no adequate idea can be conveyed of the sufferings of the people'. He writes of 'a tyranny so excessive as to deprive the peasant and artisan of the necessaries of life, and leave them to die of misery and exhaustion a tyranny, owing to which these wretched people either have no children at all, or have them only to endure the agonies of starvation, and die at a tender age-a tyranny, in fine, that drives the cultivator from his wretched home. . . As the ground is seldom tilled otherwise than by compulsion, and no person is found willing and able to repair the ditches and canals for then conveyance of water, it happens that the whole country is badly cultivated and a great part rendered unproductive from the want of irrigation. The houses, too, are left in a dilaoidated condition.'

After the old emperor had passed away, hell was let loose, and the people were ground to the dust by selfish nobles, greedy officials, and plundering armies. Hardly anyone appears on the stage of history who is worthy of remembrance for his own sake, and there is little to be said about literature or art. In most parts of the country the 'great anarchy' continued for another half-century, until the advance of the English power, in the early years of the nineteenth century, brought some measure of relief to a suffering land.

DEATH AND LEGACY

Bibi Ka Maqbara, the mausoleum of Aurangzeb's wife Dilras Banu Begum, was built by him. By 1689, almost all of Southern India was a part of the Mughal Empire and after the conquest of Golconda, Aurangzeb may have been the richest and most powerful man alive. Mughal victories in the south expanded the Mughal Empire to 3.2 million square kilometres, with a population estimated as being between 100 million and 150 million. But this supremacy was short-lived. Jos Gommans, Professor of Colonial and Global History at the University of Leiden, says that "... the highpoint of imperial centralisation under emperor Aurangzeb coincided with the start of the imperial downfall."

Aurangzeb's vast imperial campaigns against rebellion-affected areas of the Mughal Empire, caused his opponents to exaggerate the "importance" of their rebellions. The results of his campaigns were made worse by the incompetence of his regional Nawabs.

Muslim views regarding Aurangzeb vary. Most Muslim historians believe that Aurangzeb was the last powerful ruler of an empire inevitably on the verge of decline. The major rebellions organized by the Sikhs and the Marathas had deep roots in the remote regions of the Mughal Empire.

Unlike his predecessors, Aurangzeb considered the royal treasury to be held in trust for the citizens of his empire. He made caps and copied the Quran to earn money for his use. He did not use the royal treasury for personal expenses or extravagant building projects excepting perhaps the Badshahi Mosque in Lahore, which for 313 years was the world's largest mosque. Aurangzeb constructed a small marble mosque known as the Moti Masjid (Pearl Mosque) in the Red Fort complex in Delhi. However, his constant warfare, especially with the Marathas, drove his empire to the brink of bankruptcy just as much as the wasteful personal spending and opulence of his predecessors. Aurangzeb knew he would not return to the throne after his final campaign against the Maratha in 1706, in which, he was joined by newly-emerging commanders in the Mughal army such as Syed Hassan Ali Khan Barha, Saadat Ali Khan and Asaf Jah I and Daud Khan.

Aurangzeb reading the Quran

The Indologist Stanley Wolpert, emeritus professor at UCLA, says that: the conquest of the Deccan, to which, Aurangzeb devoted the last 26 years of his life, was in many ways a Pyrrhic victory, costing an estimated hundred thousand lives a year during its last decade of futile chess game warfare. The expense in gold and rupees can hardly be accurately estimated. Aurangzeb's encampment was like a moving capital

– a city of tents 30 miles in circumference, with some 250 bazaars, with a 1D 2 million camp followers, 50,000 camels and 30,000 elephants, all of whom had to be fed, stripped the Deccan of any and all of its surplus grain and wealth... Not only famine but bubonic plague arose... Even Aurangzeb, had ceased to understand the purpose of it all by the time he was nearing 90... "I came alone and I go as a stranger. I do not know who I am, nor what I have been doing," the dying old man confessed to his son, Azam, in February 1707.

The unmarked grave of Aurangzeb in the mausoleum at Khuldabad. Even when ill and dying, Aurangzeb made sure that the populace knew he was still alive, for if they had thought otherwise then the turmoil of another war of succession was likely. He died in Ahmednagar on 20 February 1707 at the age of 88, having outlived many of his children. His modest open-air grave in Khuldabad expresses his deep devotion to his Islamic beliefs. It is sited in the courtyard of the shrine of the Sufi saint Shaikh Burham-u'd-din Gharib, who was a disciple of Nizamuddin Auliya of Delhi. Brown describes that after his death, "a string of weak emperors, wars of succession, and coups by noblemen heralded the irrevocable weakening of Mughal power". She notes that the populist but "fairly old-fashioned" explanation for the decline is that there was a reaction to Aurangzeb's oppression. Aurangzeb's son, Bahadur Shah I, succeeded him and the empire, both due to Aurangzeb's over-extension and Bahadur Shah's weak military and leadership qualities, entered a period of terminal decline. Immediately after Bahadur Shah occupied the throne, the Maratha Empire – which Aurangzeb had held at bay, inflicting high human and monetary costs – consolidated and launched effective invasions of Mughal territory, seizing power from the weak emperor. Within decades of Aurangzeb's death, the Mughal Emperor had little power beyond the walls of Delhi.

8

Administration of the Mughals

THE CENTRAL GOVERNMENT

First of all, it should be recognized that the Mughals drew heavily on the past, for the organization of their government was on essentially the same lines as that of the sultanate. The principal officers of the central government were four: 1) *diwan*; 2) *mir bakhshi*; 3) *mir saman*; and 4) *sadr*. The first of these dignitaries, the diwan, often called the wazir (the chief minister), was mainly concerned with revenue and finance, but as he had a say in all matters where any expenditure was involved, the work of other departments also came under his control. All the imperial orders were first recorded in his office before being issued, and the provincial governors, district *faujdars*, and leaders of expeditions came to him for instructions before assuming their duties. All the earning departments were under his direct control, and could spend only what was allotted to them by the diwan.

The mir bakhshi performed those duties which had been the responsibility of the *ariz-i-mamalik* during the earlier period. Owing to the organization of the civil services on military lines, his power extended far beyond the war office, and some foreign travellers called him the lieutenant-general or the captain-general of the realm. The main departure from the sultanate was in respect to work relating to state karkhanas, stores, ordinance, and communications, now so important that the dignitary dealing with it, called the mir saman, ranked as an important minister often senior in rank to the sadr.

The sadr (or, more fully, sadr-i-jahan) was, as in the earlier period, director of the religious matters, charities, and endowments. Occasionally a higher dignitary, superior to the wazir and other ministers was also appointed. He was called the *vakil*, and functioned like the *naib* (deputy) of the sultanate period. This appointment, as under the sultanate, was sporadic, depending on the wish of the monarch and the requirements of the situation. During the reigns of Akbar, Jehangir, and Shah Jahan, a period of ninety-seven years (1560–1657), there were ten vakils whose terms of service totaled about thirty-nine years. Ibn Hasan, the author of the Central Structure of the Mughal Empire, argues that the post was primarily for show and honour, with the vakil as the head of the nobility but not of the administration. To a large extent this is true, and normally the vakil was less effective than the wazir, who controlled the purse, but theoretically the vakil was the king's deputy and even the wazir referred to him whatever was "beyond his own ability." Abul Fazl calls him "the emperor's lieutenant in all matters connected with the realm and the household," adding that "although the financial offices are not under his immediate superintendence, yet he receives the returns from heads of all financial offices and wisely keeps abstracts of their return."

The splendour and stability of the Mughal rule was due to a succession of very capable rulers who attempted to build up an efficient administrative system, choosing their principal officers on the basis of merit. The most famous diwan under Akbar was Raja Todar Mal, who for a time acted as the chief minister of the realm, but the contribution of Khwaja Mansur and Mir Fathulla Shirazi to the building up of Akbar's revenue administration was perhaps equally great. Under Jehangir, Itimad-ud-Daula, the father of Nur Jahan, who was a diwan even before his daughter married the emperor, remained the chief wazir and diwan until his death. He was succeeded by his son, Asaf Khan, who became the vakil just before the death of Jehangir. Itimad-ud-Daula and Asaf Khan were able, efficient officers. Asaf Khan maintained his position until his death, but his successors were selected on the basis of their scholarship and technical efficiency. Allami Afzal Khan remained Shah Jahan's diwan for ten years, and the office was held from the nineteenth to the thirtieth years of Shah Jahan's reign by the celebrated Saadulla Khan who, like his predecessor, had won his post because of his learning, wisdom, and resourcefulness.

The diwan, who can perhaps be called the finance minister, had under him two principal officers, called *diwan-i-tan* and *diwan-i-khalsa*, who were in charge of salaries and state lands respectively. It is interesting that all the assistants of the diwan-i-khalsa under Shah Jahan's reign were Hindus, and five out of the seven under the diwan-i-tan belonged to the same community. Raja Raghunath Rai, who had been diwan-i-khalsa for some years, became sole diwan in the thirty-first year of Shah Jahan's reign, and maintained this position until his death, during the reign of Aurangzeb. Aurangzeb's principal wazir, who held office for thirty-one years, was Asad Khan, originally his mir bakhshi. Next to him, the most famous mir bakhshi of the Mughal period was Shaikh Farid, who played a decisive role in the enthronement of Jehangir.

Organization of Public Services

The organization of public services was perfected during Akbar's reign, and was based on the mansabdari system, borrowed originally from Persia. Every important officer of state held a mansab or an official appointment of rank and emoluments, and, as members of an imperial cadre, were liable for service anywhere in the empire. In 1573–74 Akbar classified the office holders in thirty-three grades, ranging from commanders of ten to commanders of ten thousand. The principal categories of Mughal mansabdars, however, were three: those in command of ten to four hundred were commonly styled *mansabdars* (officers); those in command of five hundred to twenty-five hundred were *amirs* (nobles); and those in higher ranks belonged to the category of *umara-i-kabir* or *umara-i-azim* (grandees). The highest amir in the third category was honoured with the title of *amir-ul-umara*. In the eighteenth century this title was usually given to the mir bakhshi. Until the middle of Akbar's reign, the highest rank which any ordinary officer could hold was that of a commander of five thousand; the more exalted grades between commanders of seven thousand and ten thousand were reserved for princes of royal blood. Toward the end of his reign and under his successors these limits were relaxed.

MANSABDAR

Mansabdar was the generic term for the military-type grading of all imperial officials of the Mughal Empire. The mansabdars governed the empire and commanded its armies in the emperor's name. Though they were usually aristocrats, they did not form a feudal aristocracy, for neither the offices nor the estates that supported them were hereditary. The term is derived from *Mansab*, meaning 'rank'. Hence, Mansabdar literally means rank-holder.

History

The Moghals ruled India from 1526 AD, when Babar defeated Ibrahim Lodi at the Battle of Panipat, till 1707 AD when the Emperor Aurangzeb died and thereafter nominally till the Indian Mutiny in 1857 AD.

When Babar invaded India to establish his kingdom his army consisted of tribes and clans that followed him from Kabul, some joined him later, after the Battle of Panipat, he awarded the leaders of these tribes and clans in accordance to their performance in the battle and many of them who had joined Babar for the booty, chose to return to their homes.

Babar and Humayun ruled over territory that was not too far flung, after the tribes and the clans that had joined Babar for booty returned after the Battle of Panipat, their place was taken by foreign adventurers, Uzbeks, Persians, Arabs, Turks etc. who thronged to the court with contingents of troops. Since the Moghals were foreigners there were no hereditary nobles related to the rulers or ancient families to depend upon, the court consisted of adventurers from different nations, the ruler raised them to dignity or degraded them; up to the early rule of Akbar the Moghal armies consisted of contingents commanded by these adventurers.

Akbar, Babar's grandson, who ruled from 1556 to 1605, organized the 'mansabdari' system in the 19th year of his rule. The system classified the functionaries of the kingdom as fighters, 'ashab-u's-saif', (masters of the sword); clerks 'ashab-u'l-qalam' (masters of the pen); theologians, 'ashab-u'l-amamah'. The 'mansab' denoted a rank of office, it had its obligations, precedence and grade of pay; it was for life but it was not hereditary, heirs could not demand continuity of office.

The status of the 'ashab-u's-saif (military) and ashab-u'l-qalam' (clerical and administrative), was denoted by military rank, originally 66 grades but later only 33 grades existed. Every official of the empire above the rank of a sepoy or a servant held an army rank, the lowest was the commander of twenty; the highest the commander of seven thousand.

Mansabs were ranked as of 7,000, 6,000, 5,000, intervals of 500 between 5,000 and 1,000, intervals of 100 between 1,000 and 200, intervals of 50 between 200 and 100, finally intervals of 20 between 100 and 20. Mansabs were of three classes, 7,000 to 3,000- 'Amir-i-Azam' the greater nobles; 2,500 to 500-'Amir', noble; 400 to 20-'Mansabdar' office holder.

Administration of the Mughals

Commanders of higher ranks were of three classes according to the proportion of horsemen, first class if the whole command was of 'horse', second class if the 'horse' element was more than half and third class if less than half.

Compensation per annum started at rupees 350,000 with intervals of 50,000 between mansabs of 7,000 and 5,000; rupees 250,000 with intervals of 25,000 between mansabs of 5,000 and 1,000; the mansab of 20 received 1,000.

Compensation was either 'naqdi' meaning cash compensation or by the revenue of a 'jagir', an area of land which was not given to the 'mansabdar' but he could use the revenue from the land for his expenses and compensation. The 'mansab' could be increased or decreased on the wishes of the ruler and reports of performance and two lists were maintained, 'Hazir-i-rikah' present at court and 'Ta-inat' on duty elsewhere.

For a military mansab an application could be made for a mansab with troops or without troops. Those applying for a mansab with troops brought their retainers, mounted and equipped at their expense, these were known as 'silladars' and their men were known as 'bagirs'. (The system continued under the British till 1914.) When a silladar brought his men, they were paraded for inspection, their descriptive rolls were prepared and the horses were branded; these mansabdars were paid for the maintenance of horses and the salaries of the men. Men considered fit to command but lacking resources were given money to purchase horses and received the salaries of the men only. Men who could not be mansabdars but too good to be employed as soldiers were given the higher rank of a 'ahadi'.

Military mansabdars were required to maintain troops according to the mansab including beasts of burden, elephants, camels, mules, carts etc., they maintained horses for their troopers and a prescribed number in their own stables.

Military command was at the will of the emperor, Akbar held that anyone could be a military commander and often appointed commanders who had no military knowledge or experience.

Mansabdars were given control over an area of land, a 'jagir' whose revenue was to be used for maintaining troops; if not given a 'jagir' they were paid in cash through a complicated accounting system, with deductions for various things including 'the rising of the moon'; it was a normal practice to pay for only eight or ten months in the year. The mansabdars were allowed to keep five percent of the income of the 'jagir' or five per cent of the salaries received. The accounting system was complex, mansabdars usually borrowed money for expenses and when they died their private property was seized against any outstanding balances. With a corrupt system of accounting and inspection very few mansabdars kept their units up to strength. When a mansabdar was ordered to take part in an expedition, he was required to parade his unit outside the palace and the emperor inspected it from a window in the palace.

Cavalry made up the bulk of the Moghal army; they enjoyed the prestige of warriors. Individual troopers took great care to keep themselves fit, they exercised, engaged each other in mock fights, practiced horsemanship, they were personally brave and trained themselves for person to person combat, but were unwilling to endanger their mounts because their salary depended on these; there was no training for units to act collectively.

Infantry was despised as drudges, they were considered little more than watchmen to guard the baggage, labourers, porters etc. The infantry consisted of matchlock men and archers, in the ratio of one matchlock man to four archers because of the greater rate of fire of the archers since both weapons had about the same effective range; there was no infantry training, no discipline and very little reliance was placed on them.

The 'Mir Atish', the 'master gunner', was responsible for the manufacture, supply of ordnance and was the artillery commander. Gunners were called 'golandaz' (the bringer of round shot, a term also used by the British till 1857), they were paid directly from the treasury and were the most reliable part of the army. The efficiency of the Moghal artillery was poor, the rate of fire was very low and the pieces were difficult to move. Europeans as artillerymen were prized and were paid as much as ten times the amount paid to locals.

The recruitment of men was by 'classes'; it was specified that an officer from Iran could not recruit more than one third Moghals, the rest had to be Syeds or Sheikhs, Afghans could not be more than one sixth or Rajputs more than one seventh of a force. The British adopted this system of recruitment by 'classes'. The Moghal army consisted of bands of horsemen, each band linked by some personal loyalty to its leader but without any loyalty to the emperor or any national or religious loyalty. These soldiers of fortune depended on their commanders; their pay was always kept in arrears to prevent desertion. There was a theoretical pattern to which the army conformed in battle; this consisted of three divisions, the center, right and left wing, each of these had an advance guard, a screen of skirmishers and there was a rear guard to the whole force. Once a formation was adopted there was very little capability for maneuver and there was no system of communicating between the parts.

Open country was necessary for successful action by a Moghal army because it was mostly cavalry. The opposing armies deployed guns on a line protected by earthwork and tied together with chains or ropes to prevent cavalry riding through as Babar had done at Panipat. Battle started with artillery fire, the heavy guns fired one round every three hours while the others about four rounds per hour. When it was considered that the artillery had sufficiently demoralized the enemy, successive charges were delivered from one wing then the other; the cavalry first fired their matchlocks and arrows then closed with the sword, spear and the mace, fighting was series of skirmishes ending in individual combat. The cavalry was not trained to act collectively on command, once dispersed it could not be formed again but since cavalry was the bulk of the army, the object of the Moghal commander was to engage the enemy on an open plain where he could deliver a massed charge of mail clad warriors. Up to the time of Aurangzeb, the Moghals fielded much larger armies than their opponents and usually managed to defeat their enemy, either on the battlefield or after a siege.

During battle the overall commander or the king had to prominently show his presence on the battlefield, usually riding an elephant, the battle objective was usually the elephant of the opposing commander and around it raged the fiercest battle; the decisive event of a battle was the death or disappearance of the leader, if he was known to have been killed or could not be seen the troops dispersed and sought their own safety. Aurangzeb when fighting his brothers for succession, in two battles, the rival to the throne was induced by treacherous advice to dismount and their armies automatically dispersed; this was because the remuneration of the army was from individual princes. The British used this custom to their advantage by knocking off the commanders with a four-pounder artillery piece and causing the dispersion of the opponents, eventually the princes and commanders learnt to ride horses instead of elephants and not to prominently show themselves.

The Emperor usually did not personally command the army unless it was a very large force in an important campaign; when the army moved out to war with the emperor in command, the whole apparatus of government moved with it. Aurangzeb's army on the move included camels bearing treasure, one hundred loaded with gold, two hundred with silver; the emperor's hunting establishment, with hawks and cheetahs; official records, on eighty camels, thirty elephants and twenty carts, these could never be parted from the emperor; a hundred camels carried water and kitchen utensils; fifty milch-cows, a hundred cooks, each a specialist in a dish; fifty camels and a hundred carts carried the emperor's and his ladies wardrobe; thirty elephants carried the women's jewellery and presents for successful commanders.

The mass of the cavalry, the main strength of the army, led, then the way was leveled for the emperor and his women; a rear guard largely of infantry brought up the tail. When the army halted the emperor's camp was about a mile long, a square enclosure was roped off and surrounded by a ditch, heavy artillery defended the approaches, the emperor's tent was in the center, divided into four courts with the entrance facing the direction of the next day's march.

The army transport consisted of elephants, camels, packhorses, bullocks, bullock carts and porters. Every man provided for himself by buying for his needs, on a daily basis from 'banyas' who erected their shops in the camps. Supplies of grain were brought to the camp by 'banjarahs' on bullocks, which moved at two miles an hour, they formed a square in the evening with bags of grain. Either side did not attack the 'banjarahs' and the grain taken was paid for. Fodder was taken from the countryside and foragers looted the villages in the path of the army.

The armies of the Moghal times consisted of bands without military training and discipline; there was no loyalty owed to the ruler or the state; band leaders could be bought; half hearted support during battle, treachery and desertion were therefore negotiable. The two opposing armies would camp on the battlefield and for several days negotiations would be conducted to entice commanders to change sides before the battle, to refuse to act at a critical moment or to desert with their commands during a battle. The British successfully exploited this mercenary soldiering, in its worst form, when they fought the princes who had seized bits and pieces of the Moghal Empire. Insulated by the mountains and the seas, the Moghals developed a military system which, though locally successful, did not improve on the weapons, organization and tactics, failed miserably when it clashed with the European military system of the period. Instituted by the Mughal emperor Akbar, *mansabdari* was a system common to both the military and the Civil department. Basically the Mansabdari system was borrowed from Persia. It was prevalent during the reign of Babar and Humayun. Akbar made some important changes to the system and made it more efficient. Mansabdar was referred to as the official, rank, or the dignity.

Two grades delineated the mansabdars. Those mansabdars whose rank was one thousand (hazari) or below were called the Amir. Those mansabdars whose rank was above 1000, were called the Amiral Kabir (Great Amir). Some Great Amirs whose rank were above 5000 were also given the title of Amir-al Umara (Amir of Amirs)

LAND REVENUE SYSTEMS OF AKBAR

Akbar was the founder of the Mughal revenue system, which he evolved through experiments that continued till 1585. In the beginning, he adopted Sher Shah's system in which the cultivated area was measured and a central schedule was drawn up fixing the dues of peasant's crop wise on the basis of the productivity of the land. The state's share was one-third of the produce; the produce under the schedule being valued at prices fixed by the emperor. In fixing the prices, the rates current in the vicinity of Delhi were probably taken as the basis.

This arrangement created difficulties, because one uniform schedule of prices of crops could not reasonably be applied to the whole empire. Prices were lower in rural areas which were far away from the urban centres and the cultivators found it difficult lo pay in cash at the official rate.

In the tenth year of his (Akbar's) reign, prices of crops prevailing in different regions were substituted for the uniform schedule and the emperor reverted to a system of annual assessment. In 1573, the annual assessment was given up and karoris were appointed all over North India to collect a crore of dams as revenue and to check the facts and figures supplied by the qanungos regarding the actual produce, state of cultivation, local prices etc.

These karoris were also known as amils or amalguzars. On the basis of the above facts and figures, a new system was developed in 1580 called the dahsala system. This system was an improved version of the zabti system which was the standard system of revenue assessment during the greater part of the Mughal empire. The credit for developing this system goes to Todarmal who became the head of the wizarat or revenue ministry.

During the reign of Akbar and his successors four main systems of revenue assessment were prevalent: (a) zabti or dahsala system; (b) batai, ghallabakshi or bhaoli; (c) kankut and (d) nasaq. (a) Zabti or dahsala system. As stated earlier the dahsala was an improvement on the zabti system. For the purpose of assessment the land was classified in Akbar's reign in four categories: polaj (land which was cultivated every year and never left fallow); parati orparauti (land which had to be left fallow for a time to enable it to recover fertility); chachar (land which had to be left fallow for three or four years); and banjar (land which remained uncultivated for five years or more) Polaj and parauti lands were classified into three categories-good, middling and bad-and the average produce per biglia of these three categories was taken as the normal produce of a bigha. Parauti land, when cultivated, paid the same revenue as polaj land.

The chachar and banjar lands were charged a concessional rate which was progressively increased to full or polaj rate (i.e. one- third of the produce) by the fifth or the eighth year. Under the dahsala system an attempt was made to work out the revenue rates. The state demand was given in maunds\ but for the conversion of the state demand from kind to cash, a separate schedule of cash revenue rates (dasturu'l amals) for various crops was fixed.

For a period of the past ten years, 1570-71 to 1579-80, information on yields, prices, and area cultivated was collected for each locality. On the basis of the average prices of different crops in each locality over the past ten years the state demand was fixed in rupees per bigha.

Each revenue circle had a separate schedule of cash revenue rates (dasturu'l amal) for various crops. Thus the peasant was required to pay on the basis of local produce as well as local prices. The dahsala was neither a ten-year nor a permanent settlement, and the state had the right to modify it.

Since this system was associated with Raja Todarmal, it is also known as Todarmal's bandabust or settlement. This system prevailed from Lahore to Allahabad and in the provinces of Malwa and Gujarat. A major extension of it occurred in the later years of Shah Jahan's reign, when it was introduced in the Deccan by Murshid Quli Khan.

This system greatly simplified the process of assessment. The cash rates (dasturu'lamals) were not fixed by a "rule of thumb", but were based on enquiries into the yields and prices of each crop in different localities. Batai, ghalla-bakhshi or bhaoli. This was a very old system which continued during the Mughal period. This was a simple method of crop-sharing in which the produce was arranged into heaps and divided into three shares, one of which was taken by the state. Under this system the peasant had the choice to pay in cash or kind, but in the case of cash crops the state demand was mostly in cash. Kankut. This system was already in use in the fourteenth century. Under this method, instead of actually dividing the grain (kan), an estimate (kut) was made on the basis of an actual inspection on the spot.

One-third of the estimated produce was fixed as the state demand. In simple terms, it was a rough estimate of produce on the basis of actual inspection and past experience.

Nasaq. This was widely prevalent in the Mughal Empire, particularly in Bengal. In this system a rough calculation was made on the basis of the past revenue receipts of the peasants. It required no actual measurement, but the area was ascertained from the records.

The zabti system was the standard system, but other methods of assessment were prevalent in different parts of the empire. In the subahs of Ajmer, Kashmir and southern Sind, crop-sharing and in Bengal nasaq were prevalent. There was, however, a contradiction in the Mughal revenue system.

Although the assessment was made by the state of the individual cultivator, the collection of revenue was made through intermediaries like zamindars, talluqdars, muqaddams, patils etc.

RULES OF MUGHAL ADMINISTRATION

It the Mughal's rule, was introduced by Akbar and that is why, by 'Mughal Administration', we mean Akbar's Administration. Akbar was not only a brave soldier, a successful leader and a great religious reformer but also a great administrator. He introduced various reforms in all the branches of the administration, whether central, provincial, revenue, military or judicial.

Central Administration

Akbar was the overall in-charge of the central government. All the executive, judicial and legislative powers of the state were combined in him. There were no limitations on his despotism and his word was law.

But Akbar had always the welfare of his people in his mind and so his was a benevolent despotism. He himself supervised all the branches of his administration and worked hard to discharge his manifold duties. He would hold an open court, listen to the complaints of his subjects and try to pacify them.

Akbar was, however, assisted by a number of ministers in the administration. Among others, the most important ministers were – the *Vakil*, who maintained a general control over all the central departments and acted as the chief adviser of the King; *Diwan*, who was in-charge of finance and revenue; *Mir Bakshi*, who maintained the records of all the Mansabdars and distributed pay among the high officials; *Sadar-i-Sadur*, who acted as a religious adviser to the king, disbursed royal charity and discharged the function of the Chief Justice of the empire. Beside these four ministers, there were other ministers of lower rank-*Khan-i-Saman*, who was in-charge of the royal household; *Muhtasib*, who saw that the people (Muslims) led a highly moral life according to the Muslim law; and *Daroga-i-Dak Chowki*, an officer who was in-charge of the postal and intelligence department.

Provincial Administration

Akbar divided his vast empire into fifteen (15) *Subas* or provinces. In each suba or province there was a *Subedar*, a *Diwan*, a *Bakshi*, a *Sadar*, a *Qazi*, a *Kotwal*, a *Mir Bahr* and *Waqa-i-Nawis*.

The *Subedar* or Governor was the head of the provincial administration. He enjoyed vast powers and was in-charge of the provincial military, police, judiciary and the executive. The (provincial) *Diwan* was in-charge of the provincial finance and all bills of payments were signed by him. The *Bakshi* looked after the management of the provincial army. The *Sadar* was in-charge of the judicial charity department. The *Qazi* was in-charge of the judicial department of his province. He supervised the work of *Qazis* in the districts and towns. The *Kotwal* was the supreme administrator of all the '*thanas*' of the province and was responsible for the maintenance of law and order in all the cities. The *Mir Bahr* was in-charge of customs and taxation department. The *Waqa-i-Nawis* was in-charge of the secret service of the province.

The provinces were further divided into Sarkars and Sarkars into Parganas. The head of the *Sarkar* was *Faujdar* who kept his own small force and maintained law and order in his area. He was assisted by a number of other officials who collected the revenue, maintained the accounts and deposited the money into the state treasury. The head of the *Parganas* was called *Shikdar* whose functions were the same as those of the *Faujdar* in a *Sarkar*. Each *Pargana* comprised several villages. Each village was under the charge of a *Muqaddam*, a *Patwari* and a *Chowkidar* who carried on the work of administration with the help of the village *panchayat*.

Military Administration

Akbar paid much attention towards the organization, equipment and discipline of the army. For efficient military administration he introduced a new system known as the *Mansabdari* System. The Mansabdars had to maintain soldiers according to his grade or rank. There were thirty three grades of these Mansabdars who maintained soldiers ranging from 10 to 10,000. They were paid salaries in cash and the system of assignments of lands was discouraged. They were directly under the charge of the emperor and were promoted, degrade or dismissed at his will. He also revived the practice of taking the descriptive rolls of the soldiers and branding the horses.

A large number of troops were, no doubt, supplied by these Mansabdars but Akbar had maintained a standing army of his own. The Mughal army consisted of infantry, cavalry, artillery, elephants, and navy. The cavalry was the most important wing of the army and special attention was paid towards its organization and equipment.

The military organization of Akbar had no doubt certain defects (e.g., The Mansabdars cheated the government, the soldiers were more loyal to the chiefs than to the emperor, the practice of payment through the Mansabdars was precarious and often led to abuses, efficiency of one unit to unit, etc.) but still under Akbar it worked well because of his uncommon ability as a leader and an administrator, great vigilance and discipline.

Land Revenue Administration

Land Revenue was the chief sources of income of the Government. So, Akbar paid special attention towards the organization of the land revenue administration. With the help of his *Diwan* (Revenue Minister), Raja Todar Mal, Akbar introduced many reforms in his revenue department. First of all, the land was measured into *'bighas'*, secondly, all the cultivated land was classified into four divisions – *Polaj, Parauti,*

Chachar and *Banjar*. The *Polaj* land was always cultivated and was never allowed to fallow; the *Parauti* land was allowed to fallow for a year or two to recover its strength; the *Chachar* land had to be left uncultivated for three or four years and *Banjar* land had to be left fallow for five years or more. Thirdly, the total produce of each land was determined separately. Fourthly, the share of the state was fixed at one-third of the total produce. Land revenue was paid in cash or in kind, but cash payment was preferred. Loans with small interest were advanced to the cultivators. In case of famine, drought or another unexpected calamity, remission was granted and even loans were advanced for purchase of seeds and animals. The revenue collectors were asked to be friendly towards the cultivators and not to oppress them on every account. As a result of these measures the revenue of the state greatly increased, the cultivators became better off and the country became prosperous. The abundance of food also made the life of the common man better and happier than before.

Judicial Administration or Judicial Reforms

Akbar introduced various reforms in the administration of justice. Before him almost all the cases were decided according to the Islamic law. But now, for the first time, Hindu law was administered in deciding the cases where the parties Hindus, but Islamic law continued to function where the parties involved were Muslims. The king was the highest court of appeal. Capital punishment was given only in extreme cases and that too by the emperor alone.

Social Reforms

Akbar had the welfare of his people always in his mind. He had taken several measures to improve the general condition of his subjects. In 1563, the *Pilgrim Tax*, which was a great burden on the Hindus, was abolished. In 1564, *Jaziya*, a tax which was imposed on non-Muslims, was also abolished. Akbar tried to stop the practice of Sati. Child marriage was discouraged and female-infanticide was forbidden. Widow-marriage was encouraged. From the above account it is quite clear that Akbar was a great administrator and the administrative machinery that he set up continued to function throughout the Mughal period.

ADMINISTRATION OF MUGHAL DYNASTY

Administration of Mughal Dynasty was carried out by incorporating

Administration of the Mughals

certain elementary changes in the central administration structure in India. Babar, the founder of the Mughal Empire assumed the title of 'Badshaah' which was continued by his successors. Akbar enhanced further the power and prestige of the emperor. He declared himself the authority in case of disparity of opinions regarding Islamic laws. However, Mughal rule was not theocratic. Except Aurangzeb no other Mughal emperor attempted to carry his administration on the principles of Islam. A major change that they brought about in matters of administration was the principle of religious tolerance. These new innovations in polity set aside Mughal administration. It was Akbar who raised the structure of Mughal administration. It persisted till the reign of Aurangzeb with minor changes. The weak successors of Aurangzeb, however, could not maintain it.

The Omrahs or the nobles were the pillars of the imperial system. They were quick to criticize, and looked down upon anything unsophisticated. It was necessary for the sovereign to retain their support, which he did by various methods such as personal courtesy, giving presents, and bestowing honours on them such as prestigious robes, turban ornaments of precious stones or the taxation rights of a Mansab or Jagir. The hierarchy of the Omrahs was constantly getting altered and with the passage of time, new families and tribes gained ascendancy and, more significantly, there were new alliances. Many old friends became enemies and vice-versa.

POSITION OF THE EMPEROR IN MUGHAL ADMINISTRATION

The Mughal Emperors were all powerful in administration. The Mughal emperors accepted two primary duties for themselves, Jahanbani (protection of the state) and Jahangiri (extension of the empire). Besides, they tried to generate those conditions which were conducive to economic and cultural progress of their subjects. The emperor was the head of the state. He was the law-maker, the chief executive, the commander-in-chief of the army and the final dispenser of justice. Akbar enhanced further the powers of the emperor when he himself took over the power of deciding the Islamic laws in cases of dispute. His ministers and nobles, of course, could advise him but he was the final arbiter in everything. From the time of Akbar, the emperor was regarded as God's representative on earth. That is why Akbar started practices like Jharokha Darshan and Tula Dan. Even

Aurangzeb who was a religious extremist was fully aware of this duty towards his subjects.

Though there was no legal limit to the powers of the emperor, yet, there were certain limitations from the practical point of view. The emperor certainly gave due consideration to the advice given by his ministers to him and recognised the influence wielded by his powerful nobles. The Sultans of the Delhi Sultanate established their despotic rule after destroying the power of their nobles, while the Mughal emperors based their despotism on the power and loyalty of their nobles.

MINISTERS IN MUGHAL ADMINISTRATION

During the reign of Akbar there were only four ministers, namely Wakil, Diwan or Wazir, Mir Bakhsi and Sadr-us-Sadur. The posts of Wakil and Wazir were combined together afterwards and the holder of the post was called Vakil-i-Mutlaq. Akbar gave the post of the prime minister to Bairam Khan. By virtue of this office, he was the protector of the state and over and above all other ministers with the right of even appointing and dismissing them. But no other man was given these powers after the fall of Bairam Khan. The Prime Minister was given the work of the Diwan and, later on the Diwan was titled as the Wazir or the prime minister. Primarily, the Diwan looked after the income and expenditure of the state. Besides, he looked after the administration in the absence of the emperor from the capital and commanded the army on occasions. Thus, Vakil or Wazir or prime minister was the person next to the emperor in administration. The prime minister supervised the working of other departments, collected news of provinces, dispatched orders of the emperor to governors and looked after the correspondence of the state. The Sadr-us-Sadur advised the emperor on religious matters. He looked after the religious education, distribution of Jagirs to scholars and observance of the laws of the Islam by the Muslims.

Khan-i-Saman was not a minister during the reign of Akbar but was ranked as one of the ministers after him. He looked after the personal necessities of the emperor and his family and also that of the palace. Thus, he held an important office. The Muhtasib looked after the moral development of the subjects. His particular job was to see to it that the Muslims observed Islamic laws. He also checked the drinking of liquor, gambling and illegal relations between men and women. He also kept control over weights and measures and observed that articles were sold in the market at proper prices. During the reign of Aurangzeb, he was assigned the responsibility of destroying the schools and temples of the Hindus. He was assisted by provincial Muhtasibs. Though the emperor was the highest judicial authority in the state, yet, he was assisted by chief Qazi at the capital. While the Muftis interpreted Islamic laws, the chief Qazi declared the judgment. He also appointed Qazis in provinces, districts etc.

LEGAL POLICY OF AKBAR

Akbar's legal policy was reached in 1579, when, after seventeen years of rule, the *mahzar*, or "Infallibility Decree," was issued. It came with much criticism from orthodox *mullahs* in court because Akbar proclaimed himself to be the interpreter of law and no longer desired for the *mullahs* to interpret and design the law. Through his conflict with the *mullahs* he freed himself from the confines of traditional Muslim rule that was dictated by *Shari'ah* as interpreted by the *mullahs*, leading historians like Sri Ram Sharma to conclude: "Akbar's greatest achievement lay in liberating the state from its domination by the *mullahs*." This rule free from *mullah* control meant that everyone in the empire, from the sultan to the subjects, had a social freedom never experienced before under Muslim rule in Hindustan. Literally, the *mahzar* designated Akbar as "one capable of individual legal reasoning, a just ruler, the ruler of Islam, commander of the faithful, and the shadow of God over the two worlds."

The *mahzar* was that it was an official edict by Akbar proclaiming himself to be infallible. Thus, the decree has commonly been mislabeled as the "Infallibility Decree." However, the *mahzar* was not solely a despotic move to obtain ultimate power, but heavily drew upon Akbar's liberal religious views, which in turn affected his views on social leadership. By issuing the *mahzar* Akbar was not claiming to be infallible, but was claiming that when the religious divines disagreed he would become the judge and not the *mullahs*. The orthodox *mullah* historian Badayuni states: "The object of this declaration was to establish the complete superiority of the *Imam-i 'adil* (just leader) over the *Mujtahid* (chief lawyer); and to make his judgment and choice on diverse questions, so that no one could reject (his) command in either religious or political matters." In this way Akbar was proclaiming himself to be the *Mujtahid* of Hindustan in order for his vision of *sulh-i-kull* as a social policy to prosper. In effect, the decree only took away the right of orthodox *mullahs* to persecute others for their opinions. This meant that he no longer relied on the Muslim population in his empire for support; the indigenous Hindus now began to be recognized as part of the population and not just a source of revenue or exploitation. Sri Ram Sharma refers to Akbar's rule as "a despotism that left a wide margin to its citizens' choice." This decree proclaiming Akbar as the ruler of Islam, and not the current *Khalifah* over the Islamic world, upset many orthodox *mullahs* in his court. Still, it was not unique in the thought or actions of his Mughal lineage. Since the defeat of the Ottoman sultan in Baghdad in 1258, a puppet *Khalifah* had been established in Egypt, and subsequently in the subcontinent. The *khutba* had been read in the same puppet *Khalifah's* name ever since. Although not much importance was given to it, reading the *khutba* in the name of the same *Khalifah* did establish legitimacy to the rest of the Islamic world of the Indian Sultanate's rule because they were conquering in the his name. This included the two Mughal rulers prior to Akbar, Babar and Humayun, who did not attach any importance to the *khutba* being read in their courts giving reverence to the Ottoman Sultan. By Akbar's move away from this 300-year-old tradition, he was proclaiming a new era of dynastic rule in the subcontinent. Because the *khutba* proclaims the political allegiance of the region in which it is read, this action meant that Akbar was establishing the Mughal Empire's legitimacy to the rest of the Islamic world as the just rulers of the Indian subcontinent.

MONETARY POLICY OF THE MUGHAL STATE

During the reign of Akbar (1556-1605), a large part of India was unified politically and administratively through territorial conquests and bureaucratic centralization. Akbar exercised the sovereign right to issue coins of standard weight and fineness which differed from those of previous regimes. In order to ensure a high degree of uniformity and lower transaction costs in economic exchange, Akbar and his administration adopted special measures to standardize the circulation and exchange of currencies.

These involved the replacement of non-Mughal currencies by imperial issues and the implementation of uniform exchange rates. The two constant factors which determined the absolute value of a currency were weight and purity. A third factor was the cost of production (brassage) and the imperial tax on minting (seigniorage). Weight, fineness and minting cost established the exchange rate of the coin against commodities and units of account. The exchange rate of a coin could vary if any of the above factors changed. The most complex issue for Akbar's administration was the standardization of the exchange rates of imperial currencies once they lost weight in circulation.

An unknown quantity of coins that were lighter than the standard weight would always be in circulation, requiring assessment by money-changers whenever payments were made in cash. The purpose of this assessment was to levy a discount (Pers. *sarf*; Hindi *batta*) on lighter coins. The operation of the discount system required that coins be weighed rather than exchanged by tale even though the prices of goods were posted in number of coins rather than *tolas* of silver or gold per item.

However, the tedium of the continuous weighing of coins for each transaction led to the prevalence of a faster method of evaluation, in which the exchange value of a legal tender was judged from the year of mintage inscribed on the coin.

The money-changers assumed a relationship between age, velocity of circulation and weight loss in classifying coins (as *sikka*, *chalani* and *khazana*) and levied discounts to reduce their transaction costs. The system was arbitrary and open to abuse but was popular with both money-changers and state officials responsible for revenue collection for reasons of convenience and profit. Such qualitative assessments also encouraged clipping and sweating (*malish wa jaz*), which thrived on the custom of viewing rather than weighing coins.

Akbar's administration intervened in the market to standardize the exchange rates of deficient legal tenders by accepting the principle of discount. The circulation of all coins at their full exchange value, no matter how deficient they were, would have encouraged the culling of superior specie through the application of Gresham's Law, which states that bad money drives good money out of circulation. By not granting a premium to standard weight, the state would have forced the circulation of only lighter coins and a paucity of precious metal coinage. The temptation to receive payments in the new coins and get rid of the old ones was quite common in Mughal India. For the state, the acceptance of the principle of discount did not mean the acceptance of the method of applying these discounts. The method of assessing coins by age was unfair to users because it snapped the link between weight and exchange value. The intention of the administration was to strengthen the link, as is quite clear in the instructions given to the treasurer above. A discount was imposed on imperial coins (legal tenders) that were lighter than the standard weight in proportion to the loss of the metal. A number of imperial enactments during the reign of Akbar reminded the revenue collectors, money-changers and treasurers not to levy discounts on older issues of full fineness and weight (*naqd i durust aiyar tamam wazn*).

In order to discourage the system of assessment by age, Akbar's administration fixed differential rates of discount which gave credence to real loss. Moreover, to control the circulation of under-weight issues as well as the endless deterioration of its currency, the administration drew a line between the legal tender and coins deemed unfit for circulation. In most cases, the legal limit set by the monetary authority for demonetization and recoinage required a feasible balance between the total supply of currency in demand, the pressure on mint production and the level of standardization it wished to achieve. The recoinage of under-weight coins tended to reduce the physical volume of money and impinge on the minting of fresh supplies unless there was a proportional increase in the size of the mint work force or production hours. These concerns were first reflected in a set of regulations introduced in 1582 AD by Todarmal, Akbar's minister in charge of state finances. By then, revenue collection had been centralized for five years (1575-80), and the imperial administration had come face to face with the realities of metallic circulation and monetary management.

Todarmal drew up a schedule of exchange and discount rates for gold and silver coins according to fixed bands of depreciation. He also set the limits for these coins to remain legal tender (Table 1). In the case of gold coins (*akbarshahi ashrafi*), the deficiency for which discounts were charged ranged from a maximum of 9 rice grains to a minimum of 3 rice grains. Marginally deficient coins (up to 3 rice grains) exchanged at their full value, on account of tolerance or permissible deviation from the mint standard, while those which passed the maximum limit exchanged as gold bullion. In order to reduce the quantity of lighter issues, the state separated the most deficient legal tenders (7-9 grains) collected in taxes and reminted them. The regulations for silver coins were different because here, the discount system was also used to replace the old rupee (*akbarshahi*) with the new (*jalala*). Thus, the exchange rates of rupees were set out in a way that overvalued the new rupee, introduced four years before (1578 AD), against the old rupee of the same weight and fineness. While the underweight new rupee exchanged at full value up to 12 rice grains, the full weight old rupee was discounted from the start. The stock of the most deficient legal tenders reserved for reminting also had a much higher proportion of the old rupee, since the limit for its withdrawal by the treasury was kept lower (6 rice grains).

Todarmal's regulations were only partially successful in meeting the precise equivalence between weight loss and discount. A major flaw in his formula was that an underweight coin was discounted at a rate higher than the mint price of bullion. For instance, the price of 6 rice grains of gold was fixed at a level (5 *dams*) that artificially inflated the exchange rate of a full *muhr* by 80 *dams* (440 instead of 360 *dams*). Similarly, the price of 6 rice grains of silver (1 *dam*) was set at a much higher level than the exchange value of a full weight coin (92 instead of 40 *dams*).

The inconsistencies in Todarmal's regulations were addressed two years later by his successor, Fathullah Shirazi. Operating with the simple idea that discounts should serve to restore the deficient coin to its full exchange value, the new minister brought down the rates to agree with the mint price of coined bullion. Shirazi also eliminated the difference between the two types of rupee by bringing the exchange rates of the old on par with the new. The newer rupee was in circulation for about six years and there was no reason for it to be privileged with a premium. Both rupees now enjoyed a tolerance of up to 6 rice grains.

Shirazi's measures were implemented but were soon set aside. Till then, Akbar had taken little personal interest in the details of the discount business. In 1591 AD, after receiving more complaints, he looked into the matter and endorsed Shirazi's regulations. Akbar, however, decreed that the tolerance of 3 and 6 rice grains extended to gold and silver coins should be repealed since this was open to abuse. The reasons given for the repeal were that the mint officials could be encouraged by the leeway to strike lighter coins, and the treasurers would find it profitable to remit such issues to the treasury even when the actual payments were made in full weight coins.

The final implementation of Shirazi's regulations was accompanied by the standardization of the lowest unit of weight used for weighing precious metals and coins. This too was linked to the working of the discount system but had not been addressed so far. As in the case of other administrative measures, the idea of standardization stemmed from practical problems. It was reported that lighter rice grains (*birinjhai sabuk*) were used by 'thievish people' (presumably money-changers) to enhance discounts fraudulently. This was particularly serious in the case of gold coins since "the deficiency of a *muhr* was raised from 3 rice grains to 6 and from 6 rice grains to 9" and "a large amount of money was pocketed" in this way. Akbar introduced quartz grains (*baba ghuri birinj*), which were smaller than rice grains and therefore more useful in weighing precious metals and coins. The absolute weight of the higher units (*ratti, masha* and *tola*) remained unchanged.

It was one thing to decree uniform standards of currencies, weights and exchange rates for the empire, but quite another to enforce them. The imperial ordinances were generally accompanied by a warning to all 'greedy persons' (*tama' daran*), the usual beneficiaries of currency manipulation in the eyes of the state, to refrain from 'temptations' in the future. Among specific measures were sworn statements taken from the *sarrafs* to comply with the prescribed regulations. Offences were dealt with by special officers and the penalties were unremitting. The paucity of sources does not allow us to evaluate the degree of success achieved by Akbar's administration, but it seems that the principal issue behind currency depreciation and fair exchange - equivalence of weight loss and discount – was addressed, it held up well in the seventeenth century.

APPOINTMENT TO THE RANKS OF MANSABDARS

Originally each grade carried a definite rate of pay, out of which the holders were required to maintain a quota of horses, elephants, beasts of burden, and carts. But even in Akbar's days and in spite of safeguards introduced by him, the number of men actually supplied by the mansabdars rarely corresponded to the number indicated by his rank, and under Akbar's successors greater latitude was allowed. The mansabdars were paid either in cash or by temporary grant of jagirs. Theoretically, the mansabdars received enormous salaries, which appear all the more excessive when it is realised that they did not normally maintain all the troops expected of them. It was probably an awareness of this that led Shah Jahan to introduce the practice of paying salaries to the mansabdars for only four months of the year instead of twelve, the implication being that the actual income for part of the year was equivalent to what the emperor had originally intended for the whole year. Even with this reduction, the mansabdars lived extravagantly. The tendency to luxurious expenditure was undoubtedly heightened by the mansabdar's knowledge that on his death, his whole property would be taken over by the state, pending satisfaction of any outstanding claims by the treasury. But while there may have been little incentive to save within the system, the high scale of salaries enabled the state to attract the ablest and most ambitious individuals from almost the whole of southern and western Asia.

Appointment to the ranks of mansabdars was made by the emperor,

Administration of the Mughals

usually on the recommendation of military leaders, provincial governors, or court officials. In addition to the mansabdars, there was a class known as *ahadis*, who though holding no official rank, were employed in posts in the palace. They were usually young men of good families, who were not fortunate enough to secure a mansab on their first application. Given an opportunity to show their worth, they could then be promoted to the ranks of mansabdars. These mansabdars have been compared to the Civil Service during British rule in that they formed an all-India cadre of officials, liable to transfer anywhere in the empire and providing the personnel for all major offices. The existence of a single imperial cadre undoubtedly gave a cohesion and unity to the Mughal empire that was lacking during the sultanate.

POLITICAL GOVERNMENT

Akbar's system of central government was based on the system that had evolved since the Delhi Sultanate, but the functions of various departments were carefully reorganised by laying down detailed regulations for their functioning.

- The revenue department was headed by a *wazir*, responsible for all finances and management of *jagir* and *inam* lands.
- The head of the military was called the *Mir bakshi*, appointed from among the leading nobles of the court. The *Mir bakshi* was in charge of intelligence gathering, and also made recommendations to the emperor for military appointments and promotions.
- The *Mir saman* was in charge of the imperial household, including the harems, and supervised the functioning of the court and royal bodyguard.
- The judiciary was a separate organization headed by a chief *qazi*, who was also responsible for religious endowments.

Akbar departed from the policy of his predecessors in his treatment of the territories he conquered. Previous Mughals extracted a large tribute from these rulers and then leave them to administer their dominions autonomously; Akbar integrated them into his administration, providing them the opportunity to serve as military rulers. He thus simultaneously controlled their power while increasing their prestige as a part of the imperial ruling class. Some of these rulers went on to become the navaratnas in Akbar's court.

Capital of the Empire

Akbar was a follower of Salim Chishti, a holy man who lived in the region of Sikri near Agra, who later blessed him with three sons. Believing the neighbourhood to be a lucky one for himself, he had a mosque constructed there for the use of the saint. Subsequently, he celebrated the victories over Chittor and Ranthambore by laying the foundation of a new walled capital, 23 miles (37 km) west of Agra in 1569, which was named Fatehpur (*"town of victory"*) after the conquest of Gujarat in 1573 and subsequently came to be known as Fatehpur Sikri in order to distinguish it from other similarly named towns. Palaces for each of Akbar's senior queens, a huge artificial lake, and sumptuous water-filled courtyards were built there. However, the city was soon abandoned and the capital was moved to Lahore in 1585. The reason may have been that the water supply in Fatehpur Sikri was insufficient or of poor quality. Or, as some historians believe, Akbar had to attend to the northwest areas of his empire and therefore moved his capital northwest. Other sources indicate Akbar simply lost interest in the city or realized it was not militarily defensible. In 1599, Akbar shifted his capital back to Agra from where he reigned until his death.

Matrimonial Alliances

Akbar persuaded the Kacchwaha Rajput, Raja Bharmal, of Amber (modern day Jaipur) into accepting a matrimonial alliance for his daughter Harka Bai. This was the first instance of royal matrimony between Hindu and Muslim dynasties in India. Harka Bai was rechristened Mariam-uz-Zamani. After her marriage she was treated as an outcaste by her family and for the rest of her life never visited Amber. She was not assigned any significant place either in Agra or Delhi, but rather a small village in the Bharatpur district. She died in 1623. As a custom Hindus were cremated and never buried; her burial near Agra signifies that she converted to Islam. A mosque was built in her honor by her son Jahangir in Lahore.

Other Rajput kingdoms also established matrimonial alliances with Akbar. The law of Hindu succession has always been patrimonial, so the Hindu lineage was not threatened in marrying their princesses for political gain. Rajputs who married daughters to Mughals still did not treat Mughals as equals, however, they would not dine with Mughals or take Muslim wives. Two major Rajput clans remained against him, the Sisodiyas of Mewar and Hadas (Chauhans) of Ranthambore. In another turning point of Akbar's reign, Raja Man Singh I of Amber went with Akbar to meet the Hada leader, Surjan Hada, to effect an alliance. Surjan grudgingly accepted an alliance on the condition that Akbar did not marry any of his daughters. Surjan later moved his residence to Varanasi.

Other Rajput nobles did not like the idea of their kings marrying their daughters to Mughals. Rathore Kalyandas threatened to kill both Mota Raja Udai Singh (of Jodhpur) and Jahangir because Udai Singh had decided to marry his daughter Jodha Bai to Jahangir. Akbar on hearing this ordered imperial forces to attack Kalyandas at Siwana. Kalyandas died fighting along with his men and the women of Siwana committed Jauhar.

Entering into alliance with Rajput kingdoms enabled Akbar to extend the border of his Empire to far off regions, and the Rajputs became the strongest allies of the Mughals. Rajput soldiers fought for the Mughal empire for the next 130 years till its collapse following the death of Aurangzeb. To foster their compliance, Akbar kept the eldest sons of his Rajput allies as hostages.

Personality

Akbar's reign was chronicled extensively by his court historian Abul Fazal in the books *Akbarnama* and *Ain-i-akbari*. Other contemporary sources of Akbar's reign include the works of Badayuni, Shaikhzada Rashidi and Shaikh Ahmed Sirhindi.

Akbar was an artisan, warrior, artist, armourer, blacksmith, carpenter, emperor, general, inventor, animal trainer (reputedly keeping thousands of hunting cheetahs during his reign and training many himself), lacemaker, technologist and theologian.

Akbar is said to have been a wise ruler and a sound judge of character. His son and heir, Jahangir, in his memoirs, wrote effusive praise of Akbar's character, and dozens of anecdotes to illustrate his virtues. According to Jahangir, Akbar's complexion was like the yellow of wheat. Antoni de Montserrat, the Catalan Jesuit who visited his court described him as plainly white. Akbar was not tall but powerfully built and very agile. He was also noted for various acts of courage. One such incident occurred on his way back from Malwa to Agra when Akbar was 19 years of age.

Akbar rode alone in advance of his escort and was confronted by a tigress who, along with her cubs, came out from the shrubbery across his path. When the tigress charged the emperor, he was alleged to have dispatched the animal with his sword in a solitary blow. His approaching attendants found the emperor standing quietly by the side of the dead animal.

Abul Fazal, and even the hostile critic Badayuni, described him as having a commanding personality. He was notable for his command in battle, and, "like Alexander of Macedon, was always ready to risk his life, regardless of political consequences". He often plunged on his horse into the flooded river during the rainy seasons and safely crossed it. He rarely indulged in cruelty and is said to have been affectionate towards his relatives. He pardoned his brother Hakim, who was a repented rebel. But on rare occasions, he dealt cruelly with offenders, such as his maternal uncle Muazzam and his foster-brother Adham Khan.

He is said to have been extremely moderate in his diet. *Ain-e-Akbari* mentions that during his travels and also while at home, Akbar drank water from the Ganga river, which he called 'the water of immortality'. Special people were stationed at Sorun and later Haridwar to dispatch water, in sealed jars, to wherever he was stationed.

According to Jahangir's memoirs, he was fond of fruits and had little liking for meat, which he stopped eating in his later years. He was more religiously tolerant than many of the Muslim rulers before and after him. Jahangir wrote:

"As in the wide expanse of the Divine compassion there is room for all classes and the followers of all creeds, so... in his dominions, ... there was room for the professors of opposite religions, and for beliefs good and bad, and the road to altercation was closed. Sunnis and Shias met in one mosque, and Franks and Jews in one church, and observed their own forms of worship. " To defend his stance that speech arose from hearing, he carried out a language deprivation experiment, and had children raised in isolation, not allowed to be spoken to, and pointed out that as they grew older, they remained mute.

During Akbar's reign, the ongoing process of inter-religious discourse and syncretism resulted in a series of religious attributions to him in terms of positions of assimilation, doubt or uncertainty, which he either assisted himself or left unchallenged.

Such hagiographical accounts of Akbar traversed a wide range of denominational and sectarian spaces, including several accounts by Parsis, Jains and Jesuit missionaries, apart from contemporary accounts by Brahminical and Muslim orthodoxy.

Existing sects and denominations, as well as various religious figures who represented popular worship felt they had a claim to him. The diversity of these accounts is attributed to the fact that his reign resulted in the formation of a flexible centralised state accompanied by personal authority and cultural heterogeneity.

PROVINCIAL ADMINISTRATION

Provincial administration was greatly improved under Akbar, and in this respect the Mughal period differs substantially from the sultanate. The boundaries of the provincial units were more definitely fixed; and a uniform administrative pattern, with minor modifications to suit local conditions, was developed for all parts of the empire. Further, drawing upon the experiments introduced by Sher Shah, the provincial administration was strengthened, and each province was provided with a set of officials representing all branches of state activity. By the introduction of a cadre of mansabdars, liable to be transferred anywhere at the behest of the central government and by the introduction of other checks, the control over the provinces was made more effective. The principal officer was the governor, called *sipah salar* under Akbar and *nazim* under his successors, but popularly known as *subahdar* and later only as subah. Next to him in official rank, but not in any way under his control, was the provincial diwan, who was in independent charge of the revenues of the province. He was usually a mansabdar of much lower status than the governor, but he was independent of the governor's control and was directly under the imperial diwan.

The next provincial functionary was the *bakhshi*, or the paymaster. He performed a number of duties, including, occasionally, the functions of the provincial newswriter. The *diwan-i-buyutat* was the provincial representative of the khan-i-saman, and looked after roads and government buildings, supervised imperial stores, and ran state workshops. The sadr and the qadi were entrusted with religious, educational, and judicial duties. The *faujdar* and the *kotwal* were the two other important provincial officials. The faujdar, who was the administrative head of the sarkar (district), was appointed by the emperor but was under the supervision and guidance of the governor. The kotwals were not provincial officers, but were appointed by the central government in the provincial capitals and other important cities, and performed a number of executive and ministerial duties similar to the Police Commissioners during British rule in Bombay, Calcutta, and Madras. The ports were in charge of the *mir bahr*, corresponding to the modern Port Commissioner, but with powers over customs also.

The Mughals interfered very little with the local life of the village communities, for they had no resident functionary of their own in the villages. The muqaddam was normally the sarpanch (head of the village panchayat, or council) and these panchayats continued to deal with local disputes, arrange for watch and ward, and perform many functions now entrusted to the local bodies.

Finances and Tax Structure

The tax structure of the Mughal empire was relatively simple in its theoretical formulation, however much it was complicated by changing needs and local circumstances. Both revenue and expenditure were divided between the central and the provincial government. The central government reserved for itself land revenue, customs, profits from the mints, inheritance rights, and monopolies. Land revenue was the most important source of income, as it has been throughout Indian history, and more than doubled in value between the reigns of Akbar and Shah Jahan. The principal items of expenditure for the central government were defence, the general civil administration of the empire (including the religious organizations), maintenance of the court and the royal palace, and the cost of buildings and other public works. The provincial sources of income were the assignments of land revenue granted to the provincial governor and his officials as a remuneration for their services, a variety of local taxes and cesses, transit dues and duties, and fines and presents.

MUGHAL REVENUE SYSTEM

The Mughal revenue system was based on the division of the empire into subas or governorships, sarkars or districts, and parganas, consisting of number of villages which were sometimes styled mahals. (These were replaced during British rule by the somewhat large tehsils or talukas.) The revenue staff had also to perform miscellaneous administrative duties, including the keeping of the public peace, and recruitment of the military forces. The suba was modelled after the central imperial structure. The sarkar was in the charge of the faujdar, or military commander, who combined the functions of the modern district magistrate and superintendent of police. The revenue work in the sarkar was looked after by the amalguzar, who would correspond to the modern afsar-i-mal (revenue officer).

The levy of land revenue was based on survey settlements calculated after a detailed measurement and classification of the cultivated areas. The nature of the crops grown and the mean prevailing market prices were also taken into consideration in fixing the final assessment. This assessment system, evolved after many experiments, became the basis of the survey settlement of the British period. Akbar's revenue system in most areas was raiyatwari, the revenue being collected directly as far as possible from the individual cultivator, and was payable in cash. Akbar introduced the system in the greater part of northern India, and during the viceroyalty of Aurangzeb, it was extended to the Deccan. The revenue system as evolved under Akbar was thoroughly sound, but the government demand was heavy and amounted to one-third of the produce. Abul Fazl tried to justify it by referring to the abolition of many miscellaneous cesses and taxes, but it is not certain whether all the cesses abolished by royal order were given up by subordinate officials. In the settlement of the Deccan during Aurangzeb's viceroyalty, the state share was reduced to one-fourth. Mughal emperors, particularly Akbar and Aurangzeb, continued to make cautious experiments and improvements in the land-revenue system. The basic data was collected by detailed measurement of land and assessment of the yield and estimates of productivity of each pargana or assessment area. When sufficient data had been collected the system of group assessment was introduced, with the alternatives of measurement and sharing being held in reserve.

That the Mughal rulers wanted the revenue system to operate fairly is evident from the guidance to collectors of revenue given in the *Ain-i-Akbari*. "The Collector was directed to be the friend of the agriculturist; to give remissions in order to stimulate cultivation ... to grant every facility to the raiyat, and never to charge him on more than the actual area under tillage; to receive the assessment direct from the cultivator and so avoid intermediaries; to recover arrears without undue force; and to submit a monthly statement describing the condition of the people, the state of public security, the range of market prices and rents, the conditions of the poor and all other contingencies."

The specifications were high—at least on paper, but anyone who studies the procedure for giving relief to the raiyats in case of hardships, the general instructions to the collectors, and the details of the assessment system and mode of recovery is bound to be struck by the professional competence of men like Todar Mal, Shah Mansur, and Amir Fathullah Shirazi, as well as the statesmanlike benevolence motivating the state's basic policy. The British paid special attention to revenue administration, and introduced many significant improvements, but it can be said without injustice that on certain points the Mughal system compared favourably with the one that evolved over a long period in British India. As an example, one may take the assessment of lands newly brought under cultivation or reclaimed after having fallen out of cultivation. A variety of scales of assessment was applied to such lands, such as a low initial rate, rising to the full amount after five years. The collector was also able to vary the revenue demands to encourage wasteland being cultivated. Regulations under the British were neither so liberal nor so flexible for this particular kind of cultivation. Another important difference between the British and the Mughal systems was the position of the village accountant, or patwari. Throughout the Mughal period the patwari, who was responsible for the maintenance of the financial records, was an employee of the village, not of the revenue administration. Under the British system, however, he became an employee of the government. This altered his relationship to the people, because previously he had been an agent for the people, but now he became an instrument of government. This was one factor that led to the weakening of village autonomy.

Mughal theory and practice of revenue administration

The Mughal theory and practice of revenue administration must be seen as the essential elements underlying the later administrative structure of India. The great memorial to Mughal rule is not so much the great architectural monuments that fill the subcontinent, but the governments of the great successor states, India and Pakistan, which following the model of the period of British rule, have maintained an administrative pattern that derives from the Mughals. "The District system with the district officer as head of the public services and general factotum or Poo Bah, the erection of an administrative hierarchy upon the basis of land revenue collection, and the development of an involute maze of office procedure, these features of Mughal rule were all accepted as the foundation of British rule; and, indeed, to an astonishing degree, in India and Pakistan today local administration is Mughal in spirit."

MILITARY ORGANIZATION

The weakest part of Mughal administration was the military organization, precisely the area where one might have expected the most efficient centralized control. But instead of a large standing army, the emperors depended upon four different classes of troops for the maintenance of order and the defence of the empire's borders. There were, first of all, the soldiers supplied by the mansabdars; the number a mansabdar was expected to provide upon the demand of the emperor were specified in his warrant of appointment or were indicated by his rank. Another class of troops under the command of a mansabdar was known as dakhili, whose services were paid for by the state. A third class were the ahadis, or "gentlemen troopers," drawing higher pay than those in the ordinary service; according to the *Ain-i-Akbari*, they might get as much as five hundred rupees a month, in contrast to the seven or eight rupees of the regular troopers. Finally, the chiefs who had been permitted to retain a degree of autonomy were required to provide contingents under their own command.

The artillery was paid wholly out of the imperial treasury. Recognizing its importance, Akbar had given it his special attention, but his efforts to secure from the Portuguese some of their better pieces were unsuccessful. European gunners were employed later on in appreciable numbers, but no permanent improvement was effected. During the eighteenth century the Mughal army shared in the decline of the other imperial institutions, and little advantage was taken of technical improvements in weaponry. When Nadir Shah invaded India in 1739 the jazair or swivel guns employed by his troops were superior to anything the Mughals could bring against them.

There are no existing statistical records of the strength of the Mughal army. The best estimate is probably that of Sir Jadunath Sarkar, who concluded from evidence from the reign of Shah Jahan that in 1648 the army consisted of 440,000 infantry, musketeers, and artillery men, and 185,000 cavalry commanded by princes and nobles. The army could still count on the personal valor of the commander of an individual contingent, but pitted against disciplined European soldiers, or hardy, resourceful Maratha horsemen, it did not prove effective. The loose organization of the army, the paucity of officers, the failure to build up a well-knit and active pyramidical organization, reduced the efficiency of the army. There were no uniforms, and discipline was poor, particularly in lower ranks. The cavalry was the only branch which was considered respectable and fit for a gentleman to join, while the ordinary "Indian foot soldier was little more than a night watchman and guardian over baggage." The Mughal practice of taking along a great number of camp followers, including occasionally the families of the soldiers and the royal harem, made the army a very cumbersome, slow-moving organization.

Descendants of a people who knew nothing of the sea, the Mughals had little success in creating a navy. They had no large fighting vessels, and the ships that they maintained were primarily for the furtherance of the commercial operations of the state. After the conquest of Gujarat, the Mughal army reached the shores of the Indian Ocean, but Akbar failed to build a navy. He tacitly acquiesced in the Portuguese supremacy by making no effort to challenge their authority, and by taking out licenses from them for the ships which he sent to the Red Sea. To deal with the pirates in the Bay of Bengal, and also for the purpose of communication over the vast river system of Bengal, a river flotilla was maintained at Dacca. Under Akbar it consisted of 768 small armed vessels and boats, estimated to cost about 29,000 rupees a month. It was not effective against the Magh and Portuguese pirates, but it was reorganized under the efficient administration of Mir Jumla and Shayista Khan, and in 1664 the latter was able to inflict a decisive blow against the pirates.

A few years later Aurangzeb had an opportunity to make at least tentative arrangements for the defence of the seas along the west coast of India. A coastal chieftain known as the Sidi of Janjira had provided protection for the ships and ports of the sultan of Bijapur. When the Sidi's territories were attacked by Shivaji, however, the sultan did not come to his assistance, and in 1670 the Sidi offered his services to Aurangzeb. Since Aurangzeb needed all the help he could get in the Deccan, he took the Sidi into his service, placing him under the Mughal governor of Surat, and subsidizing his fleet. The Sidi was assisted by another fleet based on Surat, and in every way treated as an official of the empire, but the Mughal command of the sea was too slight to make supervision of so independent a force possible. In course of time his descendants established themselves as the rulers of the state of Janjira south of Bombay.

TAXATION OF LAND

A careful student of Indian history is very much struck by the chronic antagonism between the rent-payer and the rent-receiver from very ancient times. European travellers in India have noticed how the ryot was averse to pay even his legitimate rent and that force had to be employed to get from him the dues of the State. On the other hand, in Sanskrit literature as well as Persian Court-annals we read how the "king's men" — i.e., revenue officials and Court underlings, — preyed on the peasantry, and in both ages the sovereign is called upon to save the ryots from such bloodsuckers.

Administration of the Mughals

The Indian peasant's habitual reluctance to pay revenue was partly due to the fact that he derived little benefit from the Government in return for the revenue; but it was mainly because of the uncertainty of that Government. I have explained already how the State in Mughal India performed no socialistic duties, but simply undertook to defend the country from invaders and rebels. Even this work of national defence was badly done at times, while the policing of the villages against thieves and robbers was done by a village agency which was not remunerated out of the revenue. Thus, the ryot received nothing visible in return for which Government might fairly demand from him a share of the fruits of his labour.

Secondly, changes of dynasty were so frequent, wars of succession within the same dynasty so much the rule rather than the exception, and the invasion of neighbouring countries (in Sanskrit digvijay, in Persian mulk giri) was so universally regarded as a duty by Hindu Rajahs and Muslim Sultans alike, that the peasant in India seldom knew for certain to whom to pay the revenue, even when he was willing to pay it. He naturally wanted to avoid having to pay the same money twice over. It was (he felt) wiser to wait for some months or years, even at the risk of some beating in the meantime, and see which side became firmly planted on the throne and then pay the revenue to it. But the arrear of revenue which thus accumulated could never be paid in full after such long delays, because much of the peasant's stock was eaten up by him and much of it plundered during the unsettled state of the country.

Many centuries of political insecurity and revolution have left in the mind of the Indian peasant even of the 20th century, a sub-conscious but ingrained belief that wars of succession are quite in the nature of things and that whenever the Government is engaged in a war anywhere, a wise peasant ought to think twice before paying the revenue due. During the late war with Germany, several khas-mahal ryots in Chittagong hesitated to pay their land-tax and told the Deputy Collector, "If the Kohisur comes will he not ask for our revenue over again? Save us, Sir, from the double payment."

I was in a North Bengal village at the time of the death of King Edward VII. The first question which the local ryots asked me on hearing of His present Majesty's succession was, ' 'Are not his kinsmen disputing his accession to the throne?" We can easily imagine the long ages of disorder and oppression that lie behind this traditional belief among our villagers.

The Peasant Ever in Arrears of Payment

Hence, the collection of the revenue was always the result of a struggle between the ryot and the sarfyar, and the arrears were seldom, if ever cleared. The next logical step in this vicious circle was for the Government collectors to exact from the ryot, under the name of the never-to-be-extinguished arrears, everything except his bare subsistence. In most parts of Mughal India the ryot was, therefore, like the French peasantry in the reign of Louis XV trying to escape the unjust taille or the cottier peasantry of Ireland who were ever in debt to their land-lords.

There was this difference, however, that in pre-British times there was no eviction for de-fault, no starvation of the peasantry (except when there was a local famine, with no communication with the more fruitful parts of the country.) In the early and mediaeval times, the peasant was left in his holding and left with enough to feed him (except when the entire harvest failed.) The old custom of payment by the division of the crop (the batai system) was an advantage to him, as the payment depended on the actual harvest of the year, unlike the modern money-rent which is an amount fixed irrespective of the yield of different years. In those days of constant war and disorder, the peasant was also cherished and valued because his landlord had need for him as an armed retainer. Indeed, competition for tenants among the zamindars was the rule and the poorer peasants sometimes escaped from one zamindari to another in the hope of getting rid of their arrears with the former and of faring better under a new landlord. Cases of such fugitive ryots were very frequent in North Bengal only forty years ago.

Illegal imposts on peasants, condemned by the Government Head

The natural tendency of the ryot to with-hold or refuse the payment of revenue and the failure of the State to give him a clean slate every three or five years by writing off his arrears, were the chief causes of trouble in the Mughal revenue department. The evil was aggravated by the greed of the revenue underlings and of some of the Emperors even. When I discuss the list of abwabs or unauthorised exactions from the people in Mughal times, you will perceive the wonderful fertility of the human invention in devising means for squeezing money out of the people, — at birth, throughout life, and even after death. All these nawabs were not directly paid by the peasant; several of them affected the smaller dealers and townspeople too. But as our population is predomi-nently agricultural and most of the articles for sale came from the land, the weight of the abwabs pressed most heavily on the ryots.

It is only fair to add that in respect of the abwabs, there was a clear conflict of policy between the better sort of Emperors on the one hand and the revenue collectors on the other. These Emperors are for ever issuing orders to their officers to show leniency and consideration to the peasants in collecting the revenue, to give up all abwabs, and to relieve local distress; and the revenue officers are as often squeezing everything out of the peasants except the barest subsistence. A solemn proclamation is issued by one Emperor abolishing all abwabs and urging all his officials, at present and in future to obey these instructions. But these very abwabs crop up again and have to be abolished by his successor with another proclamation, which has exactly the same efficacy as the first. English readers will find painful illustrations of it in Thomas's Revenue Resources of the Mughal Empire published in 1871, which may be supplemented by my translation of Aurangzeb's Revenue Regulations published in the J.A.S.B. in 1906, and the list of abwabs abolished by Aurangzeb in 1673, as given in this lecture.

The policy of the supreme head of the Mughal Government not to commit any exaction on the ryot is manifest from the contemporary histories and letters, and can be proved to have been a reality and not merely a pious wish. Several instances are recorded in the reigns of Shah Jahan and Aurangzeb in which harsh and exacting revenue collectors and even provincial viceroys were dismissed on the complaints of their subjects reaching the Emperor's ears. A characteristic anecdote to the same effect is told in India Office Library Persian Manuscript No. 370, interleaf facing folio 68. It clearly illustrates Shah Jahan's eagerness to do justice and even liberality to the peasantry, and I shall narrate it here.

"One day," so runs the story, "Shah Jahan was looking through the revenue returns of his empire and discovered that in a certain village the revenue for the present year was entered as higher by a few thousands than that of past years. Immediately he ordered the High Diwan Sadullah Khan to be brought to the

Presence for explaining the difference. Sadullah Khan was then sitting in his treasury with an open bundle of revenue papers before him and his eyes dozing in consequence of his daily and nightly attention to the business of his department. The royal messengers brought him to the Emperor in exactly the same condition [and dress.] Shah Jahan asked him for the cause of the increase in the assessment. After a local inquiry it was found out that the river had receded a little and a new tract of land had risen above water-level, causing an addition to the area of the village and the income of the State. On the Emperor asking whether the land in question was halsa or aima, a further inquiry was made and it was found to adjoin a piece of rent-free grant of land (aima.) Then Shah Jahan cried out in wrath, 'The water over that tract of land has dried in response to the lamentations of the orphans, widows and poor [of the place]; it is a divine gift to them, and you have dared to appropriate it to the State ! If a desire to spare God's creation had not restrained me, 1 should have ordered the execution of that second Satan, the oppressive faujdar [who has collected revenue from this new land.] It will be enough punishment to dismiss him as a warning to others to refrain from such wicked acts of injustice. Order the excess collection to be immediately refunded to the peasants entitled to it."

This anecdote may or may not have been true in every letter, but it shows the atmosphere and the public belief in Shah Jahan's kindness to his subjects.

PROVINCIAL ADMINISTRATION

Official dislike of village life and in-difference to village interests. The administrative agency in the provinces of the Mughal empire was an exact miniature of that of the Central Government. There were the governor (officially styled the nazim and popularly called the subahdar), the diwan, the bakfishi, the qazi, the sadr, and the censor; but no Khan-i-saman and no bayutat. These provincial bakhshis were really officers attached to the contingents that accompanied the different subahdars rather than officers of the subahs as geographical units. The practical effect, however, was the same.

The administration was concentrated in the provincial capital. It was city-government, not in the Greek sense of the term, but rather as a government living and working in cities and mainly concerning itself with the inhabitants of the cities and their immediate neighbourhood. The Mughals, — after due allowance has been made for their love of hunting and laying out pleasure gardens and their frequent marches, — were essentially an urban people in India, and so were their courtiers, officials, and generally speaking the upper and middle classes of the Muhammadan population here. The villages were neglected and despised, and village-life was dreaded by them as a punishment. No doubt, the villages were the places from which their food and income came; but that was their only

Administration of the Mughals

connection with them. Life in a village was as intolerable to them as residence on 'the Getic and Sarmatian shores' away from 'the seat of empire and of the gods' was to a cultured poet of imperial Rome. This feeling comes out very clearly in a Persian couplet :

Zdgh dum su-i-shahar wa sar su-i-deh Dum-i-dn zdgh dz sar-i-u beh. The tail of a crow was turned towards the city and its head towards the village; Surely, the tail here was better than the head ! 'better/i.e., nobler or happier.

The provincial Government kept touch with the villages by means of (1) the faujdars posted to the sub-divisions, who almost always lived in the lesser towns, (2) the lower officials of the revenue department, who did the actual collection from the peasantry, (3) the visits of the zamindars to the subahdar's court, and (4) the tours of the subahdar. The contact, however, was not very intimate, and the villagers, as i have remarked in the first lecture, were left pretty much to their own devices, uninfluenced by and indifferent to the Government at the chief town of the province, so long as they paid the land-tax and did not disturb the peace.

THE JUDICIARY

The judicial system of the Mughals was very similar to that of the sultanate. It became more systematic, particularly under Aurangzeb, but as compared with the judicial structure of British India, it was very simple, being based on a different approach to many categories of disputes. Normally no lawyers were allowed to appear. The disputes were speedily settled, often on the basis of equity and natural justice, though of course in the case of Muslims the injunctions and precedents of Islamic law applied where they existed. Many crimes—including murder—were treated as individual grievances rather than crimes against society. The complaints in such cases were initiated by the individuals aggrieved, rather than by the police, and could be compounded on payment of compensation. The aim of the judicial system was primarily to settle individual complaints and disputes rather than to enforce a legal code, as is indicated by the fact that the criminal court was normally known as the *diwan-i-mazalim*, the court of complaints.

All foreign travellers have commented on the speedy justice of the Mughal courts and the comparatively few cases coming before them. The latter was partly due to the general prejudice against litigation, but even more to the fact that a large number of disputes, particularly those affecting the Hindus, were settled by the village and caste panchayats, and did not come before the official courts. The Hindus were not debarred from taking cases before the qazi or the governor—and frequently did so where other arrangements did not prove effective—but normally they had their own arrangements for settling their disputes. Badauni has recorded that according to Akbar's orders the cases of Hindus were to be decided by the Hindu judges and not by the qazis. The Jesuit Father Monserrate says that "Brachmane (Brahmans) governed liberally through a senate and a council of the common people" —referring presumably to the administration of justice by these agencies. Local usage and custom ruled in most rural areas, and, according to one estimate, perhaps not one person out of a hundred in the Punjab, for example, was governed by the provisions of either the classic Hindu or Muslim law. The judicial courts provided by the Mughals were principally of two types—secular and ecclesiastical. Except during the reign of Aurangzeb, the principal courts for settlement of disputes were presided over by the emperor, the governors, and other executive officers. Akbar used to spend several hours of the day disposing of judicial cases, and governors followed the same procedure in the provinces. In the *Ain-i-Akbari* we find the instructions issued to a governor detailing the judicial procedure he should follow.

Apart from the secular courts and the panchayats, the principal agency for the settlement of disputes was the qazis' court. The qazi, being the repository of Muslim law, attended the hearing of cases by the executive authority, whether governor, faujdar or kotwal, and assisted the latter in arriving at a decision consonant with Quranic precepts. Presumably the civil disputes of Muslims were, as a rule, left to the qazis to be settled according to the canon law. When both parties in a dispute were Hindus, the point at issue was referred to Hindu pandits for an opinion.

This principle was supported by the *Fatawa-i-Alamgiri*, the authoritative digest of Islamic law, where it is held that "Dhimmis ... do not subject themselves to the laws of Islam either with respect to things which are merely of religious nature, such as fasting or prayer, or with respect to such temporal acts, as though contrary to [Islam], may be legal by their own, such as sale of wine or of swine's flesh, because we [Muslim jurists] have been commanded to leave them at liberty in all things, which may be deemed by them to be proper according to the precepts of their own religion." These provisions presumably related to religious matters. In the case of Muslims, the secular types of criminal suits went to the kotwal, while the religious and civil cases, such as concerning inheritance, marriage, divorce, and civil disputes went to the qazis' courts. The death penalty normally had to be confirmed by the emperor, but there seem to have been departures from the rule. A Dutch resident of India states that fines represented the normal mode of settling all disputes in Mughal India. Capital punishments and mutilations were frequent, and there are records of impaling, dismemberment, and other cruel punishments. They were, however, limited in their incidence and were inflicted only under the royal orders. Furthermore, they were confined to those cases where an example was to be made of the individual concerned. Imprisonment was not a method of punishment that appealed to the Mughals. It was seldom used as a sentence in private cases, though it was sometimes resorted to for preventive purposes. Whipping was commonly used. The Muslim punishment of parading the offender in an ignominious condition seems to have been frequently used, as it coincided with the Hindu tradition as well. The assessments made by two acute British observers on Mughal government as they saw it in a period of decline may serve as summary of the Mughal achievement as administrators. Luke Scrafton, who was resident for the East India Company at the capital of Bengal in 1758, declared that until the invasion of Nadir Shah in 1739 "there was scarce a better administered government in the world. The manufactures, commerce, and agriculture flourished exceedingly; and none felt the hand of the oppression but those who were dangerous by their wealth or power."

Mughal government was despotic, and official corruption increased from the reign of Jahangir, but on the whole, the judgment of the English historian, Sidney Owen seems just: "Whatever its defects, it was ... a grandly conceived, well-adjusted, and beneficent structure of government. ... Taxation was light; and its most productive source, the land revenue, was moderately assessed, and equitably adjusted. Foreign commerce was protected and favoured; and the English East India Company throve, and multiplied its factories, under the shadow of the Imperial authority.

The judicial system, though what we should consider crude and capricious, as well as too often corruptly exercised, was not liable like our own to the tedious delays which have been its reproach, and which have so much tended to obstruct, and even defeat, the course of justice. And the right of appealing to the Emperor from inferior tribunals, though too generally a futile privilege, was sometimes really remedial, and probably was a standing check to judicial iniquity. Much the same may be said as to the provincial Governors."

THE REVENUE SYSTEM

The revenues of the Mughal Empire may be grouped under two headscentral or imperial and local or provincial. The local revenue, which was apparently collected and spent without reference to the finance authorities of the central government was derived form various minor duties and taxes levied on "production and consumption, on trades and occupations, on various incidents of social life, and most of all on transport". The major sources of central revenue were land revenue, customs, mint, inheritance, plunder and indemnities, presents, monopolies and the poll-tax. Of these, land revenue formed, as in old days, the most important source of the state income.

After securing his freedom form the influence of Baigram and that of the ladies of the harem, Akbar realized the importance of reorganizing the finances of his growing empire, which were in a hopelessly confused state. Thus in 1570-1571, Muzaffar Khan Turbati, assisted by Raja Todar mall, prepared a revised assessment of the land revenue, "based on estimates framed by the local Qanungoesx and checked by ten superior Qanungoes at headquarters". After Gujarat had been conqurere, Todar Mall effected there a regular survey of the land, and the assessment was made "with reference to the area and quality of the land". In 1575-1576. Muzaffar Khan Turbati, assisted by ragja Todar Mall, prepared a revised assessment of the land revenue, "based on estimates framed by the local Qanungoes and checked by ten superior Qanungoes at headquarters". After Gujarat had been conqrued, Todar Mall effected there a regular survey of the land, and the assessment was made "with reference to the area and quality of the land". In 1575-1576 Akbar made a new and disastrous experiment by abolishing the old revenue areas and dividing the whole of the Empire, with the exception of the provinces of Gujarat, Bengal and Bihar, into a large number of untis, each yielding one Kror (crore) a year, and placed over each of them an officer called the Krori, whose duties were to collect revenues and encourage cultivation. But the Kroris seen grew corrupt and their tyranny reduced the peasants to great misery. Their offices were, therefore, abolished and the old revenue divisions were restored, though the title of Krori continued to survive at least till the reign of Shah jahan.

Important revenue reforms were introduced in 1582, when Todar Mall was appointed the Diwani Ashraf. Hitherto assessments were fixed annually on the basis of production and statistics of current prices and the demands of the state thus varied form year to year. Todar mall established a standard

Administration of the Mughals

or "regulation" system of revenue collection, the chief features of which were (i) survey and measurement of land, (ii) classification of land, (iii) fixation of rates. Lands were carefully surveyed, and for measurement the old untis, whose length fluctuated with the change of season, were replaced by the Ilahi Gaz or yard, which was equal to about thirty three inches, tana or tent rope, and jarib of bamboes joined by iron rings, which assured a constant measure.

Land was classified into four classes according to "the continuity or discontinuity of cultivation" (i) Pelaj or land cabable of being annually cultivated, (ii) Parauti or land kept follow foursome time to recover productive capacity, (iii) chauhar or land that had lain follow for three or four years and (iv) Banjar or land uncultivated for five years of longer. Only the area actually cultivated was assed, said, in order to ascertain the average produce of land belonging to each class, the mean of the three grades into which it was divided was taken into consideration. The demand of the state was fixed at one-third of the actual produce, which the ryots could pay either in cash or in kind.

The cash rates varied according to crops. The revenue system, as applied to Northern India, Gujarat, and with some modifications, to the Deccan was rayalwad that is, "the actual cultivators of the soil were the persons responsible for the annual payment of the fixe revenue". In the outlying portions of the Empire, this system was not applied, but each of these was dealt with as local circumstances required. For purposes of administration and revenue collection, the Empire, was divided into subhas, which again were subdivided into sarkars, each of which in turn comprised number of parasanas. Each parasana was a union of several villages. The amalguzar or revenue collector incharge of a district was assisted by a large subordinate staff. As art from the village Macadam (headman) and the village pat war, the were servants of the village community and not of the state three were measures and Karkuns, who prepared the seasonal crop statistics, the Qanungo, who kept records of the revenue payable by the villages, the Biotech or accountant, and the Potter or district treasurer.

These officers were instructed to collect revenue with due care and caution and "not to extend the hand of demand out of season". The emperors were for ever" issuing orders to their officers to show leniency and consideration to the peasants in collecting the revenue, to give up all always and to relieve local distress". There are instances in the reigns of Shah Jahan and Aurangzeb of extortionate revenue officials and even provincial governors being dismissed on complaints being made against them by the subjects to the Emperors. Though the lower revenue officers, especially those in the outlying provinces and districts, were not above corruption and malpractices, "the highest were on the whole, just and statesman like" with few exceptions. The success or failure of the revenue system thus organized must have depended on the quality and nature of the administration at the centre, and evils could not lout appear when administrative machinery was getting out of fear in Aurangzeb's reign. But on the whole its principles were sound and " the practical instructions to the officials all that could be desired".

The riots get certain amount of security and the fluctuations of the state revenue were prevented, or at least minimized. Further, the riots were not evicted from their holiness for default of payment, and the "custom of payment by the division of the crop", on the basis of the actual produce of a year, was better than the modern many rent system by which one has to pay the fixed amount irrespective of the harvest of the year. The demand at the rate of one-third, through rather high, as compared with one-sixth prescribed by Hindu law and custom or with what a modern land owner gets, was not a heavy burden on the peasants, who were compensated by the State with the abolition or remission of various creases and taxes. Above analysis, has shown that the entire judicial, administrative and revenue systems during the Mughal Empires was unscientific, unmodified and some how it was a face saving divide to the king emperors. Those, who were very close to the emperors or whose approach to the palace was easy and assessable, administration and justice, was balanced and truth speaking. Obviously, those who were residents of cities and town always obtained befit and asked for justice and maintained the balance of administration but those who were residents of villages or those who were residents at a distance from the imperial palaces, they always suffered, they never obtained relief. Their thirst for justice and their tears from the eyes against the grievances were never wiped out. They always kept mum for their grievances. Certainly, it was a fact that when any irregularity or injustice and to keep strict discipline in the administration as far as possible by him, particularly the names of the Akbar and Jahangir cannot be forgotten in this respect.

JUDICIAL & ADMINISTRATIVE SYSTEM DURING MUGHAL EMPIRES

Judicial & Administrative system during Mughal empires was matchless, excellent and complete in all senses. Let us have a brief perusal

Administration of the Mughals

of Mughal system as a whole. Though the Mughal Emperors had absolute powers, they appointed a number of officers in the different departments of the Government for the transaction of its multitudinous affairs. The chief departments of the State were:

(a) the Imperial House-hold under the Khan-i-saman,

(b) the Exchequer under the Deccan

(c) the Military Pay & Accounts office under the Mir Bakshi

(d) the Judiciary under the Chief Qazi,

(e) Religious Endowments and charities under the Chief Sadr or Sadr-us-Sudur, and

(f) the Censorship of Public Morals under the Muhtasib.

The Diwan or wazir was usually the highest officer in the state, being sole incharge of revenues and finance, The Bakhshi discharged a variety of functions. While he was the Pay-master-General of all the officers of the State, who "theoretically belonged to the military department he was also responsible for the recruiting of the army, and for maintaining lists of mansabdars and other high officials, and when preparing, for a battle he has a complete muster-roll of the army before the Emperor. The Khan-i-Saman or the Lord High Steward had charge of the whole imperial household "in reference to both great and small things".

The Muhtamibs or Censors of Public Morals looked after the enforcement of the prophet's commands and the laws of morality. The other officers, somewhat inferior in status to those mentioned above, the Mir Atish or Daroga-i-Topkhana (head of the artillery), the Daroga of Dak Chowki (the correspondence department). the Daroga of the Mint, the Mir Mai or the Lord Privy Seal, the Mustayfi or the Auditer-General air the Nazir-i-luyulat or the Superintendent of the Imperial workshop, the Mushriff or the Revenue Secretary, the Mir bahri or the Lord of the Admiralty, the Mir Barr or the Superintendent of forests, the or News Reporters the Mir arz or the charge of petitions presented to the Emperor, the Mir Manzil or the Quarter master General, and the Mir Tezak or the Master of Cerensnies. We shall discuss first police, then Judicial and revenue system. The Police so far as the rural areas were concerned, Mughals introduced no new arrangement for the prevention and detection and crimes. These as from time immemorial under the headman of the village and his subordinate watchmen. The system, which afforded a fair degree of security in the local areas with only occasional disturbances in times of disorder, survived till the beginning of the nineteenth century.

NATURE OF MUGHAL ADMINISTRATION

The Mughal Empire was a centralized disposition based on military power. It rested on two pillars: the absolute authority of the emperor and the strength of the army. The emperor was the supreme commander of the armed forces, and all other commanders were appointed and-if necessary-removed by him.

He determined the rank of every mansabdar and allotted jagirs for the maintenance of the mansabdar. He was the fountain of justice as also the supreme judge. He made laws and issued administrative ordinances which had the force of laws, although the principles of the shariat (Islamic law) were generally adhered to.

Yet the Mughal system of centralization was universally effective under Akbar, Jahangir, Shah Jahan and Aurangzeb.

Like other medieval states, the Mughal empire followed "the policy of the individualistic mini-mum of interference" i.e. it contented itself with discharging only the police duties and the collection of revenue.

The Mughal administration presented a combination of Indian and extra-Indian elements, or more correctly, it was the "Perso-Arabic system in Indian setting". The bifurcation of authority in the provinces-the division of power between the subahdar and the diwan-was based on the system prevailing under the Arab rulers in Egypt. The revenue system was a resultant of two forces-the time-honoured Hindu practice, and the abstract Arabian theory. The mansabdari system was of Central Asian origin. In the days of Babur and Humayun there was a prime minister, known as vakil, who was entrusted with large powers in civil and military affairs. During the early years of Akbar's reign, Bairam Khan, as vakil, virtually served as regent for the minor sovereign.

After Bairam Khan's fall the office of vakil was not abolished, it was gradually shorn of all powers because it was not considered prudent to allow concentration of authority in a single person. At the end of Akbar's reign the office became 'more or less honorific' and continued till the reign of Shah Jahan.

The all-important department of finance, taken away from the vakil, was placed in charge of the wazir (or diwan). After the virtual disappearance of the vakil, the wazir became the emperor's 'minister par excellence' i.e. prime minister. He was the intermediary between the emperor and the rest of the official world. Among the wazirs who have left their impress on

Administration of the Mughals

the Mughal history are Raja Todarmal, Raja Raghunath, Sadullah Khan and Jalar Khan. The emperor was the commander-in-chief of the entire army. The minister who looked after the administration of the army was called mir bakshi. He was in charge of recruitment, equipment and discipline of the troops. The salary bill of all mansabdars had to be calculated and passed by his office.

Towards the end of Aurangzeb's reign the expansion of the empire necessitated the appointment of four bakhshis: the chief or first bakhsi, and the second, third and fourth bakhshis.

The khan-i-saman held independent charge of the household department and the karkhanas.

The sadr-us-sudur had three important functions. He acted as the emperor's chief adviser in ecclesiastical matters. He was in charge of the disbursement of imperial grants for religious educational and charitable purposes. He was the chief justice of the empire, and his judicial authority was subordinate to that of the emperor only.

High Officials

The muhatasib (censor of public morals) was primarily an ecclesiastical officer whose duty it was to regulate the lives of the people. He also performed certain secular duties, such as the examination of weights and measures, enforcement of fair prices in the market, recovery of debts and restoration of fugitive slaves to their owners.

There was a diwan of the khalisa in-charge of the crown lands. The diwan-i-tan looked after matters relating to the jagirs.

Apart from military and judicial officers, mention should be made of the mustaufi or the auditor-general, the daroga-i dak chauki who was in charge of the imperial post, the mir-i-arz who was in charge of petitions, the mir-i-mal or the officer in charge of the Privy Purse and the mir tuzuk or the master of ceremonies.

The central government kept itself informed of the occurrences in all parts of the country by means of public news-reporters and secret spies. There were four classes of such agents: waqianavis (news-writer), swanith-nigar (news-writers), khufia-navis (secret letter-writer), harkarah (spy and courier).

SCRIBES IN MUGHAL ADMINISTRATION

A number of scribes were delegated to keep a record of the affairs of the court and the Empire, to maintain a list of nominated officers, and to keep a record of their performance. The movements of dignitaries were also noted. Special scribes kept journals of the activities of the Emperor and the royal family. There was a Diwan of Finances to keep an account of all the expenses, and the magistrates, were responsible for justice and religious affairs, and for compiling centralized reports from all over the Empire. The Emperor was at the centre of this network of agents, functionaries, and spies, and he collected all the sifted information.

Thus the central administration of the Mughal emperors was quite an efficient one.

What was the nature of Mughal Administration in India?

The Mughals established an imperial state in the true sense free from even shadowy allegiance to an external authority like the Caliphate, and exercised unrivalled power over vast territories. The Mughal Padshah and the Turko-Afghan Sultan belonged to entirely different categories of monarchy.

Theory of Kingship

Humayun entertained exalted ideas about royal power. He considered himself entitled to do within his sphere as God did in relation to His creation. Akbar's theory of kingship is thus stated by Abul Fazl: "Kingship is a gift of God and is not bestowed till many thousand grand requisites have been gathered together in an individual." Loyalty is a light emanating from God and a ray from the Sun, the illuminator of the universe." The obligations imposed upon the monarch by his position were many. "Divine worship in monarchs consists" in Akbar's opinion, "in their justice and good administration". 'Tyranny' he holds as 'unlawful' in everyone, especially in a "sovereign who is the guardian of the world." The monarch was the well-wisher and guardian of his subject. The idea that 'Kingship is a gift of God' was thus linked with the concept of paternal government.

Aurangzeb's conception of monarchy was radi-cally different from Akbar's in one very important respect. While Akbar placed the monarchy above religious and sectarian considerations, Aurangzeb made it the handmaid of Islam.

9

Causes and Decline of Mughal Empire

THE CAUSES THAT LEADS TO DECLINE AND FALL OF MIGHTY MUGHAL DYNASTY

Descended from both Genghis Khan and Tamerlane, the Mughal dynasty originated in Central Asia. It became the strongest dynasty to rule India, lasting from 1526 to 1858. The Mughal dynasty reached its height under Akbar, who encouraged reconciliation among his subjects by encouraging intermarriage between Hindus and Muslims and appointed competent administrators. His empire stretched from the Himalayas to the Hindu Kush and included presentday India, Bangladesh, Afghanistan, and Pakistan. The Mughal Empire passed its zenith after Akbar.

Shah Jahan, although famous for the construction of the Taj Mahal, was an unsuccessful military leader. He launched three failed campaigns against the ruler of southern Afghanistan, was defeated in his attempt to regain the ancient Mughal patrimony in Central Asia, was repulsed four times in his efforts to extend rule from northern to southern Deccan, and lost an effort to oust the Portuguese from its coast.

The cumulative effect of these campaigns was the imposition of higher taxes on the peasantry, whose loyalty to the Mughals began to diminish. This became more evident under Aurangzeb. The fortunes of both the empire and the dynasty decreased in the last half of Aurangzeb's reign.

Overwhelmingly ambitious, he spent the last 28 years of his reign campaigning in the south to conquer and unite the subcontinent from the south tip to the northern Himalayas and Hindu Kush. Although initially successful, many areas quickly revolted.

Aurangzeb's wars took a toll on the empire's resources, which became strained. This led to peasant resistance and flight, thereby increasing the burden on the remaining peasants. Aurangzeb's strict Islam and intolerance toward other religions also roused opposition.

He destroyed Hindu temples and schools, dismissed Hindu officials from government, and reimposed the tax on non-Muslims. These policies led to the rise of the greatest military opponents of the Mughals—the Marathas and the Sikhs. Under the leadership of Shivaji, the Marathas in the northwest Deccan carried out resistance and by 1750 controlled large sections of central and northern India. The Sikhs, originally a peaceful sect that attempted to synthesize Hindu and Muslim beliefs, became militarized by persecution and by 1750 controlled much of the Punjab in northeast India. The Hindu Rajputs in north central India, initially won over by Akbar's policies, became hostile and began to attack the Mughals. Even within the Delhi area, Hindu peasants called the Jats became radicalized and also revolted.

After Aurangzeb's death in 1707, most of the 10 Mughal emperors who followed him between 1707 and 1857 were little more than figureheads for one of the contending parties for power in India. Court feuds and civil wars also led to disintegration as Muslim dynasties arose in south Deccan, the eastern province of Oudh, and northeast Bengal between 1704 and 1720.

One Mughal emperor, Muhammad Shah, attempted to repair some of the damage by placating the Hindus but with little success, partly due to his own indolence and foreign invasions. Mughal power never recovered from the invasion of the Persian ruler Nadir Shah, who sacked Delhi in 1739, carried away the fabled peacock throne, symbol of the dynasty, and plundered northern India. Even more devastating was the invasion of Ahmed Khan, ruler of eastern Persia, Afghanistan, Uzbekistan, and portions of northern India. He sacked Delhi, defeating the Marathas and Rajputs, but his empire disintegrated after his death in 1772.

Mughal power also suffered with the rise of European merchants, especially the British and French who replaced the earlier Portuguese and Dutch. In 1691 the British East India Company received a charter from the

Mughal government not only to trade but to collect taxes in what is now Calcutta. In time, it became progressively more involved in politics; by 1765, the company controlled all Bengal, the richest province of India. By 1800 Britain had ousted the French from India. By 1818 the company either directly or indirectly ruled most of India. By the 19th century, Mughal emperors had become mere pensioners of the company. The last Mughal emperor was deposed and exiled to Burma after the Indian Mutiny in 1857.

There were many causes for the decline and fall of the Mughal dynasty. First, the lack of tolerance shown to the non-Islamic majority by later Mughal emperors; second, the imperial overreach by emperors in terms of military expeditions which strained resources after 1680; third, the diversity of India's ethnic and religious groups as well as strong traditions of regionalism which served to weaken the centre; and fourth, the superior technological and financial expertise which the West, including England, enjoyed after 1500 gave it an advantage dealing with Islamic emperors who had fallen behind. Finally, and perhaps most important, the Mughal dynasty remained a minority in India, distinct in religion, culture, and language from the majority of subjects. Given the circumstances, its fall was perhaps inevitable.

WIDESPREAD CORRUPTION IN MUGHAL INDIA

MUGHAL rulers occupied a position of power and prestige till the time of Aurangzeb. European travellers have eulogised the all-round progress during the time of Akbar, but after his death the glory departed and it gave way to corruption on a scale unknown or unheard of before.

Things reached an alarming state during the reign of Shahjahan and Aurangzeb, and paved the way for the final annihilation of the Mughal rule. The loss of power and prestige was due amongst other causes, to the basic character of the rulers of this period, most of whom had neither the will nor the ability to guide the destinies of the state at this critical juncture of history.

Corruption in Mughal India was on an extensive scale. No social or political group was considered aboveboard those days. Corruption was a common feature even though there was an elaborate machinery to prevent corruption, and news writers were particularly instructed to keep the emperor and high officials informed about the cases of corruption. Despite all this, cases have been recorded of even high officials accepting bribe.

Sometimes even the emperor was bribed by highly placed officials to secure their continuance in office. There are many cases on record of rich presents being offered to Jahangir, Nurjahan, Khurram and Itmad-ud-Daula, father of Nurjahan, who was notorious for taking bribes and resorting to corrupt practices. Another besetting sin was embezzlement by officials, of which numerous examples can be cited. There was no moral code to guide the conduct of the government officials in those days. The officials as a rule did not care much about the general masses and led a luxurious life. They were required to give valuable presents on various accounts — so they were always in need of 'money' and the money was generated through corrupt practices.

Daulat Khan, entitled Nazur-ud-daula, the head eunuch in Akbar's time, had according to Jahangir, no equal in taking bribes. After his death, he left 10 crores of *ashrafis* and jewels worth Rs 3 crore. All the money was appropriated by the state. Banarasi Dass Jauhri of Jaunpur and a contemporary of Akbar and Jahangir had given an account of how oppressive the *hakim* of Jaunpur, Qulich Khan, was towards the diamond dealers of the city in 1595, when they failed to provide him with the 'required things'. He ordered their arrest. They were brought in his presence and were flogged with thorny whips. They were later let off in a half-dead state. Terrified and highly disturbed, they left the city and fled to different places. The poor Mughal subjects groaned under the tyrannies of the Provincial Governors who possessed immense authority to book or torture anybody not 'obliging' them.

We have sufficient evidence in the European Factory records that English caravans carrying Indian commodities like indigo, Saltpetre and other things were stopped by the customs officials and were allowed to proceed only after receiving handsome gratification from them. They were notorious for accepting bribes. Wazir Khan, a noble at Shahjahan's court, took huge bribes sometimes as much as Rs 30,000 a day. There is evidence that the decline of administrative standards set in as early as 1630, a mere 25 years after the passing away of emperor Akbar. The corrupt practices increased with each passing year, after Akbar.

During the reign of Shahjahan, Muiz-ul-Mulk, mentioned in an English letter from Ahmedabad to Surat on November 29, 1623, under the name of Mir Musa, was not averse to taking good presents from the English and harassed them to a great extent. Such a policy of expropriation drove nobles and officials to act oppressively and their most obvious victims were merchants.

Another practice was that of farming out important posts and payment of bribes for continuance in them. Muiz-ul-Mulk had to pay some three lakh *mahmudis* (about £ 15000) and a bribe of some £ 10000 to secure his post at Surat. Another report has it that Muiz had to pay 72 lakh *mahmudis* for a Surat post and even by 1641 he found himself short of his commitment by 31 lakh.

In October, 1650, he still had an uncleared debt of many lakhs of rupees. Such heavy demands for a post inevitably led the Governor to resort to oppressive measures for revenue collection. The merchants could do little but suffer at his hands and as they were utterly helpless. Muiz-ul-Mulk was only the product of the age and he was doing what he was called upon to do in order to retain his position.

Such cases were certainly not there in excess in time of Akbar, who had a galaxy of personalities like Abul Fazl, Faizi, Birbal, Man Singh, Todar Mal and many more who rose to the occasion and served the Mughal empire with utmost devotion and dedication, a rare phenomenon in medieval history. But things headed towards inevitable collapse during the time of Aurangzeb.

Historians Bhimsen and Khafi Khan have rightly painted the dismal picture of fast-declining standards of society and administration during the rule of Aurangzeb. The historians were struck by the hopeless moral degradation of the Mughal aristocracy. We find the aged emperor himself dolefully shaking his head over the prospect of the future and predicting deluge after his death. Bigotry and narrowness of outlook under Aurangzeb and vice and sloth under later Mughals ruined the administration of the empire and dragged down the Indian people along with the falling empire. Khafi Khan has pointed out that Zafar Khan, one of the early Wazirs of Aurangzeb, was offered a purse of Rs 30,000 by Jai Singh to retain him in the Deccan Campaign. Not only that, even Aurangzeb is said to have asked an aspirant to a title: "Your father gave to Shahjahan one lakh of rupees for adding alif to his name and making him Amir Khan.

How much will you pay me for the title I am giving you?" Manohar Das, a Quiledar of Sholapur, gave him Rs 50,000 for receiving the title of 'Raja'. Even officers weary of life in the Deccan used to present the emperor with large sums for a transfer to North India, especially Delhi. The inflated expenditure, continuous warfare in the Deccan, adversely affected the situation in North India. The more prosperous provinces of the empire were drained of wealth and talent by pursuing the policy set by Aurangzeb. It proved detrimental to the empire and led to its inevitable collapse.

RELIGIOUS POLICY OF AURANGZEB

The most important cause of the downfall of the Mughal Empire was the religious policy of Aurangzeb. Aurangzeb alienated the sympathy and support of the Hindus by committing all sorts of atrocities on them. He imposed Jajiya on all the Hindus in the country. Even the Rajputs and Brahmans were not spared. He dismissed the Hindu Officials from state service and allowed only those to continue who were prepared to embrace Islam. An order banning the building of new Hindu Temples in areas directly under Mughal control was promulgated early in his reign.

Though old temples were not to be destroyed under this order, it was decreed that temples built since the time of Akbar should be regarded as newly built temples and on that plea were desecrated in different parts of the Mughal Empire and those included the Temples of Vishwanath at Kashi and the Temple of Bir Singh Deo at Mathura. A number of schools attached to the temples were shut down.

In 1679, when the State of Marwarj was under direct imperial administration and the Rajputs prepared themselves to resist Mughal a Authority, old as well as new temples were destroyed in different parts of the Empire. Thousands of artisans and labourers were employed to pull down Hindu Temples and Mosques were built with their material. After the death of Raja Jaswant Singh, Aurangzeb tried to keep Ajit Singh; under his control. Durga Das managed to remove him and his Mother Rajputana in spite of all the precautions taken by the Mughal Government. That led to the Rajput War which continued from 1679 to 1681.

Although peace was made, Aurangzeb could not depend upon the Rajputs. It proved to be a great handicap when he was busy in the Deccan Wars. Instead of depending Ig upon the support of the Rajputs, he had to set apart Mughal Forces to meet any possible trouble® from their side. The execution of Guru Teg Bahadur was a blunder. That led to the alienation of the Sikhs who became a strong military power under Guru Gobind Singh. Later on, these very Sikhs gave trouble to the Mughal Emperors.

Although Banda was captured and put to death after a long resistance, the Sikh Power was not crushed. It kept on growing day by day and ultimately the Sikhs were able to out the Mughals from the Punjab. The same policy of religious persecution led to the rise of the Marathas under Shivaji. The persecution of the Hindus hardened their character and they became the bitter enemies of the Mughals. To quite Lane- Poole, "His mistaken policy towards Shivaji provided the foundation of a power that was to prove a successful rival to his own Empire.

THE DECCAN POLICY OF AURANGZEB

The Deccan policy of Aurangzeb was also partly responsible for the downfall of the Mughal Empire. Aurangzeb was bent upon crushing the power of the Marathas. He found that the States of Bijapur and Golcunda were a source of help to the Marathas who were employed in those states in large numbers. They occupied important places of trust and authority in civil administration. Maratha soldiers were welcomed in those states. They got not only money but also military training. Aurangzeb felt that if those states were annexed, the source of the strength of the Marathas will be stopped. Moreover, the rulers of those states were Shias and for a fanatical Sunni like Aurangzeb, there was no place for them in India. The Marathas were able to get a lot of booty of raiding those states. It was maintained that if those states were annexed, it will not be easy for the Marathas to gain anything because they shall have to fight against the might of the Mughal Empire.

With that object in mind, Aurangzeb himself went to the Deccan and annexed Bijapur and Golconda in 1686 and 1687 respectively. He might have claimed credit for the destruction of the Shia States, but he had committed a blunder in doing so. He should have followed a buffer state policy towards those states and subordinated his religious zeal to statesmanship. If he had helped these states against the Marathas he would have been able to keep the latter in check with much less expense and waste of energy.

After the annexation of Bijapur and Golconda, Aurangzeb tried to crush the power of the Marathas. Sambhaji, the son of Shivaji, was captured and put to death under the orders of Aurangzeb. His son, Sahu, was also captured and made a prisoner. He continued in Mughal custody up to 1707. However, the Marathas carried on their struggle against the Mughals under the leadership of Raja Ram and his widow Tara Bai. When Aurangzeb died in 1707, the power of the Marathas was still not crushed. They were stronger than before.

V. A. Smith writes about Aurangzeb and his Deccan Policy in these words, "The Deccan was the grave of his reputation as well as of his body." Aurangzeb had to remain away from the North for a quarter of a century. The result was that the whole of the Mughal administration was thrown out of gear. There was complete confusion everywhere. As the Emperor was busy in the Deccan, the Provincial Governors did not send land revenue to the Central Government. At a time when more money was required for the Deccan war, very little was coming from the provinces. When Bahadur Shah succeeded to the throne, the treasury was empty.

The Mughal Government being a centralised despotism, the absence of the Emperor from the North for a long period encouraged centrifugal tendencies among the Governors. After the death of Aurangzeb, those tendencies continued to grow and the result was that ultimately various provinces became independent of the central authority. Thus, Awadh, Bengal, the Punjab and the Deccan became independent.

The Rohillas became independent in Rohilkhand. The Rajputs also asserted their independence. Thus, gradually the Mughal Empire broke up. The failure of Aurangzeb in the Deccan wars destroyed the military prestige of the Mughals. Too much of expenditure made the Mughal Government bankrupt. The Deccan wars can be called the ulcer which destroyed the Mughal Empire.

Revolts in Provinces of the Empire

Another cause of the downfall of the Mughal Empire was the revolts in various provinces of the Empire. During the Reign of Aurangzeb, no provincial Governor could dare to defy his authority. However, there were many who were secretly hostile to him. They were all trying to build up reserves of power and secure such allies as could help them to realise their ambitions when the aged Emperor passed away. All the sons of Aurangzeb fell into this category among officers Bahadur Khan, Diler Khan and Zulfiqar Khan were all suspected of harbouring such motives. After the death of Aurangzeb, the Empire began to break up and the process of breaking up was rather rapid.

Size of the Mughal Empire Became Unwieldy

In the time of Aurangzeb, the size of the Mughal Empire became unwieldy. It became physically impossible for any man to govern the same from one centre when the means of communication and transport were not developed. A centralised despotic Government was not suited to the needs of the time. The Mughal lines of communication were open to Maratha attacks to such an extent that the Mughal Nobles found it impossible to collect their dues from the Jagirs assigned to them and sometimes made private pacts with the Marathas.

That raised the power and prestige of the Marathas, led to demoralisation in the nobility and a setback to imperial prestige. The view of Dr. Satish Chandra is that "Perhaps Aurangzeb might have been better advised to accept the suggestion put forward by his eldest son, Shah Alam, for a settlement with Bijapur and Golconda, annex only a part of their territories and let them rule over Karnatak which was away from and difficult to manage.'"

Weak Successors of Aurangzebs

Another cause of Mughal downfall was the weak successors of Aurangzeb. If they had been intelligent and brilliant, they could have stopped the decline that set in during the Reign of Aurangzeb. Unfortunately, most of them were worthless they were busy in their luxuries and intrigues and did nothing to remedy the evils that had crept into the Mughal Polity. Bahadur Shah I was 63 years of age when he ascended the throne in 1707 and did not possess the energy to perform the onerous duties of the state. He tried to keep the various parties and courtiers satisfied by offering them liberal grants, titles, rewards etc.

Rulers like Jahandar Shah (1712-13), Farrukh Siyar (1713-79), Muhammad Shah (1719-48), Ahmad Shah (1748-54), and Bahadur Shah II (1837-57) were no better. Some of them were mere puppets in the hands of their Wazirs. To quote Edwards and Garret, "The chronicles of the court of Delhi after the Heath of Aurangzeb offer an unbroken tale of plots and counter-plots on the part of powerful nobles, culminating at intervals in open disorder and fighting with the titular Emperor serving as the sport and plaything of contending groups."

Absence of the Law of Primogeniture in the Matter of Succession

Another cause was the absence of the law of primogeniture in the matter of succession to the throne. The result was that every Mughal Prince considered himself to be equally fit to become the ruler and was prepared to fight out his claim. To quote Erskine, "The sword was the grand arbiter of right and every son was prepared to try his fortune against his brothers." After the death of Bahadur Shah, the various claimants to the throne were merely used as tools by the leaders of rival factions to promote their own personal interests.

Zulfkar Khan acted as the king-maker in the war of succession which followed after the death of Bahadur Shah I in 1712. Likewise, the Sayyid Brothers acted as king-makers from 1713 to 1720.

They were instrumental in the appointment of four kings to the throne. After their disappearance from the sconce, Mir Mohammad Amin and Asaf Jah Nizam-ul-Mulk acted as king-makers. Undoubtedly, the absence of the law of succession contributed to the decline of the Mughal Empire.

DEGENERATION OF THE MUGHAL NOBILITY

There was also the degeneration of the Mughal nobility. When the Mughals came to India, they had a hardy character. Too much of wealth, luxury and leisure softened their character. Their harems became full. They got wine in plenty. They went in palanquins to the battle-fields. Such nobles were not fit to fight against the Marathas, the Rajputs and the Sikhs. The Mughal Nobility degenerated at a very rapid pace.

Sir Jadunath Sarkar writes that "No Mughal Noble family retained its importance for more than one or two generations, if the achievements of a nobleman were mentioned in three pages, the achievements of his son occupied nearly a page and the grandson was dismissed in a few lines such as "he did nothing worthy of being recorded here." The Mughal Nobility was taken from the Turks, the Afghans and the Persians and the climate of India was not suitable for their growth. They began to degenerate during their stay in India.

The truth of this argument is challenged. It is pointed out that there is no reason to believe that the people belonging to colder climates are better warriors. Among the many well-known administration and distinguished warriros produced by the Mughal Empire, there were many Hindustanis and immigrants who lived in India for a long time. The eighteenth century also produced a large number of capable nobles and distinguished generals. Their personal ambitions were unlimited and they preferred to carve out independent principalities for themselves rather than serve the Mughal Emperors loyally and devotedly.

The chief reason for the degeneration of the nobility was that gradually it became a closed corporation. It gave no opportunity of promotion of capable men belonging to other classes as had been the case earlier. The offices of the state became hereditary and the preserve of people belonging to a few families. Another reason was their incorrigible habits of extravagant living and pompous display which weakened their morale and drained their limited financial resources. Most of the Nobles spent huge sums on keeping large harems, maintaining a big staff of servants etc. and indulged in other forms of senseless show.

The result was that many of the nobles became bankrupt in spite of their large Jagirs. Dismissal from service or loss of Jagirs spelt ruin for most of them. That promoted many of them to form groups and factions for securing large and profitable Jagirs. Others turned themselves into grasping tyrant who mercilessly fleeced the peasants of their Jagirs. Many Nobles became ease-loving and soft. They dreaded war and became so much accustomed to an extravagant way of life that they could not do without many of the luxuries even when they were on military campaigns.

The Mughal Nobility was corrupt and fact-in-ridden. By giving suitable bribes, any Government rule could be evaded or any favour secured. The interests of the Mughal Empire did not appeal to them. The British regularly brided Mughal Nobles for getting their work done. Even the highest nobles took bribes which were called Peshkash or presents. That lowered the tone of administration. With the passage of time, corruption and bribery increased. Later on, even some of the Mughal.

Emperors shared the money which their favourites charged as Peshkash from people desirous of getting a post or seeking a transfer. Factionalism kept on growing till it extended to all branches of administration the two major causes of functionalism were struggle for Jagirs and personal advancement and struggle for supremacy between the Wazir and the monarch. Thus faction fights weakened the monarchy, gave a chance to the Marathas, Jats etc. to increase their power and to interfere in the court politics and prevented the Emperors from following a consistent policy. Factionalism became the most dangerous bane of the Mughal Rule from 1715 onwards. To save themselves from these faction fights, the Mughal Emperors depended upon unworthy favourites and that worsened the situation.

Sir Jadunath Sarkar writes. "All the surplus produce of a fertile land under a most bounteous Providence was swept into the coffers of the Mughal Nobility and pampered them in a degree of luxury not dreamt of even by kings in Persia or Central Asia. Hence, in the houses of the Delhi Nobility, luxury was carried to an excess. The harems of many of them were filled with immense number of women of an infinite variety of races, intellect and character.

Under Muslim Law the sons of concubines are entitled to their matrimony equally with sons born in wedlock, and they occupy no inferior position in society. Even the sons of lawfully married wives became, at a precocious age, familiar with vice from what they saw and heard in the harem, while their mothers were insulted by the higher splendour and influence enjoyed in the same household by younger and fairer rivals of servile origin or easier virtue. The proud spirit and majestic dignity of a Cornelia are impossible in the crowded harem of a polygamist; and without Cornelias among the mothers there cannot be Grachhi among the sons."

A reference may also be made to the moral degeneration among the Mughal Nobles. "In a mean spirit of jelousy, they insulted and thwarted new men drawn from the ranks and ennobled for the most brilliant public services, and yet they themselves had grown utterly worthless. We have a significant example of the moral degeneration of the Mughal peerage. The Prime Minister's grandson, Mirza Tafakhur used to sally forth from his mansion in Delhi with his ruffians, plunder the shops in the bazar, kidnap Hindu women passing through the public streets in litters or going to the river, and dishonour them; and yet there was no judge strong enough to punish him, no police to prevent such crimes.

Every time such an occurrence was brought to the Emperor's notice by the news-letters or official reports, he referred it to the Prime Minister and did nothing more."

CAUSES FOR THE DECLINE OF THE MUGHAL EMPIRE

The Mughal Empire, which had reached its zenith during the rule of Shah Jahan and his son, began to decline after the rule of Aurangzeb. In fact, the decline began during the last days of Aurangzeb. There were many causes for the downfall of this great dynasty. Let us view the causes that hastened the fall of the Mughal Empire after Aurangzeb.

Aurangzeb's Responsibility

Aurangzeb was largely responsible for the downfall of the empire. His predecessors did a lot to win over the loyalties of their subjects, particularly the Rajputs and the Hindus. But Aurangzeb was a fanatic and could not tolerate the non-Muslims. He imposed jazia and forbade the celebration of Hindu festivals. He thus lost the friendship and loyality of the Rajputs. His execution of the Sikh guru and his enmity with the Marathas forced them to raise arms against him. His excessive obsession with the Deccan also destroyed the Mughal army, the treasury and also adversely affected his health. Being a fanatic Sunni Muslim, he could not tolerate even the Shias. They too turned against him. He laid too much stress on simplicity and was against singing, dancing and drinking which were common habits of the Muslim nobles. They did not like a king who was so much against their ways. Aurangzeb, thus "himself gave a green signal to the forces of decay" and so after his death the mighty empire disintegrated into smaller states.

Weak Successors

The successors of Aurangzeb were both weak and incompetent. The later Mughals spent more time in their harems and in pleasure and soon lost control of the states.

No Definite Law of Succession

The Mughals did not follow any definite law of succession. After the death of every emperor, there ensued a bloody war of succession amongst his sons. Each one, used nobles and members of the royal family to get the throne thereby dividing the nobles who fought for their self-interest only. This created anarchy. Nobles resorted to conspiracies and made the Mughal power weak and vulnerable.

Poor Economy

The economic stability of the empire was ruined because of the constant wars. Some of the wars did not add even an inch to the Mughal Empire. Besides this, the Mughal rulers spent lavishly on buildings and monuments. Finally, the foreign invasions completely shattered the economy.

Moral Degradation of the Soldiers

An excess of wealth and luxury made the Mughal army lazy, corrupt and inefficient. The soldiers and the generals became pleasure loving and easygoing. Often they proved to be disloyal. Now they could not even go to the battlefield without their train of attendants and women. Sometimes they only fought for money and easily succumbed to bribes.

Rise of New Powers

New powers such as the Sikhs, Jats and Marathas came onto the scene. Gradually they broke off from the Mughal domination and established their own independent states.

Coming of the Europeans

The Europeans, especially the British, played an important role in putting an end to the Mughal Empire. They first obtained a freeman to trade with India, but gradually began interfering in Indian politics and gradually set up a British empire in India that lasted for 200 years.

Foreign Invasions

The invasions of Nadir Shah and Ahmad Shah Abdali proved fatal for the Mughal Empire. Not only were the Indians defeated but their weakness was exposed and India became as easy prey to other foreign powers too.

Punjab

Guru Gobind Singh, the tenth Sikh guru, had organized the Sikhs into a military force. After his death, his disciple Banda Bahadur carried on his struggle against the Mughals. However, Banda was finally captured and put to death in 1715 during the reign of Farukh Siyar. But the invasions of Nadir Shah and Ahmad Shah Abdali gave the Sikhs a fresh opportunity to once again challenge the authority of the Mughals. They organized themselves into small groups known as misls. These misls were twelve in number and each one had a leader. Although these misls could not unite for a long time, they carried on their struggle with each other's cooperation. By the end of the eighteenth century, Ranjii Singh, however, brought them together and founded a Sikh kingdom. He brought the entire area to the west of the Sutlej under his control. Under Ranjit Singh, the Sikhs power reached the zenith of its glory, but his death was followed by an internal struggle for power.

The Rajputs

The Rajputs were strong military-like warriors but they had a major drawback in that they never organized themselves into a single power. They were constantly at war with each other. Even after the fall of Aurangzeb, they failed to rise to the occasion and grab power. The royal patronage that they received during the days of Akbar was now lost. The most important ruler of this period was Sawai Raja Jai Singh of Jaipur who built the Pink city and also the astronomical observatories. But during the eighteenth century, the Rajputs became very weak due to the rise of the Sikhs, Jats and the Marathas.

CAUSES BEHIND THE DOWNFALL OF THE MUGHALS IN INDIA

In the words of Stanely Lane-Poole, "As some imperial corpse preserved for age in its dead seclusion, crowned and armed and still majestic, yet falls to the dust at the breath of heaven, so fell the Empire of the Mughals when the great name that guarded it was no more." V. A. Smith writes, "The collapse of the Empire came with a suddenness which at first sight may seem surprising. But the student who has acquired even a moderately sound knowledge of history will be surprised that the Empire lasted so long rather than it collapsed suddenly." There were many causes which were responsible for the downfall of the Mughal Empire.

DECLINE OF THE MUGHAL EMPIRE

Write your abstract here the death of auranzeb was the signal for the disintegration of the mighty mughal empire which had dazzaed the temporary world by its extensice terirrtories and cultural achievements, his three sons quarelled for the sucession of the throne. All the mughal emperors after aurangzeb were weaklings and quite incapable to meet the challenges from within and without far from stemming the tide of the decline. They failed in maintaining the integrity of the empire. The mughal nobilty degeneated at a very rapid pace. The nobles discarded hard life of military adventure and took to luxurious living. The absence of the law of primogeniture among the mughal usually meant a war of succession among the sons of the dying emperor the maraths were the most formidable to the hindu powers who made a bid for supremacy on the disemberment of the mughal empire they could not form nay strong termination of founding an empire immediately after the death of aurangzeb but were absorbed for a few years in internal quarrels. The rise of the marathas was perhaps the most powerful factor that brought about the collapse of the mughal empire. They inaugurated the policy of greater maharashtra and popularised the ideal of hindu padshahi. The mughal soldiers also cared more for their personal comforts and less for wining battles.

The army was organised more or less on the feudal basis where the common soldier owed allegiance to the mansabdar than to the emperor after the death of aurangzeb, the mughal empire faced financial bankruptcy. The deccan wars ruined the finances of the empire the marches of the inperial army damaged crops in deccan while the beasts of burden ate away all the standing crops and greenery.

The mughal government was essentially a police government and confined its attention mainly to the maintenance of internal and external order and collection of revenue. The mughals failed to effect a fusion between Hindus and muslims and create a composte nation.

Instead of reconciling the rajputs, the marathas, Sikhs . The mughal policies go ahead them to rebellion. The invasion of nadir shah gave a death blow to the tottering mughal empire.

It not only depleted the mughal treasury of its wealth but also exposed to the world the military weaknesses of the empire with the weaknesses of the central mughal authority in the eighteenth century war lordism raised its ugly head. The European companies also acted as war lords and prfited from the confused time.

The European companies outdid Indian princes in every sphere whetter it was trade and commerce or diplomacy and war. It is sad commentary on the mughal aristocracy that while they spent lakhs in importing European luxury articles none ever thought of purchasing a printing press. Infact India was left far behind the race for civilisation.

It is pointed out that Mughlas suffered from intellectual bankruptcy. That was partly due to the lack of an efficient system of education in the country which alone could produce leaders of thought.

The mughals failed to produce any political genius or leader who could teach the country a new philosophy of life another cause of the mughal downfall was the neglect of the sea power by the mughals. The result was that it could not hold its own against the foreigners who were particularly strong on the seas. Thus the inherent weaknesses of the mughal body politic and the numerous contemporary operative causes had sapped the vitality of the empire.

AURANGZEB AND THE MARATHAS

Far more serious opposition to Aurangzeb came from the Deccan, where the Marathas were beginning their long struggle with the Mughal empire. A people of whose earliest history little is known, the Marathas as a dynamic force in Indian history owe much to the Bhakti movement. By giving birth to a new literature, enriching the local language, and popularizing a religious cult which made a powerful emotional appeal to all sections of the people, the movement had infused a new life in this society. The growing self-awareness of the Marathas was also helped by the fact that the Muslim conquest of the Deccan was far less complete than that of northern India. Hindus held many offices in the revenue and finance departments of the Muslim rulers of Golkunda and Bijapur, and at times even the highest ministerial appointments were filled by Deccani Brahmans.

Life in the hill forts of the Western Ghats, never easily accessible and practically cut off from the world during the monsoon, did not appeal to the Muslim officers, and Maratha chiefs and soldiers were employed in large numbers in garrisoning these forts. Since Maratha statesmen and warriors controlled various departments of the Muslim states of Ahmadnagar, Golkunda, and Bijapur, the conflicts of the Mughals with these states provided them with an opportunity to advance their sectional interests. Amongst Maratha statesmen who rose to prominence during the days of Shah Jahan was Shahji, who served under the sultans of Ahmadnagar and Bijapur and had large estates at Poona. His importance may be judged by the fact that in 1635 he set up a Nizam Shahi boy as the nominal sultan of the kingdom of Ahmadnagar, and reoccupied in his name the whole of the western portion of the old dominion as far as the sea. Shah Jahan was able to deal with him, and Shahji, after making his submission to the Mughals, sought service with the ruler of Bijapur. Shahji's son, Shivaji, more than fulfilled the dreams of his father.

Shivaji's mother lived at Poona, and he spent his early days in the spurs and valleys of the Ghats, which were to be his battlefield. He attached to himself a number of young men, and in the disturbed conditions of the Deccan started taking control of hill fortresses. For a long time these aggressive proceedings were ignored at Bijapur, but in 1659 a strong contingent of ten thousand cavalry was sent against him under Afzal Khan. Shivaji lured Afzal to a private conference and then killed him with his dagger. The leaderless troops of Bijapur were routed by Shivaji's soldiers, who lay in ambush. The following year Shivaji came in conflict with the Mughal rulers. In 1660 Aurangzeb appointed Shayista Khan, his maternal uncle and a veteran general, viceroy of the Deccan, with instructions to suppress the activities of Shivaji. He gained a few victories and recaptured several forts, but on April 5, 1663, the Marathas made a night attack on his encampment at Poona, and although the viceroy escaped, his son was killed. Shayista Khan was recalled by Aurangzeb, who then sent Dilir Khan and Raja Jai Singh, with his son, Prince Muazzam, to the Deccan. The imperial generals forced Shivaji to sue for peace.

In 1666 he attended the court at Agra, but insulted at being given the rank of mansabdar of only five thousand horsemen, he made his displeasure public. He was kept under surveillance, but he escaped and reached the Deccan. On his return Shivaji formally assumed the title of maharaja in June, 1674, and as Aurangzeb was busy in the northwest, he was not disturbed. After his death in 1680, the mad cruelty of his unworthy son Shambhuji forcibly attracted the attention of the Mughal ruler. In 1682 Shambhuji raided Burhanpur and perpetrated such cruelties on the Muslim population that the qazis there sent a manifesto to Aurangzeb upbraiding him. The Mughal emperor, who was concerned about the developments in the Deccan since his rebel son, Prince Akbar, had taken refuge at Shambhuji's court, decided to go south. He reached Aurangabad in the third week of March, 1682, and the last twenty-five years of his life were to be spent in that part of the subcontinent. Bijapur and Golkunda, which often gave shelter to the Maratha raiders, were annexed in 1686 and 1687, and Shambhuji was captured and executed in early 1689, but this did not mean the end of Aurangzeb's troubles in the Deccan.

Aurangzeb brought up Shambhuji's son, Shahu, at the court and treated him with great consideration, but his younger brother, Rajaram, took over the Maratha leadership. On his death in April, 1700, his widow, Tara Bai, carried on the struggle. The Mughals achieved many successes against the Marathas, but these proved temporary. Often the forts won at great cost and after prolonged effort, would be lost through the treachery or the incompetence of the Muslim commanders. But even though Aurangzeb had conquered most of the Maratha forts, he was unable to suppress the powerful roving Maratha bands which challenged Mughal authority whenever they got an opportunity. In 1699, they carried their first raid in Malwa. Four years later they disrupted the communications between northern and southern India, and in 1706 they sacked Baroda. After Aurangzeb's death, the Marathas became a major factor in the downfall of the Mughal Empire.

DEMORALISATION IN THE MUGHAL ARMY

Demoralisation in the Mughal Army. The abundance of riches of India, the use of wine and comforts had very evil effects on the Mughal army. Nothing was done to stop the deterioration. The soldiers cared more for their personal comforts and less for winning battles. The importance

Causes and Decline of Mughal Empire

of the Mughal armies was declared to the world when they failed to conquer Balkh and Badakhashar in the time of Shah Jahan. Likewise the failure of Shah Jahan to recapture Kandhar inspite of three determined efforts proved to the world that the military machine of the Mughal had become important. In 1739 Nadir Shah not only murdered the people of Delhi but also ordered their wholesale massacre. When such a thing is done by a foreigners it only proves that the existing government is helpless. Such govemment forfeits the right to exact allegiance from the people as it fails to protect life and property of the people. There were inherent defects in Mughal military system.

The army was organised more or less on the feudal basis where the common soldier owed allegiance to the mansabdar rather than the Emperor. The soldier looked upon the mansabdar as their chief, not an officer. The defects of this system though evident enough in the revolts of Bairam Khan and Mahabat Khan assumed alarming proportions under the later Mughal Kings. Irvine points out thai every fault was found among the degenerate Mughals - indiscipline, want of cohesion, luxurious habits, inactivity had commissariat and cumbrous equipment. Luxury and sloth penetrated every rank of the army and the march of the spectacle of a Mughal army presented a long train of elephants, camels, carts and oxen mixed up of a crowd of camp followers women of all ranks, merchants, shopkeepers, servants, cooks and all kinds of ministers of luxury amounting to ten times the number of the fighting man. In fighting capacity, the unwieldy, Mughal armies were nothing more than an armed raffle. Bernerr compares them to a herd of animals who flud at a first shock. The Mughal artillery was crude and ineffective against the guerilla tactics of the Marathas.

The Maratha fortresses which the Mughal armies could not capture despite repeated attempts easily scummed to British arms. In 1748, the French commander Monsieur Paradise with a small detachment consisting of 230 European and 700 Indian soldiers and without any guns routed a large army of the Nawab of Carnatic consisting of 10,000 men well equipped with artillery and entrenched across a river. Dupleix wrote to the company's Directors in Paris that "500 European soldiers could reduce all Muslim strong holds and provinces this side of the Kistna". The chief defect of the Mughal armies was their composition. The soldiers were drawn from Central Asia, the soldiers and their leaders come to India to make fortunes not to toss them. The leaders of such armies changed sides without any hitch and were constantly plotting either to betray of supplant their employers. Even the Mughal Viceroys employing such hired soldiers were constantly haunted by the fear of desertion. Such hired soldiers without coherence or loyalty were unfit custodians of the interests of the empire.

MUGHALS SUFFERED FROM INTELLECTUAL BANKRUPTCY

The Mughals suffered from intellectual Bankruptcy. That was partly due to the lack of an efficient system of education in the country which alone could produce leaders of thought. The result was that the Mughals failed to produce any political genius or leader who could "teach the country a new philosophy of life and to kindle aspirations after a new heaven on earth. They all drifted and dozed in admiration of the wisdom of their ancestors and shook their heads at the gorwing degeneration of the moderns." Sir Jadunath Sarka points out that "There was no good education and no practical training of the Mughal Mobility.

They were too much patted by eunuchs and maid servants and passed through a sheltered life from birth to manhood. Their domestic tutors were an unhappy class, powerless to do any good except by love of their pupils, brow-beaten by eunuchs, disobeyed by the lads themselves and forced to cultivate the arts of the courtier or to throw up their thankless office. Not much could be expected from such teachers and their wards."

Mughal Empire Faced Financial Bankruptcy

After the death of Aurangzeb, the Mughal Empire faced financial bankruptcy. The beginning had already been made in the time of Aurangzeb and after his death; the system of farming of taxes was resorted to. Although the Government did not get much by this method, the people were ruined. They were taxed to such an extent that they lost all incentive to production. Shah Jahan had increased the state demand to one-half of the produce. The extravagant expenditure by Shah Jahan on buildings was a crushing burden upon the resources of the country.

Bibliography

Ali, M. Athar Ali: *The Mughal Nobility Under Aurangzeb*. Bombay: Asia Publishing House, 1968.
Archer, Mildred : *Indian Architecture and the British,* Delhi, Delhi,1968.
Ashton, S.R. : *British Policy Towards the Indian States, 1905-1939,* London, Curzon, 1982.
Atul Chandra: *History of Bengal: Mughal Period (1526-1765 A.D.).* Calcutta, 1968.
Baer, Eva : *Islamic Ornament,* New York: New York University Press, 1998.
Beach, Milo Cleveland: *Mughal and Rajput Painting.* Cambridge: Cambridge University Press, 1992.
Chaudhary, M.: *Partition and the Curse of Rehabilitation,* Calcutta, Bengal Rehabilitation Organization, 1964.
Das, Kamal Kishore: *Economic History of Moghul India: An Annotated Bibliography, 1526-1875.* Calcutta: Santiniketan, 1991.
Deak, Istvan: *The Lawful Revolution: Louis Kossuth and the Hungarians 1848-1849,* Columbia University Press, 1979.
Fisher, Michael H.: *The Politics of British Annexation of India - 1757-1857,* Oxford, 1996.
Garrett, H. L. O. : *Mughal Rule in India,* Delhi, 1956.
Gascoigne, Bamber : *The Great Moghuls*. London: Jonathan Cape, 1971.
Gommans, Jos: *Mughal Warfare: Indian Frontiers and High Road to Empire 1500-1700.* London, 2002.
Goradia, Nayana: *Lord Curzon: The Last of the British Moghuls,* New Delhi, Oxford University Press, 1993.
Grousset, Rene : *The Empire of the Steppes,* New Brunswick: Rutgers University press, 1994.
Gulbadan Begum : *Humayun Nama,* London 1902, Indian Reprint, Delhi, 1972.
Guy, John & Deborah Swallow : *The Arts of India 1550-1900,* Delhi, 1990.
Habib, Irfan : : *An Atlas of the Mughal Empire,* New York: Oxford University Press, 1982.
Hasan, Murhirul: *Legacy of a Divided Nation: India's Muslims Since Independence,* New Delhi, Oxford, 1997.

Henry Beveridge : *The Akbarnama of Abul-Fazl*, Bibliotheca Indica Series, 1897.
Husain, ABM : *Architecture : A History Through the Ages*, Asiatic Society of Bangladesh, 2007.
Ibn Hasan, *The Central Structure of the Mughal Empire*, Macmillan, London, 1936.
James, Lawrence: *The Rise and Fall of the British Empire*, St. Martin's, 1997.
Kishore, Kamal: *Economic History of Moghul India: An Annotated Bibliography, 1526-1875*. Calcutta: Santiniketan, 1991.
Koch, Ebba : *Mughal Architecture: An Outline of Its History and Development (1526-1858)*, Munich, Delhi, 1991.
Krishnamurti, R.: *Akbar: The Religious Aspect*. Baroda, 1961.
Lal, K.S. : *The Mughal Harem*. New Delhi: Aditya Prakashan, 1988.
Leach, Linda York : *Paintings from India*, Delhi, 1998.
Major, R.H. : *India in the Fifteenth Century*, London, 1857.
Mehra, Parshotam: *A Dictionary of Modern Indian History, 1707-1947*, New Delhi, Oxford University Press, 1985.
Moreland, W.H.: *From Akbar to Aurangzeb*, London, 1923.
Moynihan, E. : *Moonlight Garden: New Discoveries at the Taj Mahal*, Delhi, 2001.
Mukhia, Harbans : *The Mughals of India*, New Delhi: Wiley-Blackwell 2004.
Owen, Sidney J. : *The Fall of the Moghul Empire*, London, 1912,
Preston, Diana: *The Boxer Rebellion*, Berkley Books, 2000.
Qureshi, I. H.: *The Administration of the Mughals*. Lahore, 1944.
Rafiabadi, Naseem : *Islam and Sufism in Kashmir : Some Lesser Known Dimensions*, Sarup, Delhi, 2009.
Richard C. Foltz : *Mughal India and Central Asia*, Oxford University, 1998).
Richards, John F.: *The Mughal Empire*. Cambridge: Cambridge University Press, 1993.
Sanjay Subrahmanyan : *The Mughal State 1526-1750*, Delhi. 1998.
Saran, Parmatma: *The Provincial Governments of the Mughals*, Allahabad, 1941.
Satyamurthy, T.V.: *Region, Religion, Caste, Gender and Culture in Contemporary India*, Delhi, OUP, 1996.
Savarkar, Vinayak Damodar : *The Indian War of Independence* 1857 Rajdhani Granthagar, Delhi, 1988.
Sidney J. Owen: *The Fall of the Moghul Empire*, London, 1912,
Skelton, Robert : *The Indian Heritage: Court Life & Arts under Mughal Rule*, Delhi, 1982.
Smith, Edmund W. : *The Mughal Architecture of Fathpur Sikri*, Delhi, 1985.
Stuart, C.: *The Art of Mughal India*. New York, 1964.
Thackston, M., *The Baburnama: Memoirs of Babur, Prince and Emperor*, Oxford UP, 1996.
Tillotson, G. H. R. : *Mughal India*, New York: Penguin Books, 1990.
Westcoat, James : *Mughal Gardens*, Delhi, 1996.
William Irvine : *The army of the Indian Moghuls*, London, 1902.

Index

A
Administration of Babur, 69, 70.
Administration of Justice, 204, 228.
Akbar the Great, 56, 88, 166, 167.

B
Battle of Chanderi, 47.
Battle of Ghaghra, 49, 56, 63.
Battle of Khanwa, 3, 49, 55, 56, 64, 65, 67, 105.
Battle of Panipat, 1, 3, 4, 40, 43, 45, 46, 49, 56, 57, 67, 94, 95, 96, 97, 110, 111, 187, 194.

C
Coins of Akbar, 116, 117, 118, 135.
Court of Shah Jahan, 149.

D
Deccan Policy of Aurangzeb, 243.
Deccan Policy of Jahangir, 133.
Deccan Policy of Shah Jahan, 144.
Decline of Empire, 7.
Decline of the Mughal Empire, 246, 248, 251.

F
Founder of Mughal Empire, 40.

I
Islamic Architecture, 74, 154.

L
Land Revenue Systems, 199.
Legal Policy of Akbar, 207.
Lodi Empire, 42, 67.

M
Military Administration, 203.
Military Career of Babur, 68.
Military Innovations, 96.
Military Organization, 203, 220.
Mughal Administration, 201, 205, 206, 233, 235, 236.
Mughal Revenue System, 199, 201, 218.

N
Nature of Mughal Administration, 233, 236.

P
Persians in the Mughal Empire, 22.
Political Government, 213.
Provincial Administration, 202, 217, 226.

R
Rajput, 3, 5, 10, 28, 45, 53, 65, 77, 78, 79, 102, 109, 110, 111, 112, 121, 125, 127, 128, 129, 135, 136, 137, 138, 146, 148, 149, 150, 157, 162, 163, 175, 202, 236, 237, 238, 256.

Rajput Policy, 113, 114, 115, 128.
Reign of Akbar, 2, 4, 94, 117, 138, 141, 200, 206, 208, 209.
Reign of Aurangzeb, 7, 171, 179, 193, 205, 206, 228, 244, 245.
Reign of Babur, 2.
Reign of Humayun, 4, 73.
Reign of Shah Jahan, 139, 142, 143, 144, 145, 148, 155, 221, 234.
Reigns of Jahangir, 6.
Religious Policy, 115, 134, 166, 172, 179, 242.
Religious policy of Jahangir, 134.
Retreat to Kabul, 81, 95.
Revenue System, 70, 199, 201, 218, 219, 231, 233, 234.
Revolt of Sikhs, 143.
Rise of Mughal Empire, 1.
Rules of Mughal Administration, 201.

S

Sculptures During Akbar Era, 119.
Sher Shah Suri, 76, 80.
Structure of Government, 229.
Successors of Aurangzeb, 180, 205, 245, 249.

W

War of Succession, 145, 180, 182, 190, 245, 249, 251.

❏❏❏

Printed in the USA
CPSIA information can be obtained
at www.ICGtesting.com
LVHW040804110924
790758LV00001B/24

9 789395 034364